McGraw-Hill Education

500

Regulation

Questions

for the CPA Exam

Also in the McGraw-Hill Education 500 Questions Series

McGraw-Hill Education

500
Regulation
Questions

for the CPA Exam

Denise M. Stefano, CPA, CGMA, MBA, and Darrel Surett, CPA

New York Chicago San Francisco Athens London Madrid
Mexico City Milan New Delhi Singapore Sydney Toronto

1 2 3 4 5 6 7 8 9 10   QFR/QFR   1 0 9 8 7 6 5 4

ISBN   978-0-07-182094-3
MHID   0-07-182094-9

e-ISBN   978-0-07-182095-0
e-MHID   0-07-182095-7

Library of Congress Control Number 2014932388

McGraw-Hill Education products are available at special quantity discounts to use as premiums and sales promotions or for use in corporate training programs. To contact a representative, please visit the Contact Us pages at www.mhprofessional.com.

This book is printed on acid-free paper.

CONTENTS

INTRODUCTION

Congratulations! You've taken a big step toward CPA exam success by purchasing *McGraw-Hill Education: 500 Regulation Questions for the CPA Exam*. This book gives you 500 multiple-choice questions that cover all the most essential material for the Regulation section of the CPA exam. Each question is clearly explained in the answer key. The questions will give you valuable independent practice to supplement your other studies.

You might be the kind of student who needs to study extra a few weeks before the exam for a final review. Or you might be the kind of student who puts off preparing until the last minute before the exam. No matter what your preparation style, you will benefit from reviewing these 500 questions, which closely parallel the content, format, and degree of difficulty of the questions on the actual CPA exam. These questions and the explanations in the answer key are the ideal last-minute study tool for those final weeks before the test.

If you practice with all the questions and answers in this book, we are certain you will build the skills and confidence needed to excel on the CPA exam. Good luck!

—Editors of McGraw-Hill Education

CHAPTER 1

Taxation of Individuals

1. Theresa and John were single for all of Year 12 and lived mostly apart until December 31 when they flew to Las Vegas and were married shortly before midnight. What is Theresa and John's filing status for Year 12?

   (A) married filing jointly
   (B) head of household
   (C) single
   (D) married filing separately

2. Gil Gallon's wife died in Year 1. Gil Gallon did not remarry. He continued to maintain a home for himself and his dependent infant child during Year 1 and Year 2, providing full support for himself and his child during these years. Gil Gallon's filing status for Year 2 is

   (A) single
   (B) head of household
   (C) married filing jointly
   (D) qualifying widower with dependent child

3. Bonnie's husband died in Year 1. She did not remarry. She continued to maintain a home for herself and her dependent infant child during Year 2, Year 3, and Year 4, providing full support for herself and her child during these three years. For Year 4, Bonnie's filing status is

   (A) single
   (B) head of household
   (C) qualifying widow with dependent child
   (D) married filing jointly

4. In Year 8, Kathleen and Lee were married and had four dependent children. On May 1, Year 8, Lee packed his bags and abruptly deserted his family. His whereabouts were still unknown to Kathleen at the time she filed her Year 8 income tax return in February of Year 9. What is the most advantageous filing status that Kathleen is legally allowed for Year 8?

   (A) single
   (B) married filing separately
   (C) head of household
   (D) qualifying widow with dependent child

5. Shari is 22 years old, is a full-time student, and earned $6,000 in Year 10. Which of the following is CORRECT?

   I. Shari cannot earn more than the exemption amount if claimed as a dependent on her parents' tax return in Year 10.
   II. Shari must claim herself as a dependent if her parents furnish less than 50% of her support for Year 10.

   (A) I only
   (B) II only
   (C) both I and II
   (D) neither I nor II

6. Ben and Freeda, both age 62, filed a joint return for Year 7. They provided all the support for their daughter Susan, who is 19, legally blind, mostly deaf, and has no income. Their son, Harold, age 21 and a full-time university student, had $6,200 in income and provided 40% of his own support during Year 7. Ben and Freeda can claim how many exemptions on their Year 7 joint tax return?

   (A) 2
   (B) 3
   (C) 4
   (D) 5

7. Walter is 86 years old but still files an income tax return because he works part-time at a nearby amusement park. Which of the following is TRUE?

   (A) Because of his age, Walter receives an additional amount if he claims itemized deductions.
   (B) Because of his age, Walter receives an additional amount of personal exemptions.
   (C) Because of his age, the first $6,200 of Walter's salary is nontaxable.
   (D) Because of his age, Walter receives an additional amount for his standard deduction.

8. Erin and Mars are married cash-basis taxpayers. The couple had interest income as follows:

$500 interest on federal income tax refund
$600 interest on state income tax refund
$800 interest on US Treasury (i.e., federal government) obligations
$300 interest on Puerto Rico government obligations
$700 interest on state government obligations

    What amount of interest income is taxable on the couple's joint income tax return?

(A) $500
(B) $1,100
(C) $1,900
(D) $2,900

9. Griffin received the following interest payments during the current year:

Interest of $500 on a refund of federal income tax for last year
Interest of $400 on an award for personal injuries sustained in a car accident three years ago
Interest of $1,600 on municipal bonds
Interest of $1,100 on US savings bonds (Series HH)

    What amount, if any, should be reported as interest income on Griffin's current year tax return?

(A) $3,600
(B) $2,000
(C) $900
(D) $0

10. Which of the following is a condition required for accumulated interest on Series EE US savings bonds to be exempt from tax?
    I. The bonds must have been purchased by the taxpayer or taxpayer's spouse and put in the name of a dependent child.
    II. Redemption proceeds from the bonds are used to fix up the taxpayer's home.

(A) I only
(B) II only
(C) both I and II
(D) neither I nor II

11. Kleinman bought Series EE US savings bonds. Redemption proceeds from the bonds will be used to pay for the college tuition of his dependent daughter. One of the conditions that must be met for tax exemption of accumulated interest on these bonds is that
    I. Kleinman must be the sole owner of the bonds (or joint owner with his spouse).
    II. The bonds must have been purchased by Kleinman before Kleinman reached the age of 24.
    III. The bonds must be transferred to the college for redemption by the college rather than by Kleinman.
    (A) I only
    (B) II only
    (C) I and III only
    (D) II and III only

12. Which of the following dividends are taxable?
    I. dividend on a listed stock where the taxpayer reinvests the dividend into additional shares
    II. dividend on a life insurance policy
    III. dividend of a Chinese corporation listed on a foreign stock exchange
    (A) I and III only
    (B) I, II, and III
    (C) I and II only
    (D) II and III only

13. Tatum owned 1,000 shares of common stock in Cyrus Corp. for which she paid $50 per share. The company distributed a 5% common stock dividend to all holders of common stock. The fair market value of the stock on the date of distribution was $60. With respect to this dividend, what amount must be included in Tatum's gross income?
    (A) $0
    (B) $1,000
    (C) $2,500
    (D) $3,000

14. On Form 1040, which of the following schedules are used to report interest and dividend income?

	Interest Income	Dividend Income
(A)	Schedule B	Schedule D
(B)	Schedule D	Schedule B
(C)	Schedule B	Schedule E
(D)	Schedule B	Schedule B

15. In Year 2, Stegman had a passive gain of $1,000 and a passive loss of $5,000. Stegman also earned a salary of $50,000 from her employer in Year 2 and had interest income of $100 on a certificate of deposit. What is Stegman's net passive income or loss for Year 2?

    (A) loss of $4,000
    (B) 0
    (C) loss of $3,900
    (D) income of $46,100

16. Adrian, an unmarried individual, had an adjusted gross income (AGI) of $190,000 for Year 6. Adrian incurred a loss of $29,000 from rental real estate activity she participated in during Year 6. What amount of the $29,000 loss can be used (in Year 6) to offset income from nonpassive sources?

    (A) $0
    (B) $12,500
    (C) $25,000
    (D) $30,000

17. Cindy, an unmarried individual, had an adjusted gross income (AGI) of $75,000 for Year 9. Cindy incurred a loss of $30,000 from a rental real estate activity in which she actively participated during Year 9. What amount of loss attributable to this rental activity can Cindy use in Year 9 to offset income earned from nonpassive sources?

    (A) $0
    (B) $12,500
    (C) $25,000
    (D) $30,000

18. In Year 10, Shan, a single taxpayer, received $160,000 in salary from his employer; received $15,000 in income from an S corporation in which he did not actively participate during Year 10; and incurred a $35,000 loss from a rental real estate activity in which he did actively participate during Year 10. Shan's adjusted gross income (AGI) amounted to $165,000 for Year 10. What amount of the $35,000 loss associated with the rental real estate activity was deductible in Year 10?

    (A) $0
    (B) $15,000
    (C) $20,000
    (D) $25,000

19. Skorecki owns a two-family house that has two identical apartments. He lives in one unit and rents out the other. In Year 4, the rental apartment was fully occupied and Skorecki received $10,000 in rent. Skorecki owned no other real estate during Year 4 and paid the following:

Mortgage interest	$3,000
Real estate taxes	$5,000
Repairs of rental apartment	$800

Skorecki is preparing his Year 4 income tax return. Depreciation for the entire house was determined to be $2,000. What amount should Skorecki include in his income for the rental property for Year 4?

(A) ($800)
(B) $4,200
(C) $3,800
(D) $1,000

20. Rudnick became a general partner in Wolinsky Associates partnership on January 1, Year 6, with a 5% interest in profits, losses, and capital. Wolinsky Associates is a distributor of test prep software. Rudnick does not actively participate in the partnership business. For the year ended December 31, Year 6, Wolinsky had an operating loss of $50,000. In addition, Wolinsky earned interest of $20,000 on US Treasury obligations. Rudnick's passive loss for Year 6 is

(A) $0
(B) $1,500
(C) $2,500
(D) $5,000

21. Benson, an individual taxpayer, reported the following items for Year 7: $70,000 of ordinary income from partnership A: operating a bowling alley in which she materially participates; $9,000 passive loss from partnership B: operating an equipment rental business in which she does not materially participate; $7,000 of rental income from a building rented to a third party; and $4,000 of interest and dividend income. What is Benson's adjusted gross income (AGI) for Year 7?

(A) $70,000
(B) $72,000
(C) $74,000
(D) $77,000

22. Shapiro, an individual taxpayer, reports the following items for Year 9:

    $40,000 of ordinary income from partnership A: operating a pinball arcade in which Shapiro materially participates

    $9,000 net gain from partnership B: operating a bike rental business in which Shapiro does not materially participate

    $17,000 loss from Shapiro's rental of a building to a third party

    How much of Shapiro's $17,000 building rental loss is deductible in Year 9?

    (A) $0
    (B) $9,000
    (C) $8,000
    (D) $17,000

23. Jonathan, age 22, is a full-time student at Randolph College and a candidate for a bachelor's degree. During Year 9, he received the following payments:

State scholarship for tuition	$4,200
Loan—college financial aid	$1,000
Cash support from parents	$2,000
Cash dividends on stocks	$500
Cash prize awarded in contest	$300
Unemployment compensation	$1,000
Interest income on tax refund	$10

    Jonathan's adjusted gross income (AGI) for Year 9 is

    (A) $700
    (B) $800
    (C) $810
    (D) $1,810

24. During Year 5, Tammy accepted and received a $10,000 humanitarian award. Tammy was selected to win this award without any action on her part, and no future services are expected of her as a condition of receiving the award. Which of the following is CORRECT?

    I. If Tammy never took possession of the $10,000 but instead had the amount sent directly to a charity, the $10,000 would be excluded from gross income.

    II. If Tammy first took the $10,000 check and later donated it to a charity, the $10,000 would be included in gross income.

    (A) I only
    (B) II only
    (C) both I and II
    (D) neither I or II

25. Carl owns a machine shop and provides life insurance for each of his employees. The amount of life insurance provided is equal to the employee's annual salary (under a qualified plan). Bob works for Carl and is covered by the life insurance policy. How much of the premium (paid by Carl to the insurance company) is taxable to Bob as income?

(A) none

(B) all of the premium

(C) an amount equal to the premium paid for the first $50,000 of coverage provided

(D) an amount equal to the premium paid for coverage provided in excess of $50,000

26. Cobbs works for the Johnson Regional Bank. He is covered by a $90,000 group-term life insurance policy, which lists his brothers as the beneficiaries. Johnson Regional Bank pays the entire cost of the policy, for which the uniform annual premium is $8 per $1,000 of coverage. How much of this premium is taxable to Cobbs?

(A) $0

(B) $360

(C) $320

(D) $720

27. Olney, an accrual basis taxpayer, operates an office building. He received the following payments during the current year:

Current rents	$30,000
Rents for next year	$10,000
Security deposits held in a segregated account	$5,000
Lease cancellation payments	$15,000

What amount can be included in Olney's current gross income?

(A) $60,000

(B) $55,000

(C) $40,000

(D) $30,000

28. Jay, a dentist, billed Lou $600 for dental services. Lou paid Jay $200 cash for these services and catered a party for Jay's office staff in full settlement of the bill. Lou caters comparable parties for $350 and makes a profit of approximately $250 per party. What amount should Jay include in taxable income as a result of this transaction?

(A) $200

(B) $450

(C) $550

(D) $600

29. Which of the following conditions must be present in a divorce agreement for a payment to qualify as deductible alimony?
    I. Payments must be in cash or property.
    II. Payments can be made to a third party on behalf of a spouse.

    (A) I only
    (B) II only
    (C) both I and II
    (D) neither I or II

30. Karen and Terry were divorced in Year 3. The divorce decree provides that beginning in Year 4, Terry pay alimony of $20,000 per year, to be reduced by 30 percent on their child's 18th birthday. Karen and Terry's child is currently 13 years old. During Year 4, Terry paid $9,000 to Karen's landlord, $6,000 directly to Karen, and $5,000 to Wildwood College for Karen's college tuition. What amount of these payments should be reported as income in Karen's Year 4 income tax return?

    (A) $6,000
    (B) $14,000
    (C) $15,000
    (D) $20,000

31. Buddy is a cash-basis, self-employed handyman. He files Schedule C as a sole proprietor. His cash receipts and disbursements for Year 2 were as follows:

Gross income	$30,000
Plumbing supplies	$2,500
Web page hosting	$300
Depreciation of business equipment	$400
Advertising	$1,700
Estimated federal income tax	$4,000
Charitable contribution to Red Cross	$500
Buddys' regular weekly salary—$100 per week	$5,200

    What amount can Buddy deduct on his Form 1040 Schedule C for Year 2?

    (A) $4,900
    (B) $8,900
    (C) $9,400
    (D) $14,600

32. Dr. Bernstein is a cash-basis taxpayer. The following items pertain to Dr. Bernstein's medical practice in Year 4:

Cash received from patients in Year 4	$270,000
Cash received in Year 4 from insurance companies for services provided by Dr. Bernstein in Year 3	$30,000
Salaries paid to employees in Year 4	$50,000
Year 4 bonuses paid to employees in Year 5	$4,000
Other expenses paid in Year 4	$25,000

What amount of taxable net income should Dr. Bernstein report from his medical practice for Year 4?

(A) $255,000
(B) $216,000
(C) $221,000
(D) $225,000

Use the following facts to answer Questions 33 and 34: Anita earned consulting fees of $8,000 and directors' fees of $1,800 last year. Also last year, Anita had a net profit on her gift business of $1,000, which she reported on Form 1040 Schedule C. Anita also had interest income of $2,400 from PNC Bank and she received alimony of $1,500.

33. Anita's income from self-employment last year was

(A) $10,800
(B) $10,000
(C) $9,800
(D) $0

34. Will Anita pay federal income or self-employment tax on her net earnings from self-employment?

	Federal Income Tax	Self-Employment Tax
(A)	Yes	No
(B)	No	Yes
(C)	Yes	Yes
(D)	No	No

35. Freedson is a self-employed literary agent and is required to pay self-employment tax as a result. On Freedson's current year tax return, the self-employment tax is

(A) one-half deductible from gross income in arriving at adjusted gross income (AGI)

(B) not deductible

(C) fully deductible as an itemized deduction

(D) fully deductible in determining net income from self-employment

36. Truncale is a landlord with an adjusted gross income (AGI) of $75,000 for 2013. What taxes would Truncale pay if he shows a profit from net rental activities on Form 1040 Schedule E?

(A) federal income tax only

(B) self-employment tax only

(C) both federal income tax and self-employment tax

(D) neither federal income tax nor self-employment tax, because rental income is passive

37. Which of the following would be considered a capital asset?
   I. land operated as a small outdoor marketplace
   II. a large shed on the land used for table storage when the marketplace is not open

(A) I only

(B) II only

(C) both I and II

(D) neither I nor II

38. Ratner recently purchased land to be held as a long-term investment. On that land was an abandoned building that will soon need to be torn down. Should Ratner classify the land and the building as Section 1231 assets?

	Land	Building
(A)	No	Yes
(B)	Yes	No
(C)	Yes	Yes
(D)	No	No

39. Rocky owns the following assets: recreational skis and a limousine that is used in her personal limousine service business for transporting passengers to and from airports. Which of these assets should Rocky classify as part of capital assets?

(A) the recreational skis only
(B) the limousine only
(C) both the recreational skis and the limousine
(D) neither the recreational skis or the limousine

40. During Year 6, Angie sold a painting for $25,000 that she had bought for her personal use in Year 1 at a cost of $10,000. Angie sold the painting in Year 6 and had a gain on the sale. In Angie's Year 6 income tax return, Angie should treat the sale of the painting as a transaction resulting in

(A) ordinary gain
(B) long-term capital gain
(C) Section 1231 gain
(D) short-term capital gain

41. Andrea and Ken are a married couple filing a joint return. A current year capital loss incurred by them

(A) can be deducted only to the extent of capital gains
(B) may be carried forward up to a maximum of three years
(C) cannot be deducted unless the capital loss is from an asset held for personal use
(D) can be deducted to the extent of capital gains, plus to $3,000 of ordinary income

42. Which of the following statements is TRUE with respect to capital assets for individual taxpayers?

(A) Gains and losses for both investment and personal property are reported on Form 1040, Schedule D.
(B) The taxpayer must report gains and losses on investment property, but should report only gains on personal property.
(C) Losses on personal property are deductible only to the extent of gains on personal property.
(D) Losses on investment property are deductible only to the extent of gains on investment property.

43. When exchanging "like-kind" property, which of the following terms has essentially the same meaning as "realized gain"?
    I. recognized gain
    II. accounting gain
    III. economic gain
    (A) I only
    (B) II only
    (C) II and III only
    (D) III only

44. Saralee exchanged commercial real estate that she owned for other commercial real estate. Saralee also received $50,000 cash as part of the exchange. The following additional information pertains to this transaction:

    Property Given Up by Saralee
    Fair market value $500,000
    Cost basis $300,000

    Property Received by Saralee
    Fair market value $450,000
    Cost basis $50,000

    Based on these facts and additional information, what is Saralee's recognized gain?
    (A) $200,000
    (B) $50,000
    (C) $100,000
    (D) $0

Use the following facts to answer Questions 45 and 46: Pollack exchanged an apartment building having an adjusted cost basis of $375,000 and subject to a mortgage of $100,000 for $25,000 cash and another apartment building with a fair market value of $550,000 and subject to a mortgage of $125,000. The property transfers were made subject to the outstanding mortgages.

45. What amount of gain would Pollack **realize** on this exchange?
    (A) $25,000
    (B) $100,000
    (C) $125,000
    (D) $175,000

46. What amount of gain should Pollack **recognize** on this exchange?
    (A) $25,000
    (B) $100,000
    (C) $125,000
    (D) $175,000

47. Hymanson exchanged investment real property with an adjusted cost basis of $160,000, which was subject to a mortgage of $70,000, and received (from Poppel) $30,000 cash and other investment real property having a fair market value of $250,000. Poppel assumed Hymanson's old mortgage in this exchange. What is Hymanson's recognized gain on this exchange?
    (A) $100,000
    (B) $90,000
    (C) $70,000
    (D) $30,000

Use the following facts to answer Questions 48 and 49: In Year 7, Jerry paid $15,000 for shares of ABC stock. In Year 9, Jerry sold all of the ABC stock shares to his son, Evan, for $11,000.

48. Considering these facts, which of the following is a CORRECT statement?
    I. Jerry may NOT deduct any of the $4,000 loss on the sale to Evan, since it is a related party loss.
    II. Evan may use Jerry's previously disallowed loss if Evan sells the ABC stock shares at a gain to an unrelated party.
    (A) I only
    (B) II only
    (C) both I and II
    (D) neither I or II

49. Now assume in Year 9 that Evan sells the ABC company shares to an unrelated party for $16,000. As a result, what amount of gain (from the sale of these shares) should Evan recognize in his Year 9 income tax return?
    (A) $0
    (B) $1,000
    (C) $4,000
    (D) $5,000

50. On July 1 of Year 4, Mitch owned stock (held for investment) having a fair market value of $7,000 that had been purchased two years earlier at a cost of $10,000. On this date (July 1, Year 4), Mitch sold the stock to his brother Glen for $7,000. Glen then sold the stock for $6,000 to an unrelated party on November 1, Year 4. Glen should report the effects of this stock sale on his Year 4 tax return as a

(A) short-term capital loss of $1,000
(B) long-term capital loss of $1,000
(C) short-term capital loss of $4,000
(D) long-term capital loss of $4,000

51. Phil died on December 31, Year 2, bequeathing shares of stock to his son, Jeff. All of the stock was distributed to Jeff on March 31, Year 3. Phil's estate executor elected the alternative valuation date for Phil's estate. The value of the stock on December 31, Year 2, was $210,000. The value on March 31, Year 3, was $240,000. The value on June 30, Year 3, was $270,000. Jeff's basis for this stock is

(A) $210,000
(B) $240,000
(C) $270,000
(D) $300,000

52. Fanny died on April 1, Year 1. Because of the size of Fanny's estate, no distributions were made until after July 1, Year 2. For estate valuation purposes, the executor of the estate selected the alternative valuation date. On what date must the estate assets be valued?

(A) April 1, Year 1
(B) October 1, Year 1
(C) December 31, Year 1
(D) April 1, Year 2

53. Andy sold 500 shares of XYZ Corp. stock on June 1, Year 2. He had received this stock on June 1, Year 1, as a bequest from the estate of his uncle Bart, who died on March 1, Year 1. Andy's basis was determined by reference to the stock's fair market value on March 1, Year 1. Andy's holding period for this stock was

(A) long-term
(B) short-term
(C) short-term if sold at a gain; long-term if sold at a loss
(D) long-term if sold at a gain; short-term if sold at a loss

54. Denise, a single individual, sold her personal residence in Year 15 for $390,000. She had purchased the home in Year 12 for $105,000. In Year 13, she added a patio to the home at a cost of $25,000. She has always used the home as her principal residence. Back in Year 8, she sold a different personal residence and excluded $100,000 of gain earned on that sale from her tax return in that year. What amount of gain must Denise recognize on her Year 15 tax return from the Year 15 sale of her personal residence?

   (A) $10,000
   (B) $110,000
   (C) $250,000
   (D) $260,000

55. Which of the following is a requirement for a taxpayer filing single to exclude (from income) up to $250,000 of realized gain on the sale of a home?
   I. The home must be considered a vacation home.
   II. The taxpayer must buy another residence for an amount in excess of the proceeds the taxpayer received from the sale of the current residence.

   (A) I only
   (B) II only
   (C) both I and II
   (D) neither I nor II

56. Barry and Saralee are a married couple filing jointly for Year 12. They purchased their principal residence for $300,000 back in Year 2. The couple spent $40,000 on improvements to the home. After living in the home for 10 years, Barry and Saralee sold the home for $650,000 and paid $36,000 in real estate commissions. What amount of gain should the couple recognize on their Year 12 joint return?

   (A) $0
   (B) $60,000
   (C) $274,000
   (D) $500,000

Use the following facts to answer Questions 57 and 58: Koshefsky owned a building condemned by the state. The building had a tax basis of $200,000, but was worth $250,000. The state paid him $260,000 for the condemned property.

57. If Koshefsky bought similar replacement property for $170,000, what was Koshefsky's taxable gain?

   (A) $10,000
   (B) $30,000
   (C) $60,000
   (D) $90,000

58. If Koshefsky bought similar replacement property for $230,000, what amount of gain would Koshefsky be required to recognize on this transaction?

(A) $0
(B) $30,000
(C) $60,000
(D) $90,000

59. An office building owned by Brad was condemned by the state on January 2, Year 2. Brad received proceeds for the condemnation, from the state, on March 1, Year 2. In order to qualify for nonrecognition of gain on this involuntary conversion, what is the last date for Brad to acquire qualified replacement property?

(A) December 31, Year 4
(B) January 2, Year 4
(C) December 31, Year 5
(D) March 1, Year 5

60. In Year 4, Frank gave a painting to his friend Stan. Frank originally paid $200 for the painting. At the time of the gift, the painting was worth $150. Stan sold the painting in Year 5 to Rizzo for $360, its fair market value at that time. Which of the following is CORRECT?

  I. Stan's basis in the painting is NOT determinable until he sells the painting.

  II. At the time of sale, Stan recognizes a $160 gain.

(A) I only
(B) II only
(C) both I and II
(D) neither I nor II

61. Property is purchased by Harry for $150,000 and later gifted to Barry when the value of the property is $147,000. If Barry then sells the property to Larry, an unrelated party, for $144,000, which of the following is CORRECT?

  I. Barry's basis in the property is NOT determinable until he sells the property.

  II. Barry is precluded from reporting a loss on the sale of the property to Larry since Barry had originally received the property as a gift.

(A) I only
(B) II only
(C) both I and II
(D) neither I nor II

62. Property is purchased by Keri for $150,000 and later gifted to Jeri when the value of the property is $147,000. Jeri then sells the property to Meri, an unrelated party, for $149,000. What amount of gain or loss should Jeri report on this transaction?

(A) $0
(B) $1,000 loss
(C) $2,000 gain
(D) $3,000 gain

63. In June, Year 4, Debbie gifted her grandson, Craig, 100 shares of a listed stock. Debbie's basis for this stock, which she bought in Year 2, was $4,000 and the fair market value of the stock on the date of the gift was $3,000. Craig sold this stock in July Year 4 to an unrelated party for $3,500. What was Craig's basis when he sold the 100 shares in Year 4?

(A) $4,000
(B) $3,500
(C) $3,000
(D) $0

Use the following facts to answer Questions 64 and 65: Grace bought a diamond necklace in Year 1 for her own use at a cost of $10,000. In Year 9, when the fair market value was $12,000, she gave this necklace to her daughter, Rochelle.

64. Assuming that Rochelle sells the diamond necklace in Year 9 for $13,000, Rochelle's recognized gain would be

(A) $3,000
(B) $2,000
(C) $1,000
(D) $0

65. For tax purposes, Rochelle's diamond necklace and the sale thereof are considered a(n)

(A) Section 1231 asset
(B) capital asset
(C) involuntary conversion
(D) passive activity

66. During the current year, Lois, an unmarried US citizen, made a $5,000 cash gift to an only child and also paid $25,000 in tuition expenses directly to a grandchild's university on the grandchild's behalf. Lois made no other lifetime transfers. For gift tax purposes, what was Lois's taxable gift?

(A) $30,000
(B) $25,000
(C) $17,000
(D) $0

67. Micki, a single taxpayer, gave the following outright gifts during the current year: $16,000 cash to her grandson for a down payment on a house, $14,000 cash to her friend's son for his college tuition, and $6,000 cash to her cousin for a vacation trip. What amount of the gifts Micki gave would be excluded from the gift tax?

(A) $28,000
(B) $34,000
(C) $14,000
(D) $2,000

68. Jeffrey and Alice have been married for 25 years. Alice inherited $1,000,000 from her father. What amount of the $1,000,000 can Alice give to Jeffrey without incurring a gift tax liability?

(A) $0
(B) $26,000
(C) $500,000
(D) $1,000,000

69. During the holiday season, Luchentos Restaurant gave business gifts to 16 customers. The value of the gifts, which were not of an advertising nature, were as follows: four customers at $10; four customers at $20; four customers at $60; four customers at $80. What amount of these gifts can Luchentos deduct as a business expense?

(A) $0
(B) $340
(C) $320
(D) $400

70. For which of the following asset sales would the seller's tax basis NOT be known until the time of actual sale?
    I. sale in Year 3 of property received by gift back in Year 1
    II. sale in Year 3 of property received as an inheritance back in Year 1

    (A) I only
    (B) II only
    (C) both I and II
    (D) neither I nor II

71. Which of the following are deductible to arrive at adjusted gross income (AGI)?
    I. moving expenses
    II. student loan interest

    (A) I only
    (B) II only
    (C) both I and II
    (D) neither I nor II

72. Which of the following are deductible to arrive at adjusted gross income (AGI)?
    I.   alimony paid
    II. child support paid
    III. contribution to a health savings account

    (A) I only
    (B) I and II only
    (C) I and III only
    (D) II and III only

73. Which of the following penalties can a taxpayer deduct from gross income to arrive at adjusted gross income (AGI)?
    I. penalty on early withdrawal of savings
    II. penalty for late payment of federal income tax

    (A) I only
    (B) II only
    (C) both I and II
    (D) neither I nor II

74. Corey was transferred from New Jersey to Massachusetts by his employer. In connection with this transfer, Corey incurred the following moving expenses: moving his household goods: $2,000; temporary living expenses in Massachusetts: $400; lodging on the way to Massachusetts: $100; meals on the way to Massachusetts: $40; and a penalty for breaking his lease on his residence in New Jersey: $50. What amount of these moving expenses can Corey deduct on his tax return if his employer reimburses him $2,000 for these expenses?

(A) $0
(B) $100
(C) $150
(D) $500

75. A single taxpayer, age 42, wishes to contribute and deduct $5,500 into a traditional IRA for the current year. Which of the following types of income combinations would enable the taxpayer to qualify for the full $5,500 deduction?

(A) alimony received of $2,000 and wages earned of $3,500
(B) self-employment income (Schedule C profit) of $2,000, alimony of $1,000, and interest income of $2,500
(C) interest income of $3,000 and dividend income of $2,500
(D) wages earned of $4,500 and rental income of $1,000

Use the following facts to answer Questions 76 and 77: Koslow is 45 years old and has a dependent daughter, Lily. During Year 2, Koslow took three premature distributions from his IRA account. The first distribution was $6,000 and was used to pay medical expenses. The second distribution was $10,000 and was used to pay off his credit card balances. The third distribution was $8,000 and was used to pay for tuition for his daughter, Lily, who is attending Western City University.

76. How much is the 10% penalty tax that Koslow will be subject to?

(A) $0
(B) $1,000
(C) $1,600
(D) $2,400

77. How much increase in **taxable income** will Koslow have as a result of the three premature IRA distributions?

(A) $6,000
(B) $8,000
(C) $16,000
(D) $24,000

78. Which of the following is CORRECT regarding IRA limits in 2014?
  I. The maximum IRA deduction is $5,500 for those under age 50.
  II. The maximum IRA deduction is $6,500 for those ages 50 or older.
  (A) I only
  (B) II only
  (C) both I and II
  (D) neither I nor II

79. Audrey takes a qualifying distribution from her **Roth IRA**. Such distributions are
  (A) fully taxable
  (B) taxable only to the extent of the income element distributed
  (C) not taxable
  (D) not taxable, but subject to the alternative minimum tax

80. By what age must a taxpayer begin to withdraw at least minimum distributions from a retirement account such as a traditional IRA?
  (A) 59½
  (B) 65
  (C) 70½
  (D) whatever age the taxpayer first begins to collect social security benefits

81. Contributions to a health savings account (HSA) are
  (A) deductible as an itemized medical expense deduction if made by the employee
  (B) not available to self-employed individuals
  (C) excluded from the employee's income if made by the employer
  (D) not available to employees

82. Anzalone, a self-employed taxpayer, had a gross income of $57,000. Anzalone made a contribution of $4,000 to a health savings account, paid health insurance premiums of $6,000, and paid $5,000 of alimony and $3,000 in child support. Anzalone also contributed $2,000 to a traditional IRA and contributed $1,000 to an educational IRA for his nephew, age 10. What is Anzalone's adjusted gross income?
  (A) $55,000
  (B) $50,000
  (C) $46,000
  (D) $40,000

83. Cindy and Dan are married and file a joint income tax return. Both were employed during the year and earned the following salaries: Dan: $128,000; Cindy: $134,000. In order to enable Cindy to work, she incurred at-home child care expenses of $16,000 for their two-year-old daughter and elderly grandfather. Cindy and Dan can claim what amount of the dependent care credit?

(A) $1,200
(B) $600
(C) $960
(D) 0

84. Mike qualified for the earned income credit in Year 2. This credit could result in a

(A) refund only if Mike had tax withheld from wages
(B) carry back or carry forward for any unused portion
(C) refund even if Mike had no tax withheld from wages
(D) refund provided Mike had at least one child

85. Which is CORRECT regarding tax credits?

I. Most credits will reduce tax dollar for dollar and then provide a tax refund if the remaining credit is greater than the total tax.

II. The earned income credit is a refundable credit.

(A) I only
(B) II only
(C) both I and II
(D) neither I nor II

86. Ziga is single with no dependents. He showed a loss on his Schedule C of $8,000. He has dividend income of $200 and interest income of $100. He also has a profit of $500 from a rental activity on Schedule E. Which is CORRECT?

I. Because Ziga's income is very low, he should qualify for the earned income credit.

II. Ziga's income from rental activities of $500 is considered passive income.

(A) I only
(B) II only
(C) both I and II
(D) neither I nor II

87. The American Opportunity Credit

    (A) may be taken in addition to the tuition deduction for the same student in the same tax year

    (B) is limited to $2,500

    (C) is limited to $1,800

    (D) is limited to the first two years of postsecondary education

88. The American Opportunity Credit

    I. can be taken for the first four years of postsecondary education

    II. can be taken regardless of a taxpayer's adjusted gross income (AGI), but the student must be enrolled on at least a half-time basis

    (A) I only

    (B) II only

    (C) both I and II

    (D) neither I nor II

89. Benny is single and has a modified adjusted gross income (AGI) of $64,000. He paid $8,000 in tuition for his daughter Melissa to attend Richmond University. What is the amount of Benny's Lifetime Learning Credit for the year?

    (A) $2,500

    (B) $1,800

    (C) $1,600

    (D) $0

90. "Student must be enrolled on a half-time basis at least" is a characteristic of the

    I. American Opportunity Credit

    II. Lifetime Learning Credit

    (A) I only

    (B) II only

    (C) both I and II

    (D) neither I nor II

91. In 2013, Joe and Jean Riley, married and filing jointly, paid a solar contractor $80,000 to have solar panels installed on their roof. Their state of residence gave them a $20,000 instant rebate toward the purchase. If their adjusted gross income (AGI) is $150,000, how much is their solar energy tax credit for the current year?

    (A) $18,000

    (B) $45,000

    (C) $12,000

    (D) $40,000

92. Which of the following personal tax credits are **refundable**?
   I. Lifetime Learning Credit
   II. Foreign Tax Credit

(A) I only
(B) II only
(C) both I and II
(D) neither I nor II

93. The Monahans incurred the following expenses during 2013 when they adopted a child from the Ukraine:

Child's medical expenses $13,000
Legal expenses $14,000
Agency fee $15,000

   Without regard to the limitation of the credit or adjusted gross income limit, what amount of the preceding expenses are qualifying expenses for the adoption credit?

(A) $29,000
(B) $28,000
(C) $42,000
(D) $27,000

94. Which of the following statements is CORRECT regarding tax credits?
   I. If a child is adopted who has "special needs," the taxpayer would be entitled to an additional adoption credit.
   II. In order to qualify for the retirement savings contribution credit, the taxpayer must NOT be a full-time student.

(A) I only
(B) II only
(C) both I and II
(D) neither I nor II

95. Foreign taxes paid by US taxpayers may be taken on Form 1040 as
   I. a credit against the taxpayer's US tax
   II. an adjustment to arrive at adjusted gross income (AGI)

(A) I only
(B) II only
(C) both I and II
(D) neither I nor II

96. Luke made the following expenditures this year. Which of the following qualifies as a deductible medical expense for tax purposes?
    I. vitamins for general health NOT prescribed by a physician
    II. health club dues
    III. transportation to a physician's office for required medical care
    (A) I and II only
    (B) I, II, and III
    (C) III only
    (D) II and III only

97. Scotti, an individual, paid the following expenses:

    Premiums on an insurance policy against loss of $1,000
    earnings due to sickness or accident
    Physical therapy after surgery $2,000
    Premium on an insurance policy that covers $600
    reimbursement for the cost of prescription drugs

    Scotti recovered $1,500 of the $2,000 that she paid for physical therapy through an insurance reimbursement from a group medical policy paid for by her employer. Disregarding the adjusted gross income percentage threshold, what amount could be claimed on Scotti's income tax return for medical expenses?
    (A) $2,100
    (B) $2,600
    (C) $600
    (D) $1,100

98. Which of the following is CORRECT regarding medical expenses?
    I. For taxpayers under age 65, medical expenses must exceed 10% of the taxpayer's adjusted gross income (AGI) in order to be deductible.
    II. For taxpayers 65 and older, medical expenses must exceed 7.5% of the taxpayer's AGI in order to be deductible.
    (A) I only
    (B) II only
    (C) both I and II
    (D) neither I nor II

99. Which of the following is CORRECT regarding medical expenses in 2014?
    I. If a taxpayer swipes her credit card for medical expenses in early December of 2013, she must pay the credit card company by December 31, 2013, in order to claim the deduction in 2013.
    II. Taxpayers may NOT deduct the medical costs paid on behalf of elderly parents unless the elderly parent qualifies as a dependent of the taxpayer.

    (A) I only
    (B) II only
    (C) both I and II
    (D) neither I nor II

100. Imhoff, a 67-year-old cash-basis taxpayer, had an adjusted gross income of $40,000 in Year 5. During the year, he incurred and paid the following medical expenses:

Medicines prescribed	$300
Health insurance premiums	$500
Dental surgery	$4,000

    Imhoff received $1,000 as reimbursement for a portion of the dental surgery. If Imhoff were to itemize his deductions, what is his allowable net medical expense deduction in Year 5?

    (A) $0
    (B) $800
    (C) $900
    (D) $1,200

101. Keith, a 35-year-old unmarried taxpayer with an adjusted gross income (AGI) of $70,000, incurred and paid the following unreimbursed medical expenses for the year:

Doctor bills resulting from a serious fall	$3,500
Eyeglasses	$500
Cosmetic surgery that was necessary to correct a birth defect considered a congenital deformity	$16,000

    For regular income tax purposes, what is Keith's MAXIMUM allowable medical expense deduction, after the applicable AGI threshold limitation, for the year?

    (A) $20,000
    (B) $4,000
    (C) $0
    (D) $13,000

102. O'Connor was a single taxpayer, age 72, with an income of $95,000 reported on his W-2 form for Year 3. He was not covered by an employer-sponsored retirement plan but contributed $5,000 to his own traditional IRA in June of Year 3. His medical costs for Year 3 include two surgeries: September Year 3, surgery to correct hearing loss, $10,000; November Year 3, hair transplant, $8,000. How much is O'Connor's medical deduction in Year 3?

(A) 0
(B) $1,000
(C) $2,250
(D) $3,250

103. Labuono was a cash-basis taxpayer whose records show the following:

Year 1 state income taxes withheld	$1,500
Year 1 city taxes withheld	$200
Year 1 state and local income taxes paid April 17, Year 2	$300

Labuono is entitled to claim what amount for taxes on his Year 1 Schedule A of Form 1040?

(A) $0
(B) $1,700
(C) $2,000
(D) $1,500

104. Singer was a cash-basis taxpayer whose records show the following:

Year 1 state and local income taxes withheld	$1,500
Year 1 state and local estimated income taxes paid December 30, Year 1	$400
State and local sales tax paid in Year 1	$900
Year 1 state and local income taxes paid April 17, Year 2	$100

Singer is entitled to claim what amount for taxes on his Year 1 Schedule A of Form 1040?

(A) $1,900
(B) $2,000
(C) $2,900
(D) $2,800

105. Which of the following is a Schedule A itemized deduction?
  I. real estate taxes paid on a vacation home that is not rented out
  II. personal property tax paid on an automobile

(A) I only
(B) II only
(C) both I and II
(D) neither I nor II

106. In Year 10, Ben pays real estate taxes and medical expenses out of his own funds for his elderly mother, Sabina, who has very little income and slightly more income than the exemption amount, but who would otherwise qualify as Ben's dependent. Sabina, however, is NOT Ben's dependent. Which of the following is deductible by Ben in Year 10?

    I. the medical expenses

   II. the real estate taxes

(A) I only

(B) II only

(C) both I and II

(D) neither I nor II

107. Simberg, a self-employed individual, paid the following taxes this year:

Personal property tax on value of car	$10
State income tax	$2,000
Real estate tax on land in the Netherlands	$900
State unincorporated business tax	$300
Real estate taxes on his mother's house	$400

    Simberg can claim what amount as an itemized deduction for taxes paid?

(A) $7,500

(B) $4,400

(C) $2,930

(D) $2,910

108. If a taxpayer owns four houses and does not rent out any, on how many of the homes can the taxpayer deduct the real estate taxes?

(A) 4

(B) 3

(C) 2

(D) 1

109. If a taxpayer owns three houses and does not rent out any, on how many of the homes can the taxpayer deduct the mortgage interest?

(A) 4

(B) 3

(C) 2

(D) 1

110. Which of the following interest payments are deductible on Form 1040 Schedule A itemized deductions?
    I. interest paid in connection with acquiring a taxpayer's main home or second home
    II. interest paid on a home equity loan where the loan proceeds are used to buy a car
    (A) I only
    (B) II only
    (C) both I and II
    (D) neither I nor II

111. On January 2, Year 5, Briscese paid $40,000 cash and obtained a $300,000 mortgage to purchase a home. In Year 8, he borrowed $10,000 secured by his home, and used the cash to add a new pool to the residence. That same year, he took out a $25,000 auto loan from GMAC Finance. Briscese paid credit card interest in Year 8 and also was assessed by the Internal Revenue Service (IRS) and had to pay interest in regard to late payment of federal income taxes from Year 7. The following information pertains to interest paid by Briscese in Year 8:

Mortgage interest	$15,000
Interest on home equity loan	$1,500
Auto loan interest	$500
Credit card interest	$2,000
Interest on late paid Year 7 federal income tax	$200

    How much interest is deductible in Year 8, prior to any itemized deduction limitations?
    (A) $16,500
    (B) $17,000
    (C) $19,000
    (D) $19,200

112. Fein earned $120,000 in investment income, $100,000 in noninterest investment expenses, and $50,000 in investment interest expense. What amount can Fein deduct on his current year's tax return for investment interest expenses?
    (A) $0
    (B) $20,000
    (C) $30,000
    (D) $50,000

113. Jerry and Elaine Newman made the following payments during the tax year:

Interest on bank loan (loan proceeds were used to purchase taxable US Treasury bonds)	$4,000
Interest on home mortgage	$5,000

During the year, income of $4,300 was received on savings bonds. What is the MAXIMUM amount of interest expense that the Newmans can utilize in calculating their current year's itemized deductions?

(A) $4,000
(B) $5,000
(C) $5,300
(D) $9,000

114. Kyle and Ann made the following payments during the tax year:

Interest on bank loan (loan proceeds were used to purchase taxable US Treasury bonds)	$4,000
Interest on home mortgage	$5,000
Points to obtain mortgage	$2,500
Interest on credit cards	$100

During the year, income of $4,300 was received on savings bonds. What is the MAXIMUM amount of interest expense that Kyle and Ann can utilize in calculating their current year's itemized deductions?

(A) $7,500
(B) $9,000
(C) $11,500
(D) $11,600

115. Donna and Jeff made the following payments during this taxable year:

Interest on home mortgage	$3,600
Late payment penalty for mortgage	$2,100
10% penalty on IRA distribution	$1,000
Personal property tax	$500

What amount of these expenses can Donna and Jeff utilize in calculating their current year's itemized deductions?

(A) $3,600
(B) $4,100
(C) $5,100
(D) $7,200

116. Pollack, who itemizes deductions, had an adjusted gross income (AGI) of $70,000 in Year 5. He made a contribution to his church in the amount of $4,000 and a cash contribution to a friend's son in the amount of $1,300. He made a donation of his used car to charity (fair market value evidenced by receipt received: $600). What is the MAXIMUM amount Pollack can claim as a deduction for charitable contributions in Year 5?

(A) $5,900
(B) $5,200
(C) $5,000
(D) $4,600

117. Foltz itemizes his deductions and had an adjusted gross income (AGI) of $60,000 in Year 5. That same year he donated $4,000 to his church. His church has a tradition: all members who donate over $3,000 in one single donation receive tickets to a ballgame. Foltz's tickets were worth $200 when he received them in Year 5. Also that same year, Foltz purchased jewelry at the church bazaar for $1,900. The fair value of the jewelry was $1,500 on the date of purchase. Foltz had no other charitable deductions or carryovers in Year 5. What is the MAXIMUM amount Foltz can claim as a deduction for charitable contributions in Year 5?

(A) $4,200
(B) $4,400
(C) $5,700
(D) $5,900

118. Naomi, a single taxpayer, had $50,000 in adjusted gross income (AGI) for Year 2. During the year, she contributed $18,000 to her church. She had a $10,000 charitable contribution carryover from her Year 1 church contribution. What is the MAXIMUM amount of properly substantiated charitable contributions that Naomi could claim as an itemized deduction for Year 2?

(A) $10,000
(B) $18,000
(C) $25,000
(D) $28,000

119. O'Keefe, an unmarried taxpayer, qualified to itemize Year 3 deductions. O'Keefe's Year 3 adjusted gross income (AGI) was $20,000. In Year 3, O'Keefe donated stock, valued at $3,000, to her church. O'Keefe had purchased the stock **seven months** earlier for $1,400. What was the MAXIMUM amount of the charitable contribution allowable as an itemized deduction on O'Keefe's Year 3 income tax return?

    (A) $0
    (B) $1,400
    (C) $1,600
    (D) $3,000

120. Berman, an unmarried taxpayer, qualified to itemize Year 3 deductions. Berman's Year 3 adjusted gross income (AGI) was $40,000. Berman donated art in Year 3, valued at $11,000, to a local art museum. Berman had purchased the artwork two years earlier for $2,000. What was the MAXIMUM amount of the charitable contribution allowable as an itemized deduction on Berman's Year 3 income tax return?

    (A) $2,000
    (B) $9,000
    (C) $11,000
    (D) $12,000

121. Brian, an unmarried taxpayer, qualified to itemize Year 3 deductions. His Year 3 adjusted gross income (AGI) was $20,000. He donated art in Year 3, valued at $15,000, to a local art museum. He had purchased the artwork two years earlier for $6,000. What was the MAXIMUM amount of the charitable contribution allowable as an itemized deduction on Brian's Year 3 income tax return?

    (A) $2,000
    (B) $6,000
    (C) $9,000
    (D) $15,000

122. Teri, an unmarried taxpayer, qualified to itemize Year 3 deductions. Teri's Year 3 adjusted gross income (AGI) was $25,000. Teri donated art in Year 3, valued at $11,000, to a local art museum. Teri had purchased the artwork two years earlier for $2,000. She also gave a cash contribution of $7,000 to her temple. What was the MAXIMUM amount of the charitable contribution allowable as an itemized deduction on Teri's Year 3 income tax return?

    (A) $7,500
    (B) $12,500
    (C) $14,500
    (D) $18,000

123. Harold had adjusted gross income (AGI) of $60,000 in the current year, donated artwork to a museum held for five years worth $20,000, and also donated $5,000 in cash to a recognized charity. How much is Harold's total deduction in the current year for charitable contributions?

    (A) $5,000
    (B) $18,000
    (C) $23,000
    (D) $25,000

124. Casualty losses are deductible if they exceed what percentage of an individual taxpayer's adjusted gross income (AGI)?

    (A) 2%
    (B) 7.5%
    (C) 10%
    (D) 30%

125. In Year 2, Boniguen's residence was totally destroyed by fire. The property had an adjusted basis and a fair market value of $130,000 before the fire. During Year 2, she received an insurance reimbursement of $120,000 for the destruction of her home. Boniguen's Year 2 adjusted gross income (AGI) was $70,000. Boniguen is entitled to claim what amount of the fire loss as an itemized deduction on her Year 2 tax return?

    (A) $2,900
    (B) $8,500
    (C) $8,600
    (D) $10,000

126. In Year 8, Grande's adjusted gross income (AGI) is $50,000, including $3,000 in gambling winnings. Grande has gambling losses totaling $7,000 in the current year and had gambling losses from last year that he could NOT deduct on his Year 7 tax return of $1,000. Grande can itemize the deductions. What amount of gambling losses is deductible by Grande in Year 8?

    (A) $0
    (B) $4,000
    (C) $3,000
    (D) $7,000

127. Which of the following unreimbursed employee expenses are considered miscellaneous itemized deductions subject to 2% of adjusted gross income (AGI)?
  I. small tools
  II. nurse's uniforms
  III. unreimbursed business car expense

(A) I and III only
(B) I, II, and III
(C) I and II only
(D) II and III only

128. Which of the following is included in the category of miscellaneous itemized deductions that are deductible only to the extent that the aggregate amount of such expenses exceeds 2% of the taxpayer's adjusted gross income (AGI)?

(A) funeral expenses
(B) union dues
(C) preparation of a will
(D) credit card interest expense

129. Which of the following are deductible subject to 2% of AGI?
  I. preparation of a will
  II. gambling losses
  III. safe-deposit box rental

(A) I, II, and III
(B) I and III only
(C) II and III only
(D) III only

130. Which item can be claimed as an itemized deduction subject to the 2% of AGI floor?
  I. tax return preparation fee
  II. foreign taxes paid
  III. penalty on early withdrawal of savings (from a non-retirement account)
  IV. penalty for late payment of mortgage

(A) I, II, and III only
(B) I, II, and IV only
(C) I only
(D) I and III only

131. Wes, 49 years of age, incurred the following expenses in the current year: $500 for the preparation of a personal income tax return, $100 for custodial fees on an IRA, $150 for professional publications, and $2,000 for union dues. His current year adjusted gross income (AGI) is $85,500 before consideration of a $5,500 IRA contribution. Wes, who is NOT covered by any retirement plan at work, NOT self-employed, and NOT married, itemizes deductions. What will Wes's deduction be for miscellaneous itemized deductions after any limitations in the current year?

    (A) $0
    (B) $850
    (C) $1,150
    (D) $2,250

132. Landi earned $6,000 in wages, incurred $1,000 in unreimbursed employee business expenses, paid $400 in interest on a student loan, contributed $100 to a charity, and received $10 in jury duty pay. What is Landi's adjusted gross income (AGI)?

    (A) $6,010
    (B) $4,600
    (C) $5,600
    (D) $5,610

133. During the current year, Pelosi was assessed a deficiency on a prior year's federal income tax return. As a result of this assessment, he was required to pay $2,750 determined as follows:

Additional federal income tax	$2,350
Late filing penalty	$150
Negligence penalty	$50
Interest on late paid taxes	$200

    What portion of the $2,750 paid by Pelosi would qualify as an itemized deduction on Schedule A?

    (A) $0
    (B) $200
    (C) $350
    (D) $2,750

134. For an individual taxpayer, which of the following is includable in income?

    I. damages awarded for breach of contract

    II. fees received for jury duty services

    III. workers' compensation monies received

    IV. forgiveness of debt

    (A) I, III, and IV only

    (B) I, II, and IV only

    (C) I and II only

    (D) I, II, and III only

135. The calculation of alternative minimum tax (AMT)

    (A) begins with taxable income, then adds back adjustments, and subtracts out preferences

    (B) begins with taxable income, then adds back adjustments and preferences, and subtracts an AMT exemption

    (C) does not involve the addition or subtraction of itemized deductions, except for charitable contributions and miscellaneous itemized deductions that exceed 2% of AGI

    (D) does not involve the addition or subtraction of municipal bond interest income from private activity bonds

136. In Year 4, Reynolds, a single taxpayer, had $70,000 in taxable income. Her itemized deductions were as follows:

State income tax	$3,500
Local income tax	$1,500
Home mortgage interest on loan to acquire a residence	$6,000
Miscellaneous deductions in excess of 2% of AGI	$2,000
Gambling losses	$1,000

    What amount should Reynolds report as alternative minimum taxable income before the alternative minimum tax (AMT) exemption?

    (A) $72,000

    (B) $75,000

    (C) $77,000

    (D) $83,000

137. Shirley, a single taxpayer, reported the following items in her regular federal income tax for Year 6:

Personal exemption	$3,100
Interest on a home equity loan, the proceeds of which were used for son's college expenses.	$1,200
Cash charitable contribution	$1,250
Net long-term capital gain	$700

What amount of the preceding items represents alternative minimum tax (AMT) adjustments for Shirley?

(A) $4,300
(B) $5,000
(C) $6,250
(D) $3,100

138. Betty has the following items:

Straight line depreciation	$600
Tax-exempt interest income on private activity bonds	$400
Personal exemption	$3,100
Itemized deduction for state income taxes	$1,500
Cash charitable contributions	$1,250
Net long-term capital gain	$1,000

What amount of tax preference items should be added back to Betty's regular income in determining alternative minimum tax (AMT)?

(A) $400
(B) $1,000
(C) $1,900
(D) $3,700

139. For an individual computing his or her alternative minimum tax (AMT), which of the following are considered AMT adjustments?
  I. standard deduction
  II. personal exemption
(A) I only
(B) II only
(C) both I and II
(D) neither I nor II

140. For an individual taxpayer, interest income from which of the following bond investments is considered a tax preference item for the computation of the alternative minimum tax (AMT)?

    I. private activity bonds issued by the State of Arizona

   II. general obligation bonds issued by the State of Florida

(A) I only

(B) II only

(C) both I and II

(D) neither I nor II

CHAPTER 2

Taxation of Entities

141. During March of Year 8, Steelman and Schechter contribute cash equally to form the Glenwood Partnership. Steelman and Schechter share profits and losses of 75% and 25%, respectively. The Glenwood Partnership's ordinary income was $60,000 in Year 8. A distribution of $5,000 was made to Steelman. No distribution was made to Schechter. What is Steelman's share of taxable income from the Glenwood Partnership in Year 8?

    (A) $5,000
    (B) $30,000
    (C) $45,000
    (D) $50,000

142. The Daltrey Partnership has sales revenues of $450,000, operating expenses of $350,000, dividend revenue of $8,000, charitable contributions of $6,000, and a $12,000 capital loss. Therefore, the partnership has a net income of $90,000. What is the Daltrey Partnership's ordinary income for tax purposes?

    (A) $90,000
    (B) $100,000
    (C) $102,000
    (D) $104,000

143. Which is CORRECT regarding partnership tax returns?
    I. A partnership tax return is due March 15th, or two and a half months after year end.
    II. Each partner in a partnership is given a Schedule K-1 to report all items of income and loss on their personal tax returns.

    (A) I only
    (B) II only
    (C) both I and II
    (D) neither I nor II

144. Which of the following is CORRECT regarding partnership tax returns?
- I. No tax is due with the filing of a partnership tax return even if the partnership earned profits in excess of $50,000.
- II. A partnership tax return is filed on Form 1065.

(A) I only
(B) II only
(C) both I and II
(D) neither I nor II

145. In a partnership, a fixed payment made to a partner for services provided to the partnership is known as a
- I. normal distribution
- II. guaranteed payment

(A) I only
(B) II only
(C) both I and II
(D) neither I nor II

146. A guaranteed payment by a partnership to a partner for services rendered may include an agreement to pay
- I. a salary of $15,000 monthly without regard to partnership income
- II. a 17% interest in partnership profits

(A) I only
(B) II only
(C) both I and II
(D) neither I nor II

147. Barry, CPA, is computing the ordinary income of a client's partnership. A deduction is allowed for
- I. contributions to recognized charities
- II. short-term capital losses
- III. guaranteed payments to partners

(A) I and III only
(B) II and III only
(C) III only
(D) I and II only

Use the following facts to answer Questions 148 and 149: Disston, a 25% partner in Witness Partnership, received a $40,000 guaranteed payment for deductible services rendered to the partnership. Guaranteed payments were not made to any other partner. Witness Partnership income consisted of

Net business income *before* guaranteed payments	$100,000
Net long-term capital gains	$10,000

148. How much is ordinary income of the Witness Partnership?

(A) $40,000
(B) $60,000
(C) $100,000
(D) $140,000

149. Disston should report how much income from the Witness Partnership on his Form 1040?

(A) $20,000
(B) $67,500
(C) $55,000
(D) $57,500

150. The partnership of Marty and Walter sustained an ordinary loss of $104,000. The partners share profits and losses equally. Walter had an adjusted basis of $36,000 on December 31, before consideration of the loss. Walter can deduct what amount on his individual tax return?

(A) ordinary loss of $36,000
(B) ordinary loss of $52,000
(C) ordinary loss of $36,000 and a capital loss of $16,000
(D) capital loss of $52,000

Use the following facts to answer Questions 151 and 152: Norris is a 25% partner in Clark Partnership. Norris's tax basis in Clark on January 1 was $20,000. At the end of the year, Norris received a cash distribution of $8,000 from Clark Partnership. The partnership reported ordinary income of $40,000.

151. Norris's basis in Clark on December 31 is

(A) $15,000
(B) $22,000
(C) $25,000
(D) $30,000

Assume the same fact as in Question 151 but that, in addition, Clark Partnership also received a municipal bond interest income of $12,000 during the year.

152. As a result of the municipal bond interest income addition, how much is Norris's basis in Clark Partnership on December 31?
    (A) $15,000
    (B) $23,000
    (C) $25,000
    (D) $30,000

153. Tax-exempt interest income received by a partnership will have what effect on the basis of each partner in the partnership?
    (A) increase the basis, thereby making the tax-exempt income taxable
    (B) decrease the basis
    (C) have no effect on the basis
    (D) increase the basis although the tax-exempt income is not taxable

154. Krin is a partner in Prager Partnership. Which of the following represents a **decrease** in Krin's partnership basis?
     I. distributions of cash from Prager Partnership to Krin
     II. loans made to the partnership from Krin
    (A) I only
    (B) II only
    (C) both I and II
    (D) neither I nor II

155. Cuciti and Lussier Partnership had a $10,000 increase in partnership liabilities. The partnership will treat that increase in which of the following ways?
    (A) increases each partner's basis in the partnership by $5,000
    (B) increases the partner's basis only if the liability is nonrecourse
    (C) increases each partner's basis in proportion to his or her ownership
    (D) does not change any partner's basis in the partnership, regardless of whether the liabilities are recourse or nonrecourse

156. Andy is a 50% partner in the London Ale House, a US partnership. Andy's tax basis on January 1, Year 2, was $5,000. London Ale House recorded the following:

Ordinary income	$20,000
Tax exempt income	$8,000
Taxable interest income	$4,000
Cash distribution	$1,000

What is Andy's tax basis in the London Ale House Partnership on December 31, Year 2?

(A) $21,000
(B) $20,000
(C) $10,000
(D) $12,000

Use the following facts to answer Questions 157 through 159: Mike and Luke formed Stratomatic Partnership as equal partners by contributing the following assets: Mike contributed cash of $45,000. Luke contributed land with a basis of $30,000 and a fair value of $53,000. The land was held by Luke as a capital asset.

157. Luke's initial basis in his partnership was

(A) $30,000
(B) $45,000
(C) $37,500
(D) $15,000

158. Assume that the land was subject to a $12,000 mortgage, which was assumed by Stratomatic Partnership. Because of the mortgage, Luke's initial basis would be

(A) $53,000
(B) $30,000
(C) $24,000
(D) $18,000

159. Assuming the $12,000 mortgage on the land is assumed by Stratomatic Partnership, what was Mike's initial basis in this partnership?

(A) $51,000
(B) $45,000
(C) $39,000
(D) $33,000

160. In 2012, Adimak, Singer, and Klein formed Olympic General Partnership by contributing the assets that follow:

Adimak contributed cash of $40,000 for a 50% partnership interest.
Singer contributed land with a $12,000 basis and a $21,000 fair market value (FMV) for a 20% partnership interest. The land was a capital asset to Singer, subject to a $5,000 mortgage, which was assumed by the partnership.
Klein contributed inventory with both a $24,000 basis and FMV for a 30% partnership interest.

    Klein's initial basis in Olympic Partnership is

(A) $25,000
(B) $24,000
(C) $25,500
(D) $29,000

161. The adjusted basis of Chris's interest in Dean Partnership was $240,000 immediately before receiving two distributions in complete liquidation of Dean Partnership. One distribution was a cash amount of $150,000. The other distribution was real estate with a fair market value of $110,000 and basis of $91,000. What is Chris's basis in the real estate?

(A) $0
(B) $150,000
(C) $91,000
(D) $90,000

162. In Year 1, Anita acquired a one-third interest in Party Basket Associates, a partnership. In Year 12, when Anita's entire interest in the partnership was liquidated, Anita's adjusted basis for her one-third interest was $52,000. Anita received cash of $50,000 in liquidation of her entire interest. What was Anita's recognized loss in Year 12 on the liquidation of her interest in Party Basket Associates?

(A) $2,000 long-term capital loss
(B) $0
(C) $2,000 short-term capital loss
(D) $2,000 ordinary loss

163. If a partnership is being liquidated, which of the following is CORRECT?

(A) A partner may report a gain but not a loss on liquidation.
(B) A partner may report a loss but not a gain on liquidation.
(C) The partnership may report a gain but not a loss on liquidation.
(D) The partnership may report neither a gain nor a loss on liquidation.

164. Carol received $30,000 in cash and an automobile with an adjusted basis and market value of $20,000 in a proportionate liquidating distribution from Zeta Partnership. Carol's basis in the partnership interest was $70,000 before the distribution. What is Carol's basis in the automobile received in the liquidation?

    (A) $70,000
    (B) $40,000
    (C) $30,000
    (D) $20,000

Use the following facts to answer Questions 165 and 166: Ryan's basis in Bruder Partnership was $70,000 at the time he received a nonliquidating distribution of partnership capital assets. These capital assets had an adjusted basis of $65,000 to the Bruder Partnership and a fair market value of $83,000.

165. Ryan would value the capital assets when received from the partnership at what amount?

    (A) $65,000
    (B) $70,000
    (C) $83,000
    (D) $0

166. Assuming Ryan's basis was $40,000 prior to the distribution of the capital assets, what would Ryan's basis be in the capital assets distributed to him?

    (A) $40,000
    (B) $65,000
    (C) $70,000
    (D) $83,000

167. Tyler's basis in Aero Partnership was $80,000 at the time he received a nonliquidating distribution of partnership capital assets. These capital assets had an adjusted basis of $75,000 to the partnership and a fair market value of $93,000. What is Tyler's recognized gain or loss on the distribution?

    (A) $18,000 ordinary income
    (B) $13,000 capital gain
    (C) $0
    (D) $5,000 capital gain

Use the following facts to answer Questions 168 and 169: Yimeny is a 50% partner is Victoria Partnership. Yimeny's basis in the partnership is $50,000 immediately before Yimeny received a current nonliquidating distribution of $20,000 cash and property with an adjusted basis to the partnership of $40,000 and a fair market value of $35,000.

168. What is the amount of taxable gain that Yimeny must report as a result of this distribution?
    (A) $0
    (B) $5,000
    (C) $10,000
    (D) $20,000

169. Based on the same facts, what is Yimeny's basis in the distributed property?
    (A) $0
    (B) $30,000
    (C) $35,000
    (D) $40,000

Use the following facts to answer Questions 170 and 171: Robyn is a partner in the Seena Partnership. Her basis in the partnership at the time she received a nonliquidating distribution of land was $5,000. The land had an adjusted basis of $6,000 and a fair value of $9,000 to Seena Partnership.

170. What is Robyn's basis in the land?
    (A) $9,000
    (B) $6,000
    (C) $5,000
    (D) $1,000

171. How much gain will Robyn recognize on the distribution?
    (A) $0
    (B) $1,000
    (C) $5,000
    (D) $9,000

172. Kelvin's basis in his KB Partnership interest is $50,000 at the beginning of the current year. During the current year Kelvin received a nonliquidating distribution of $25,000 cash plus land with an adjusted basis of $15,000 to KB and a fair market value of $20,000. Kelvin's basis in the land is
    (A) $10,000
    (B) $15,000
    (C) $20,000
    (D) $25,000

173. Lesnik, a 50% partner in Lesnik and Condon, received a distribution of $12,500 in the current year. The partnership's income for the year was $25,000. What is the character of the payment that Lesnik received?

    (A) partial liquidating distribution
    (B) full liquidating distribution
    (C) disproportionate distribution
    (D) current distribution

174. Which of the following are generally includable as income by a partner in a partnership?
    I. partnership distributions of cash that are NOT in excess of basis
    II. guaranteed payments to partners

    (A) I only
    (B) II only
    (C) both I and II
    (D) neither I nor II

175. Which of the following items does a partnership entity pay taxes on?
    I. ordinary business income
    II. municipal bond interest income

    (A) I only
    (B) II only
    (C) both I and II
    (D) neither I nor II

176. Which of the following cash distributions from partnership to partner would require a partner to recognize a gain for tax purposes?
    I. a liquidating distribution that is NOT in excess of basis
    II. a nonliquidating distribution that is NOT in excess of basis

    (A) I only
    (B) II only
    (C) both I and II
    (D) neither I nor II

177. On February 1, Year 4, Stefano Corp. was formed. Stefano Corp. met all eligibility requirements for S corporation status during the pre-election portion of the year. What is the last date that Stefano Corp. can file their S election and be recognized as an S corporation in Year 4?

    (A) December 31, Year 4
    (B) April 15th, Year 4
    (C) March 15th, Year 4
    (D) February 1, Year 4

178. Hanson Corp., a calendar-year corporation, began business in Year 2. Hanson made a valid S corporation election on August 25th, Year 5, with the unanimous consent of all shareholders. The eligibility requirements for S corporation status continued to be met throughout Year 5. On what date did Hanson's S corporation status become effective?

    (A) January 1, Year 5
    (B) January 1, Year 6
    (C) August 25, Year 5
    (D) August 25, Year 6

179. Capell Corporation, a calendar-year S corporation, has two equal shareholders. For the year ended December 31, Year 1, Capell Corporation had income of $90,000, which included $60,000 from operations, $20,000 from investment interest income, and $10,000 from municipal bond interest income. There were no other transactions that year. Basis in the stock of Capell Corporation for each shareholder will increase by

    (A) $90,000
    (B) $45,000
    (C) $40,000
    (D) $15,000

180. If an S corporation receives municipal bond interest income of $50,000 and has two equal shareholders,

    (A) each shareholder would increase their basis by $25,000 and report $25,000 each in taxable income
    (B) since interest income is municipal, the S corporation rather than the individual shareholders would recognize all the tax on the interest
    (C) each shareholder will report a basis decrease of $25,000
    (D) each shareholder will report a basis increase of $25,000

181. Morgan is the sole shareholder of Corinthos, Inc., an S corporation. Morgan's adjusted basis in Corinthos, Inc., stock is $60,000 at the beginning of the year. During the year, Corinthos, Inc., reports the following income items:

Ordinary income	$30,000
Tax-exempt income	$5,000
Capital gains	$10,000

    In addition, Corinthos makes a nontaxable distribution to Morgan of $20,000 cash during the year. What is Morgan's adjusted basis in the Corinthos stock at the end of the year?

    (A) $105,000
    (B) $125,000
    (C) $80,000
    (D) $85,000

182. Crellin is considering forming an S corporation. Which of the following conditions will prevent a corporation from qualifying as an S corporation?

    (A) The corporation has one class of stock with different voting rights.
    (B) The corporation has 75 shareholders.
    (C) The corporation was formed before 1991.
    (D) The corporation has both common and preferred stock.

183. Bagel Bazaar, Inc., has been an S corporation since inception. In each of Year 1, Year 2, and Year 3, Bagel Bazaar, Inc., made distributions in excess of each shareholder's basis. Which of the following statements is CORRECT concerning these three years?

    (A) In Year 1 and Year 2 only, the excess distributions are taxed as a capital gain.
    (B) In Year 1 only, the excess distributions are tax free.
    (C) In Year 3 only, the excess distributions are taxed as a capital gain.
    (D) In all three years, the excess distributions are taxed as capital gains.

Use the following facts to answer Questions 184 and 185: Wilson owns 100% of an S corporation and materially participates in its operations. The stock's basis at the beginning of Year 7 is $5,000. During Year 7, the S corporation makes a distribution of $3,500 and passes through a loss from operations of $2,000 for the year.

184. How much of the $3,500 distribution will be taxable to Wilson in Year 7?

    (A) $3,500
    (B) $2,000
    (C) $1,500
    (D) $0

185. How much loss can Wilson deduct on Wilson's personal tax return in Year 7?

    (A) $0
    (B) $1,500
    (C) $2,000
    (D) $5,500

186. Wolfson, Inc., an S corporation, reported in Year 1 $50,000 of income from operations and a $20,000 long-term capital gain for a total profit of $70,000. The corporation has 10 equal shareholders, and each one received a cash distribution during the year of $4,000. Wolfson shareholders report what with respect to ownership of the S corporation for tax purposes?

    (A) $5,000 ordinary income and $2,000 long-term capital gain
    (B) $4,000 ordinary income
    (C) $5,000 ordinary income
    (D) $4,000 ordinary income and $7,000 long-term capital gain

187. An S corporation is NOT permitted to take a deduction for
   I. charitable contributions
   II. compensation of officers
   III. short-term capital losses

   (A) I and II only
   (B) III only
   (C) I and III only
   (D) II and III only

188. Dauber, Inc., a calendar-year S corporation, reported the following items of income and expense in the current year:

Revenue	$44,000
Operating expenses	$20,000
Long-term capital loss	$6,000
Charitable contributions	$1,000

   What is the amount of Dauber's ordinary income?

   (A) $17,000
   (B) $18,000
   (C) $24,000
   (D) $28,000

189. Party Basket Corp. is a calendar-year S corporation. If Party Basket Corp. does not request an automatic six-month extension of time to file its income tax return, the return is due by

   (A) January 31
   (B) April 15
   (C) June 30
   (D) March 15

190. What are the requirements to form an S corporation?
   I. must have at least two shareholders
   II. must adopt a calendar year (December 31) as its year end

   (A) I only
   (B) II only
   (C) both I and II
   (D) neither I nor II

191. For the taxable year ended December 31, Rothstein, Inc., an S corporation, had net income per books of $80,000, which included $62,000 from operations and a $18,000 net long-term capital gain. During the year, $9,000 was distributed to Rothstein's three equal stockholders, all of whom are on a calendar-year basis. On what amounts should Rothstein, Inc., compute its income tax and capital gain taxes?

(A) income tax of $31,500, capital gain tax of $0
(B) income tax of $0, capital gain tax of $0
(C) income tax of $22,500, capital gain tax of $0
(D) income tax of $0, capital gain tax of $9,000

192. For tax purposes, which of the following entities are considered pass-through entities?
   I. S corporation
  II. partnerships

(A) I only
(B) II only
(C) both I and II
(D) neither I nor II

193. With regard to S corporations, unanimous consent of all shareholders is required to
   I. elect S corporation status
  II. voluntarily revoke the S corporation election

(A) I only
(B) II only
(C) both I and II
(D) neither I nor II

194. Krepps owns 100% of RK Incorporated, which is an S corporation for income tax purposes. Krepps's basis in the company at the beginning of the year is $60,000. During the year the company had ordinary income of $39,500, municipal bond interest income of $10,000, and short-term capital losses of $17,000. Krepps also received a dividend distribution of $20,000. What is his basis in this corporation at year end?

(A) $92,500
(B) $82,500
(C) $72,500
(D) $62,500

195. Owen incorporated a sole proprietorship by exchanging all the proprietorship's assets for the stock of Millstone Corporation, a new corporation. To qualify for tax-free incorporation, Owen must be in control of Millstone Corporation immediately after the exchange. What percentage of Millstone Corporation's stock must he own to qualify as control for this purpose?

    (A) 50%
    (B) 51%
    (C) 100%
    (D) 80%

196. In the current year, Hametz decides to form a corporation. Cash of $120,000 is transferred to the business along with equipment having a tax basis of $100,000 but a fair value of $165,000. Hametz received all of the stock of this new corporation. What is his tax basis in this new business, and what tax basis does the new business use for this equipment?

    (A) $220,000 and $100,000
    (B) $270,000 and $165,000
    (C) $220,000 and $165,000
    (D) $270,000 and $100,000

Use the following facts to answer Questions 197 through 202: Laura and Micki organized the Minder Binder Corporation, which issued voting common stock with a fair market value (FMV) of $120,000. Laura transferred a building with a basis of $40,000 and a FMV of $82,000 for 60% of the stock. Micki contributed equipment with a basis of $45,000 and a FMV of $48,000 in exchange for 40% of the stock.

197. How much is Laura's basis in Minder Binder Corporation stock?

    (A) $35,000
    (B) $40,000
    (C) $30,000
    (D) $50,000

198. Now assume that Laura's building had a mortgage of $10,000, and Minder Binder Corporation assumed the $10,000 mortgage. What is Laura's basis in Minder Binder Corporation stock?

    (A) $35,000
    (B) $40,000
    (C) $30,000
    (D) $50,000

199. Assume the same fact as Question 198 and that the Minder Binder Corporation assumed the $10,000 mortgage remaining on Laura's building. What gain did Laura recognize on the exchange?

(A) $0
(B) $10,000
(C) $42,000
(D) $52,000

200. Assume the same fact regarding the assumption of the $10,000 mortgage noted in Questions 198 and 199, what was the newly formed corporation's basis in the building transferred by Laura?

(A) $30,000
(B) $40,000
(C) $72,000
(D) $82,000

201. Assume that Laura's building had a mortgage of $10,000 and the mortgage is being assumed by Minder Binder Corporation. What is Micki's basis in her stock?

(A) $45,000
(B) $48,000
(C) $50,000
(D) $53,000

202. How much is the newly formed corporation's basis in the equipment transferred by Micki?

(A) $45,000
(B) $48,000
(C) $60,000
(D) none of the above

Use the following facts to answer Questions 203 and 204: During Year 5, Adrian, Barry, and Corey formed David Corp. Pursuant to the incorporation agreement, Adrian transfers property with a basis of $30,000 and a fair market value of $45,000 for 40% of David Corp. stock. Barry transfers cash of $35,000 in exchange for 30% of the stock, and Corey performed legal services valued at $25,000 (exchanged no property) and received 30% of the stock.

203. How much does David Corp. value the property received from Adrian?

(A) $0
(B) $30,000
(C) $45,000
(D) $65,000

204. Adrian would recognize a gain of
(A) $0
(B) $15,000
(C) $10,000
(D) $5,000

Use the following facts to answer Questions 205 and 206: Parker, Broussard, and Monti organized Kenpo Corp. Parker received 10% of the capital stock in payment for the organizational services that he rendered for the benefit of the newly formed corporation. Parker did not contribute property and was not receiving payment for the services. Broussard and Monti contributed property as follows:

Broussard contributed assets with a basis of $5,000 and a fair market value (FMV) of $20,000 for 20% of the stock.

Monti contributed assets with a basis of $60,000 and FMV of $70,000 for 70% of the stock.

205. What amount of gain did Monti recognize from this transaction?
(A) $0
(B) $5,000
(C) $10,000
(D) $3,333

206. How much does Kenpo Corp. value the asset contributed by Broussard?
(A) $65,000
(B) $20,000
(C) $5,000
(D) $0

Use the following facts to answer Questions 207 and 208: The Ashbrook Corporation is an accrual-based taxpayer. The company generates credit revenues in Year 1 of $400,000 and estimates that 4%, or $16,000, of these accounts will prove to be uncollectible. In Year 2, $23,000 of these accounts turn out to be uncollectible and are written off the company's records.

207. For tax purposes, how much is bad debt expense for Year 1?
(A) $16,000
(B) $0
(C) $23,000
(D) $7,000

208. For tax purposes, how much is bad debt expense for Year 2?

(A) $16,000
(B) $0
(C) $23,000
(D) $7,000

209. Fascination Corp. is a small fashion-consulting firm. The company operates as a cash-basis taxpayer. In January of the current year, the firm did work for a client, Twin Spin, Inc., and accepted a note for $40,000 plus interest at a 10% annual rate in lieu of immediate payment. After exactly one month, Twin Spin, Inc., went bankrupt and the note was judged to be worthless. What is the amount of the bad debt expense deduction that Fascination Corp. is entitled to report?

(A) $0
(B) $40,000
(C) $42,000
(D) $44,000

Use the following facts to answer Questions 210 and 211: In October of Year 1, Solar Express Corporation sells 100,000 solar panels with a warranty to fix any that break. Based on Year 1 sales, the company expects 1,500 to break in the first two years and cost $100 each to fix. None break in Year 1. During Year 2, 800 panels break and cost $120 each to fix.

210. What amount can Solar Express deduct for tax purposes for warranty expenses in Year 1?

(A) $150,000
(B) $96,000
(C) $0
(D) $12,000

211. What amount can Solar Express deduct for tax purposes for warranty expenses in Year 2?

(A) $150,000
(B) $96,000
(C) $0
(D) $12,000

212. Life insurance premiums paid by a corporation on behalf of its employees
    I. are deductible for financial reporting purposes to arrive at book income, regardless of who the beneficiary of the policy is
    II. are NOT deductible for tax purposes if the corporation pays the premiums on behalf of employees and the employees can name the beneficiary of the policy

    (A) I only
    (B) II only
    (C) both I and II
    (D) neither I nor II

213. Marlboro Freedom, Inc., had book income of $200,000. $5,000 was deducted to arrive at book income to pay for life insurance to cover the lives of key employees. The face amount of the policy, $500,000, gets paid to the family members of the employees. No employees died during the year. In addition, the company incurred warranty costs of $10,000. An estimated $4,000 was expensed for warranty costs on the financial statements. How much is taxable income for this year?

    (A) $194,000
    (B) $199,000
    (C) $203,000
    (D) $205,000

214. Spence Corporation has sales revenues of $400,000, normal and necessary operating expenses of $300,000, short-term capital gain of $7,000, and a long-term capital loss of $10,000. What is the amount of capital loss that can be deducted by Spence Corporation for this year?

    (A) $0
    (B) $3,000
    (C) $7,000
    (D) $10,000

215. Blue Chip Industries is a C corporation. How does Blue Chip, Inc., treat its net capital losses for federal income tax purposes?

    (A) deducted from the corporation's ordinary income only to the extent of $3,000 per year
    (B) carried back 3 years and carried forward 5 years
    (C) deductible in full from the corporation's ordinary income
    (D) carried forward 15 years

216. Drake Corporation, a calendar-year C (regular) corporation, had the following capital gains and capital losses during Year 5:

Short-term capital gain	$7,500
Short-term capital loss	5,000
Long-term capital gain	2,500
Long-term capital loss	2,500

   In addition, Drake realized taxable income of $56,000 from its regular business operations for calendar Year 5. What is Drake Corporation's total taxable income for Year 5?

(A) $56,000
(B) $62,000
(C) $60,500
(D) $58,500

217. Linden Corporation, a calendar-year C (regular) corporation, realized taxable income of $66,000 from its regular business operations for calendar Year 5. In addition, the corporation had the following capital gains and capital losses during Year 5:

Short-term capital gain	$5,000
Short-term capital loss	(4,000)
Long-term capital gain	1,000
Long-term capital loss	(9,000)

   With $66,000 in ordinary income before capital gains and losses, what is Linden Corporation's taxable income for Year 5?

(A) $59,000
(B) $66,000
(C) $72,000
(D) $53,000

218. For the year ended December 31, Year 8, Breitbart Corp. had book net income of $227,000. Included in the computation of net income were the following items:

Net long-term capital loss	$5,000
Utility expense	$4,000
Key-person life insurance premiums (company is beneficiary)	$3,000

   Breitbart Corp.'s Year 8 taxable income was

(A) $227,000
(B) $230,000
(C) $232,000
(D) $235,000

219. In Year 4, Adams Corporation, an accrual-basis, calendar-year C corporation, reported book income of $480,000. Included in that amount were

$5,000	rent expense
$50,000	municipal bond interest income
$170,000	federal income tax expense
$2,000	interest expense on the debt incurred to carry the municipal bonds

    How much is Adams Corporation's taxable income as reconciled on Schedule M-1 of Form 1120, US corporation income tax return?

    (A) $607,000
    (B) $600,000
    (C) $602,000
    (D) $650,000

220. On December 31, Year 5, Hampton Corporation reported book income (financial accounting) of $240,000 for the year. Included in that amount was $50,000 for meals and entertainment expense, $11,000 for advertising expense, and $40,000 for federal income tax expense. In Hampton Corporation's Schedule M-1 of Form 1120, which reconciles book income and taxable income, what amount should Hampton Corporation report as taxable income?

    (A) $240,000
    (B) $265,000
    (C) $280,000
    (D) $305,000

221. Tailgate Studios, Inc., is a C corporation and has the two expense items listed. Which of the two items will be reported on Schedule M-1 of Tailgate's corporation income tax return in order to reconcile book income to taxable income?

    I. interest incurred on a loan to carry municipal bonds
    II. provision for federal income tax

    (A) I only
    (B) II only
    (C) both I and II
    (D) neither I nor II

222. Which of the following items are reportable on a corporation's Schedule M-1 book to taxable income reconciliation?

   I. interest expense on a loan to carry US savings bonds

  II. state income tax provision

  (A) I only

  (B) II only

  (C) both I and II

  (D) neither I nor II

223. Which of the following costs incurred to organize a corporation are considered amortizable organizational expenditures?

  (A) professional fees to issue the corporate stock

  (B) printing costs to issue the corporate stock

  (C) legal fees for drafting the corporate charter

  (D) commissions paid by the corporation to an underwriter

224. Mobile Tech was organized and began doing business on July 1 of Year 6. Amounts that Mobile Tech paid for organizational costs included $3,000 to Barry Surett & Co. CPAs for services the firm provided to assess which business structure was most advantageous for Mobile Tech and then to file various documents needed to incorporate Mobile Tech. Mobile Tech also paid the State of New Jersey $7,500 in fees to incorporate. In additions Mobile Tech paid the law firm of Gerald S. Hymanson $3,500 to draft the corporate charter. Other organization costs in Year 6 included $2,000 to print the stock certificates and $5,000 to sell the initial shares. For tax purposes, Mobile Tech would like to take as much of a deduction for these costs as possible. How much can Mobile Tech deduct in Year 6 for organizational expenditures?

  (A) $5,300

  (B) $5,000

  (C) $5,534

  (D) $14,000

225. A company is filing its Year 2 income tax return. The company bought another company in Year 1, and $300,000 of the purchase price was allocated to goodwill. For financial reporting (book) purposes, that amount was not amortized nor viewed as impaired. Which of the following is CORRECT?
    I. The goodwill should be recorded as a capital asset and amortized over 15 years for tax purposes.
    II. For Year 2, a deduction of $20,000 should be reported on the company's corporate tax return.
    (A) I only
    (B) II only
    (C) both I and II
    (D) neither I nor II

226. Which of the following assets are amortized for tax purposes over a 15-year life (180 months)?
    I. trademarks and trade names that are purchased
    II. covenants NOT to compete
    III. goodwill
    (A) I and II only
    (B) II and III only
    (C) I and III only
    (D) I, II, and III

227. Davis owns land that is operated as a parking lot. A shed was erected on the lot for the purpose of conducting business with customers. How should the land and shed be classified?
    (A) land and shed both as capital assets
    (B) land as a capital asset, shed as a Section 1231 asset
    (C) shed as a capital asset, land as a Section 1231 asset
    (D) land and shed both as Section 1231 assets

228. For a corporation, which of the following is a capital asset?
    (A) a machine used in the business
    (B) land used in the business
    (C) goodwill
    (D) treasury stock

229. Which of the following is CORRECT?
  I. Since land does not depreciate, land cannot be a Section 1231 asset.
  II. For a corporation, capital assets are assets used in the production of ordinary income.

  (A) I only
  (B) II only
  (C) both I and II
  (D) neither I nor II

230. Regina Corp. sells treasury stock to an unrelated broker in Year 9 and receives proceeds of $50,000. The treasury stock cost Regina Corp. $30,000 to acquire. The total par value of the treasury shares sold is $9,000. What amount of capital gain should Regina Corp. recognize on the sale of the treasury stock in Year 9?

  (A) $0
  (B) $8,000
  (C) $20,000
  (D) $30,500

231. On May 1, Year 1, Laughlin, Inc., purchased and placed into service an office building costing $304,000, including $70,000 for the land. What was Laughlin, Inc.'s Modified Accelerated Cost Recovery System (MACRS) depreciation deduction for Year 1?

  (A) $3,750
  (B) $6,000
  (C) $4,000
  (D) $2,250

232. On August 1, Year 1, Bachman, Inc., purchased and placed into service an apartment building costing $225,000, including $25,000 for the land. What was Bachman, Inc.'s Modified Accelerated Cost Recovery System (MACRS) deduction for Year 2?

  (A) $7,273
  (B) $8,182
  (C) $2,727
  (D) $5,128

Use the following facts to answer Questions 233 through 235: On February 1, Year 1, Griffin Corporation buys an asset considered a "light truck" for tax purposes on that has a cost of $40,000 and an expected salvage value of $6,000. Griffin Corporation estimates that the truck will last eight years.

233. What method of depreciation should be used for tax purposes according to the Modified Accelerated Cost Recovery System?
     (A) double declining balance over eight years
     (B) double declining balance over five years with half year taken in Year 1
     (C) straight line method over eight years
     (D) straight line method over five years with depreciation for Year 1 starting on February 15th of Year 1

234. What amount of depreciation should be recognized by Griffin Corporation for Year 2 based on the Modified Accelerated Cost Recovery System (MACRS)?
     (A) $16,000
     (B) $12,800
     (C) $8,000
     (D) $6,800

235. What amount of depreciation should be recognized for Year 3 based on the Modified Accelerated Cost Recovery System?
     (A) $7,680
     (B) $12,800
     (C) $19,200
     (D) $8,000

236. The Carson Company bought a piece of equipment on September 4 of the current year. The company's tax return is filed on a calendar-year basis. The Modified Accelerated Cost Recovery System (MACRS) is used to determine depreciation for income tax purposes. Which of the following is TRUE as to the amount of depreciation that can be recognized in this initial year?
     (A) Carson should take depreciation for four-twelfths of the year.
     (B) Carson should take a full year of depreciation.
     (C) Carson can take depreciation for three-twelfths of the year.
     (D) Carson can take depreciation for one-half of the year.

237. The allowable depreciation deduction taken in Year 3 for a commercial building that was placed in service in Year 1

(A) is calculated based on a 27.5-year straight line
(B) depends upon the amount of depreciation taken in Year 1
(C) depends upon what month in Year 1 the building was originally purchased
(D) is calculated based on a 39-year straight line

238. Which of the following statements is NOT true in connection with Section 179 asset acquisitions and the immediate expense thereof?

(A) The cost spent for off-the-shelf computer software qualifies for Section 179 expense as long as the software has a useful life of more than one year.
(B) There is a maximum amount that can be taken as a Section 179 expense.
(C) If the company buys a large quantity of qualifying Section 179 property, the immediate expense is reduced, eventually to zero.
(D) Buildings are qualifying property for Section 179 expense, but land is not.

239. A taxpayer purchased 14 acres of land for $30,000 and placed in service other tangible business property that cost $100,000 in the current year. Disregarding business income limitations and assuming that the annual Section 179 expense limit is $108,000, what is the MAXIMUM amount of expense associated with Section 179 property that the taxpayer can claim this year?

(A) $130,000
(B) $108,000
(C) $100,000
(D) $30,000

240. For the year ended December 31, Year 1, Bentley, Inc., had gross business income of $160,000 and dividend income of $100,000 from unaffiliated domestic corporations that are AT LEAST 20% owned. Business operating expenses for Year 1 amounted to $170,000. How much is Bentley's dividends received deduction (DRD) for Year 1?

(A) $0
(B) $72,000
(C) $80,000
(D) $90,000

241. Jandersit Corporation, in the current year, had sales revenues of $380,000 and normal and necessary operating expenses of $390,000. In addition, the company received a $50,000 cash dividend from another domestic corporation, a company in which it held a 17% ownership. What is Jandersit Corporation's taxable income?

(A) $0
(B) $5,000
(C) $8,000
(D) $12,000

242. Belfer Corporation, a calendar-year C corporation, contributed $80,000 to a qualified charitable organization. Belfer had taxable income of $820,000 before the deduction for current year charitable contributions and after a $40,000 dividends received deduction (DRD). Belfer Corporation also had carryover charitable contributions of $10,000 from the prior year. What amount can Belfer Corporation deduct as charitable contributions?

(A) $90,000
(B) $86,000
(C) $82,000
(D) $80,000

243. Markware Corporation contributed $40,000 to a qualified charitable organization in the current year. Markware Corporation's taxable income before the deduction for charitable contributions was $410,000. Included in that amount was a $20,000 dividends receivable deduction (DRD). Markware Corporation also had carryover charitable contributions of $5,000 from the prior year. What amount can Markware Corporation deduct as charitable contributions in the current year?

(A) $40,000
(B) $41,000
(C) $43,000
(D) $45,000

244. Christie Corporation, an accrual-basis, calendar-year corporation, was organized on January 2, Year 4. The following information pertains:

Taxable income before charitable contributions for the year ended December 31, Year 4	$419,000
Gifts in Year 4 directly to families in need following hurricane disaster	$20,000
Contributions to recognized charities after hurricane disaster	$10,000
Board of directors' authorized contribution to a qualified charity (authorized December 1, Year 4, made February 1, Year 5)	$30,000

What is the MAXIMUM allowable deduction that Christie Corporation may take as a charitable contribution on its tax return for the year ended December 31, Year 4?

(A) $30,000
(B) $40,000
(C) $41,900
(D) $60,000

245. Czonka, Inc., is preparing its consolidated tax return. Which of the following statements is CORRECT?
  I. The common parent must directly own 51% or more of the total voting power of all corporations included in the consolidated return.
  II. Operating losses of one group member may be used to offset operating profits of the other members included in the consolidated return.

(A) I only
(B) II only
(C) both I and II
(D) neither I nor II

246. The accumulated earnings tax can be avoided by
  I. paying dividends late where the calendar-year corporation pays the dividend by March 15th of the following year
  II. consent dividends where the taxpayer (stockholder) agrees to include the dividend on his or her Form 1040 even though he or she never received the money
  III. demonstrating that the reasonable needs of the business include retention of all or part of the earnings

(A) I and II only
(B) II and III only
(C) I and III only
(D) I, II, and III

247. The personal holding company tax can be imposed

(A) regardless of the number of shareholders in a corporation

(B) on companies that make distributions in excess of accumulated earnings

(C) on corporations that have paid the accumulated earnings tax in the same year

(D) on small C corporations that do not pay sufficient dividends

248. An accumulated earnings tax can be imposed

(A) regardless of the number of shareholders in a corporation

(B) on companies that make distributions in excess of accumulated earnings

(C) on personal holding companies

(D) on both partnerships and corporations

249. For a corporation, removing which of the following benefits would be considered an alternative minimum tax (AMT) adjustment?

   I. installment sales method

  II. completed contract method

(A) I only

(B) II only

(C) both I and II

(D) neither I nor II

250. For a corporation, which of the following represents an alternative minimum tax (AMT) preference item?

(A) municipal bond interest income from private activity bonds

(B) the 80% dividends received deduction

(C) the 70% dividends received deduction

(D) all of the above

251. For a corporation that invests in municipal bonds, which of the following is TRUE regarding the alternative minimum tax (AMT) and municipal bond interest income?

  I. Interest income from general obligation municipal bonds is considered a tax preference item for a corporation when computing their alternative minimum taxable income prior to the adjusted current earnings (ACE) adjustment.

  II. Interest income from private activity municipal bonds is considered a tax preference item for a corporation when computing their alternative minimum taxable income prior to the ACE adjustment.

  (A) I only
  (B) II only
  (C) both I and II
  (D) neither I nor II

252. In computing the alternative minimum tax (AMT) for a corporation, which of the following is TRUE?

  (A) If the corporation has any tax-exempt private activity bond interest, taxable income will be increased in arriving at the alternative minimum taxable income.
  (B) If the corporation has any municipal bond interest, that interest must be added to taxable income in arriving at the alternative minimum taxable income.
  (C) All corporations are allowed to subtract an exemption.
  (D) If the corporation has any life insurance proceeds, taxable income will be increased by that amount in arriving at the alternative minimum taxable income.

253. Which of the following is part of the calculation of the adjusted current earnings (ACE) adjustment used to calculate a corporation's alternative minimum tax (AMT)?

  I. interest income from general obligation municipal bonds
  II. life insurance proceeds received by the corporation
  III. the 70% dividends received deduction

  (A) I and III only
  (B) I, II, and III
  (C) I and II only
  (D) II and III only

254. The number of shareholders in a corporation is a factor in determining whether a corporation is subject to which of the following?
    I.   the alternative minimum tax (AMT)
    II. the accumulated earnings tax
    III. the personal holding company tax
    (A) I, II, and III
    (B) II and III only
    (C) I and III only
    (D) III only

255. Which of the following is subject to the alternative minimum tax (AMT) adjusted current earnings (ACE) adjustment?
    I.   C corporations
    II. S corporations
    III. individuals
    IV. partnerships
    (A) I and III only
    (B) I and II only
    (C) I and IV only
    (D) I only

Use the following facts to answer Questions 256 and 257: Lemoi, a single individual, had a $60,000 investment in qualified Section 1244 stock that became worthless in Year 7. He had no other capital gains or losses in Year 7.

256. How much total loss can Lemoi deduct in Year 7?
    (A) $50,000
    (B) $53,000
    (C) $60,000
    (D) $3,000

257. Assuming Lemoi were married filing jointly, how much total loss could he deduct in Year 7?
    (A) $50,000
    (B) $53,000
    (C) $60,000
    (D) $3,000

Use the following facts to answer Questions 258, 259, and 260: Aquilino, married filing jointly, sells 2,000 shares of his qualified Section 1244 small business stock for a loss of $110,000 in Year 5 and sells his remaining 600 shares for a loss of $35,000 in Year 6. Aquilino had no other capital gains or losses in either year.

258. How much total loss can Aquilino deduct in Year 5?

   (A) $100,000
   (B) $103,000
   (C) $50,000
   (D) $53,000

259. How much total loss can Aquilino deduct in Year 6?

   (A) $100,000
   (B) $35,000
   (C) $3,000
   (D) $38,000

260. How much total loss can Aquilino deduct in Year 7?

   (A) $0
   (B) $30,000
   (C) $100,000
   (D) $3,000

261. Junior, a single individual, inherited Rainbow Corp. common stock from his parents. Rainbow is a qualified small business corporation under code Section 1244. The stock cost Junior's parents $120,000 and had a fair market value of $225,000 at the parents' date of death. During the year, Rainbow Corp. declared bankruptcy and Junior was informed that the stock was worthless. What amount may Junior deduct as an **ordinary loss** in the current year?

   (A) $0
   (B) $3,000
   (C) $120,000
   (D) $225,000

262. Which of the following entities may operate on a fiscal year rather than a calendar year?
    I. C corporation
    II. S corporation
    III. partnership
    (A) I, II, and III
    (B) I and II only
    (C) I and III only
    (D) II and III only

263. An income tax return for a trust is filed on Form
    (A) 990
    (B) 1040
    (C) 1041
    (D) 706

264. The party who creates the trust and funds the trust with assets is known as the
    (A) trustee
    (B) beneficiary
    (C) grantor
    (D) remainderman

265. If NOT expressly granted, which of the following implied powers would a trustee have?
    I. power to sell trust property
    II. power to borrow from the trust
    III. power to pay trust expenses
    (A) I and III only
    (B) I and II only
    (C) II and III only
    (D) I, II, and III

266. Grace is the creator of an inter vivos trust naming Rochelle as beneficiary. Which of the following would generally be allocated to trust principal rather than to Rochelle?
    I. cash dividend
    II. stock dividend
    (A) I only
    (B) II only
    (C) both I and II
    (D) neither I nor II

267. Aragona transferred assets into a trust under which Cain is entitled to receive the income for life. After Cain's death, the remaining assets are to be given to Clark. In Year 1, the trust received rent of $1,000, stock dividends of $6,000, interest on certificates of deposit of $3,000, municipal bond interest of $4,000, and proceeds of $7,000 from the sale of bonds. Both Cain and Clark are still alive. What amount of the Year 1 receipts should be allocated to the trust principal?

(A) $15,000
(B) $8,000
(C) $13,000
(D) $7,000

268. Haley is the grantor of a trust over which Haley has retained a discretionary power to receive income. Blanche, Haley's child, receives all taxable income from the trust, unless Haley exercises the discretionary power. To whom is the income earned by the trust taxable?

(A) to the trust to the extent it remains in the trust
(B) to Haley because she has retained a discretionary power
(C) to Blanche as the beneficiary of the trust
(D) to Blanche and Haley in proportion to the distributions paid to them from the trust

269. Generally, which of the following parties would have the first priority to receive the estate of a person who dies without a will?

(A) the state
(B) a parent of the deceased
(C) a spouse of the deceased
(D) a child of the deceased

270. Which of the following is CORRECT regarding a trust?
  I. a trust that begins upon the creator's death is known as a testamentary trust
  II. assets held in trust are known as trust corpus or trust res

(A) I only
(B) II only
(C) both I and II
(D) neither I nor II

271. Which of the following types of trusts are allowed to distribute more than their current earnings for the year?
   I. complex trusts
   II. simple trusts

   (A) I only
   (B) II only
   (C) both I and II
   (D) neither I nor II

272. The standard deduction for a simple trust in the fiduciary income tax return (Form 1041) is

   (A) $800
   (B) $300
   (C) $0
   (D) $750

273. Which of the following is CORRECT regarding a simple trust?
   I. If a simple trust properly distributes all its income for a year, the simple trust will pay no tax for that year.
   II. A simple trust receives an exemption of $300.
   III. A simple trust can use a fiscal year or calendar year.

   (A) I and II only
   (B) II and III only
   (C) I and III only
   (D) I, II, and III

274. For an estate tax return, a number of specific expenses and other costs can be deducted from the gross estate value. These deductions include
   I. administrative expenses
   II. debts and mortgages

   (A) I only
   (B) II only
   (C) both I and II
   (D) neither I nor II

275. The following are the fair market values of Richard's assets at the date of his death:

Personal effects and jewelry	$150,000
Land bought by Richard's funds five years prior to his death and held with Rita	$800,000

If Rita was Richard's spouse, the amount includable in Richard's gross estate in the federal estate tax return (Form 706) would be

(A) $950,000
(B) $550,000
(C) $475,000
(D) $800,000

276. When Beth and Matt became engaged in April of Year 3, Matt gave Beth a ring that had a fair market value of $50,000. After their wedding in July of Year 6, Matt gave Beth $75,000 in cash, which Beth used to open her own bank account. Beth and Matt are US citizens. What was the amount of Matt's marital deduction?

(A) $0
(B) $75,000
(C) $115,000
(D) $125,000

277. Castellano died on March 1 of Year 1. He had total assets of $2 million and liabilities of $400,000. He had funeral expenses of $30,000. In the will, he donated $290,000 to a charitable organization and gave his spouse another $400,000. The remaining amount is divided evenly between his daughter and his father. Without regard for any exclusion, what is the taxable amount of Castellano's estate?

(A) $880,000
(B) $440,000
(C) $460,000
(D) $900,000

278. Sylvia died early in Year 1 with an estate that had a considerable value. The executor of her estate is currently determining the value of her estate for taxation purposes. Which of the following CANNOT be deducted in arriving at the estate value?

(A) debts owed at death
(B) a bequest made to her only daughter
(C) funeral expenses
(D) charitable bequests

279. Gordon died early in Year 1 with an estate valued at several million dollars. In his will, he left a considerable amount of money (approximately 72% of his asset value) to his spouse, Grace. In determining the amount of his taxable estate for federal estate tax purposes, what amount is subtracted in connection with this bequest to his spouse?
    (A) $600,000
    (B) $1 million
    (C) 50% of the value of the estate assets
    (D) no limitation

280. Within how many months after the date of a decedent's death is the federal estate tax return (Form 706) due if no time extension for filing is granted?
    (A) 9
    (B) 6
    (C) 4.5
    (D) 3.5

281. Which of the following is CORRECT regarding estates?
    I. Estates may adopt a fiscal year or calendar year.
    II. Estates are exempt from paying estimated tax during the estate's first two taxable years.
    (A) I only
    (B) II only
    (C) both I and II
    (D) neither I nor II

282. An executor of a decedent's estate that has only US citizens as beneficiaries is required to file a fiduciary income tax return if the estate's gross income for the year is AT LEAST
    (A) $100
    (B) $600
    (C) $300
    (D) $1,000

283. Which of the following is a valid deduction from a decedent's gross estate?
    I. federal estate taxes
    II. unpaid income taxes on income received by the decedent before death
    (A) I only
    (B) II only
    (C) both I and II
    (D) neither I nor II

CHAPTER 3

Other Taxation Areas

284. Mac opened a brokerage account with Vanguard Bank in Year 1. Mac was instructed to provide his social security number on the application. Mac failed to provide the social security number to the financial institution. The investment earned interest and dividend income of $2,000 in Year 1.

   I. Mac will be limited to receiving only $500 of the interest income since he failed to provide his social security number to the bank.

   II. Mac will be subject to backup withholding tax on any investment income earned in this new brokerage account until he provides his social security number to the brokerage company.

(A) I only
(B) II only
(C) both I and II
(D) neither I nor II

285. Stefano Inc., has sales of inventory in excess of $10,000,000 for the past three tax years. Which of the following costs are subject to uniform capitalization?

   I. repackaging
   II. research
   III. advertising and marketing

(A) I and II only
(B) I and III only
(C) I only
(D) II and III only

286. Which of the following is CORRECT regarding uniform capitalization rules?
  I. Officers' compensation NOT attributed to production would be expensed even if a company were subject to uniform capitalization.
  II. Service companies, like accounting and law firms, are NOT subject to uniform capitalization.

  (A) I only
  (B) II only
  (C) both I and II
  (D) neither I nor II

287. Maskell, an individual taxpayer, had Year 2 taxable income of $195,000 with a corresponding tax liability of $40,000. For Year 3, Maskell expects taxable income of $264,000 and a tax liability of $50,000. In order to avoid a penalty for underpayment of estimated tax, what is the minimum amount of Year 3 estimated tax payments that Maskell can make?

  (A) $40,000
  (B) $44,000
  (C) $45,000
  (D) $50,000

288. Selzer Corp.'s taxable income for the year ended December 31, Year 7, was $2,000,000, on which its tax liability was $680,000. In order for Selzer to escape the estimated tax underpayment penalty for the year ending December 31, Year 8, Selzer's Year 8 estimated tax payments must equal at least

  (A) 90% of the Year 8 tax liability
  (B) 93% of the Year 8 tax liability
  (C) 100% of the Year 8 tax liability
  (D) the Year 7 tax liability of $680,000

289. Which of the following entities must make their final payment of Year 4 taxes by December 15, Year 4?
  I. C corporation
  II. individuals
  III. S corporation

  (A) II only
  (B) I and II only
  (C) I only
  (D) I, II, and III

290. Quirk filed his Year 1 tax return on March 12, Year 2, and paid a small tax due for the prior year. What is the statute of limitation for this return?

(A) three years from the date filed because it was filed on time

(B) three years from the due date for the return

(C) three years from the date filed regardless of whether it was filed on time or not

(D) three years from December 31, Year 1

291. Gabriel, a self-employed individual, had income for Year 4 as follows:

$436,000	gross receipts
$(316,000)	deductions
$120,000	net business income

In March of Year 6, Gabriel discovers that he had inadvertently omitted some income on his Year 4 return and retains Rutherford and Banks CPAs to determine his position under the statute of limitations. Rutherford and Banks CPAs should advise Gabriel that the six-year statute of limitations would apply to his Year 4 return only if he omitted from gross income an amount in excess of

(A) $109,000

(B) $30,000

(C) $29,000

(D) $120,000

292. A calendar-year taxpayer files an individual tax return for Year 9 on March 20, Year 10. The taxpayer neither committed fraud nor omitted amounts in excess of 25% of gross income on the tax return. What is the latest date that the Internal Revenue Service (IRS) can assess tax and assert a notice of deficiency?

(A) April 15, Year 13

(B) March 20, Year 13

(C) March 20, Year 12

(D) April 15, Year 12

293. Strauss, a sole practitioner CPA, prepares individual income tax returns. According to the Internal Revenue Service (IRS) Circular 230, approximately how long is Strauss required to keep copies of the tax returns that he prepared?

(A) 2 years

(B) 3 years

(C) 5 years

(D) permanently

294. Which of the following is CORRECT regarding Circular 230?

    I. A dispute over fees does NOT generally relieve the practitioner of responsibility to return the client's records.

    II. A contingent fee is allowed in connection with the filing of a client's **amended** tax return but not when filing an original tax return.

    III. A paid preparer is required to sign a tax return and include their preparer tax identification number (PTIN) on the client's return.

    (A) I and II only

    (B) I and III only

    (C) II and III only

    (D) I, II, and III

295. According to the AICPA's "Statements on Standards for Tax Services" and Internal Revenue Service (IRS) Circular 230, which of the following is CORRECT?

    I. When considering whether to give oral or written advice to a client, a CPA should consider the tax sophistication of the client and whether the client will seek a second opinion.

    II. If new legislation will have an impact on advice previously given a year ago, a tax preparer need NOT advise the client of the new legislation even if the original advice was given in writing.

    III. A tax return preparer is NOT permitted to endorse a taxpayer's refund check.

    (A) I and II only

    (B) II and III only

    (C) I and III only

    (D) I, II, and III

296. According to Circular 230, which of the following individuals may represent taxpayers before the Internal Revenue Service (IRS)?

    I. registered tax return preparers

    II. attorneys

    III. CPAs and enrolled agents

    (A) I, II, and III

    (B) I and III only

    (C) II and III only

    (D) I and II only

297. Which of the following is CORRECT regarding Internal Revenue Service (IRS) tax procedures?
  I. In general the tax court, including the small tax case procedures, hears a case before any tax is paid.
  II. If the assessed tax has already been paid and a claim for refund has been filed, a suit may generally be filed in the district court or the claims court.

(A) I only
(B) II only
(C) both I and II
(D) neither I nor II

298. Which of the following is CORRECT regarding the State Board of Accountancy?
  I. ultimately grants the successful CPA candidate a license to practice public accounting
  II. has the power to suspend but not the power to revoke the CPA license

(A) I only
(B) II only
(C) both I and II
(D) neither I nor II

299. Brenner, a CPA, discovers material noncompliance with a specific Internal Revenue Code (IRC) requirement in the prior-year return of a new client. Which of the following actions should Brenner take?
  I. Contact the prior CPA and discuss the client's exposure.
  II. Contact the Internal Revenue Service (IRS) and discuss courses of action.

(A) I only
(B) II only
(C) both I and II
(D) neither I nor II

300. If a tax preparer knowingly deducted the expenses of the taxpayer's personal domestic help as wages paid in the taxpayer's business on the taxpayer's income tax return,

(A) the Internal Revenue Service (IRS) will examine the facts and circumstances to determine whether the reasonable cause exception applies

(B) the IRS will examine the facts and circumstances to determine whether the good faith exception applies

(C) the tax preparer's action does not constitute an act of tax preparer misconduct

(D) the tax preparer's action constitutes an act of tax preparer misconduct subject to the IRC penalty

301. Before a tax preparer is assessed a penalty, the Internal Revenue Service (IRS) will sometimes examine the facts and circumstances to determine whether the reasonable cause or the good faith exception applies. In which of the following situations would the IRS examine the facts further to determine whether the good faith or reasonable cause exception applies?

I. The tax preparer relied on the advice of an advisory preparer to calculate the taxpayer's tax liability. The tax preparer believed that the advisory preparer was competent and that the advice was reasonable. Based on the advice, the taxpayer had understated income tax liability.

II. The tax preparer endorses and cashes the taxpayer's refund check and within 24 hours then gives the taxpayer the remainder of the refund after deducting the tax preparer's fee.

III. The tax preparer reveals confidential client information while being evaluated by a quality or peer review team from the state society of CPAs.

(A) I only

(B) I and III only

(C) I, II, and III

(D) III only

302. The Perry Corporation sells inventory costing $15,000 to a customer for $20,000. Because of significant uncertainties surrounding the transaction, the installment sales method is viewed as proper. In the first year, Perry Corporation collects $5,700. In the second year, Perry Corporation collects another $8,000. What amount of profit should the Perry Corporation recognize in the second year?

(A) $2,000

(B) $3,000

(C) $4,000

(D) $5,000

303. Desimone Corp. began operations on January 1, Year 1 and appropriately uses the installment method of accounting for financial reporting purposes. The following information pertains to operations for Year 1:

Installment sales	$1,200,000
Collections on installment sales	$500,000
General and administration expenses	$180,000
Cost of goods sold minus installment sales	$720,000

The balance in Desimone's deferred gross profit account at December 31, Year 1, should be

(A) $160,000
(B) $175,000
(C) $200,000
(D) $280,000

304. In Year 1 Krohn, Inc., sells $5,000 of goods with a total cost of $2,500 on installment. During Year 1, Krohn, Inc., collects $2,000 and then collects $3,000 in Year 2. Using the cost recovery method, how much will Krohn, Inc., report as gross profit in Year 1 and Year 2 respectively?

	Year 1	Year 2
(A)	$0	$2,500
(B)	$1,500	$1,000
(C)	$1,000	$1,500
(D)	$1,250	$1,250

305. Mitchell, Inc., has a contract to build a building for $1,000,000, with an estimated completion time of three years. A reliable cost estimate for the project will be $600,000. In the first year, Mitchell, Inc., incurred costs totaling $240,000. No cash was received from the customer in Year 1. Under the percentage of completion method, in the first year, Mitchell, Inc., will report a profit of

(A) $0
(B) $160,000
(C) $400,000
(D) $760,000

306. Binstock Construction Co. has consistently used the percentage of completion method. On January 10, Year 1, Binstock began work on a $3,000,000 construction contract. At the inception date, the estimated cost of construction was $2,250,000. The following data relate to the progress of the contract:

Income recognized at December 31, Year 1	$300,000
Costs incurred January 10, Year 1 through December 31, Year 2	$1,800,000
Estimated costs to complete at December 31, Year 2	$600,000

In its income statement for the year ended December 31, Year 2, what amount of gross profit should Binstock Co. report?

(A) $450,000
(B) $300,000
(C) $262,500
(D) $150,000

307. Cash collection is a critical event for income recognition in the
  I. percentage of completion method
  II. installment method
  III. cost recovery method

(A) II only
(B) II and III only
(C) I, II, and III
(D) III only

308. In October 1 of Year 4, Everlast Builders receives $250,000 as an advance payment from the State of New Jersey for a contract to build an express roadway connecting the interstate highway to a section of the Jersey Shore. The contract is for $4,000,000 and expected to last three years. Total costs incurred over the life of the contract are expected to be $3,500,000. No costs have yet been expended by Everlast by December 31, Year 4. Everlast will recognize at least some of the $250,000 as profit in Year 4 if they use which of the following methods to account for the long-term construction contract?

  I. percentage of completion method
  II. completed contract method

(A) I only
(B) II only
(C) both I and II
(D) neither I nor II

309. Which of the following tax-exempt organizations must file annual information returns (Form 990)?

(A) those with gross receipts of less than $10,000 in each taxable year
(B) private foundations
(C) internally supported auxiliaries of churches
(D) churches

310. Which of the following is required information of a not-for-profit that files Form 990-N?

(A) name and address of major contributors
(B) highest employee salaries
(C) name and address of a principal officer
(D) all of the above

311. Most tax-exempt organizations are required to file an annual return. Which form an organization must file generally depends on its

  I. gross receipts for the year
 II. total assets at year end

(A) I only
(B) II only
(C) both I and II
(D) neither I nor II

312. The Olney Group is a not-for-profit organization formed under Section 501c of the Internal Revenue Code. Total assets are $350,000 for the current year. Barnes, CPA, and a director of the Olney Group are wondering whether he needs to file Form 990 on behalf of the Olney Group and if so, which Form 990 to file. The following are the figures for the current year.

Revenues	$350,000
Cost of sales	$200,000
Gross profit	$150,000
Salary expenses	$70,000
Net income	$80,000

    Assuming these figures closely approximate the most recent three prior years, which 990 form is Barnes likely to file on behalf of the Olney Group?

(A) Form 990-N
(B) Form 990-EZ
(C) Form 990 (long form)
(D) Even if the Olney Group was a church, they would have to file Form 990.

313. A tax-exempt organization must still pay income taxes on any unrelated business income in excess of

(A) $1,000
(B) $5,000
(C) $10,000, after allowing for three prohibited transactions
(D) $25,000

Use the following facts to answer Questions 314 through 316: The Benning Museum, a not-for-profit art gallery, offers art appreciation summer courses to high school students for a fee.

314. Since the museum's mission involves the education of the public about art, the proceeds from such courses are

(A) fully taxable
(B) tax exempt
(C) taxable for the amount in excess of $1,000 per student
(D) tax exempt if the high school students receive high school credit, otherwise taxable

315. Assume that the Benning Museum maintains a website that sells advertising to restaurants and hotels located near the museum. The income from advertising on its website is

 I. taxable at the corporate tax rate after a $1,000 exemption
 II. considered unrelated business income

(A) I only
(B) II only
(C) both I and II
(D) neither I nor II

316. The time for filing Form 990-N for a not-for-profit (NFP) organization is normally

(A) two and a half months after the close of the tax year
(B) three and a half months after the close of the tax year
(C) four and a half months after the close of the tax year
(D) five and a half months after the close of the tax year

CHAPTER 4

Business Law, Ethics, and Professional Responsibilities

317. Which is CORRECT regarding contract law?
   I. a legally enforceable agreement can result even if an offer is not accepted
   II. a contract can be for any legal purpose

(A) I only
(B) II only
(C) both I and II
(D) neither I nor II

318. On November 20, Sheran, Inc., an appliance dealer, placed a television advertisement stating that Sheran would sell 300 high-end smartphones at its store for a special discount only on November 25, Year 13. On November 22, Ragofsky called Sheran and expressed an interest in buying one of the advertised phones.

Ragofsky was told that there will probably be long lines and to come to the store as early as possible.

Ragofsky went to Sheran's store on November 25 and demanded the right to buy the phone at the special discount.

Sheran had sold the 300 phones and refused Ragofsky's demand. Ragofsky sued Sheran for breach of contract.

   Sheran's best defense to Ragofsky's suit would be that Sheran's

(A) offer was unenforceable
(B) advertisement was not an offer
(C) mentioning of the long lines in the phone call effectively revoked the offer
(D) offer had not been accepted

319. Which of the following communications sent by an offeree must be received to be effective?
  I. counteroffers
  II. rejections
  (A) I only
  (B) II only
  (C) both I and II
  (D) neither I nor II

320. An offer that is irrevocable for an agreed time and is supported by consideration
  I. is called an option or an option contract
  II. is NOT allowed in a real estate contract
  (A) I only
  (B) II only
  (C) both I and II
  (D) neither I nor II

321. Poznok offers to sell Lavroff his pizza place for $50,000. Lavroff would like to think about it for a while and offers Poznok $500 for a 30-day option. If Poznok takes Lavroff's $500 check:
  I. Lavroff has 30 days to make offers to Poznok but does not have to buy the store
  II. then on day 18, Lavroff offers Poznok less than $50,000 and Poznok refuses, the option contract has been terminated by counteroffer and Poznok could immediately place the store back on the open market
  (A) I only
  (B) II only
  (C) both I and II
  (D) neither I nor II

322. The mailbox rule generally makes acceptance of an offer effective at the time the acceptance is dispatched. The mailbox rule does not apply if
  (A) both the offeror and offeree are merchants
  (B) the offer provides that an acceptance should not be effective until actually received
  (C) the offer proposes a sale of real estate
  (D) the duration of the offer is not in excess of three months

323. An offer is made on July 2 that calls for acceptance to be in writing and received by August 10. Which of the following is CORRECT regarding the acceptance of this offer?

  I. An acceptance that is mailed August 3 and is received on August 6 is valid on August 3.

  II. An acceptance that is mailed July 8 and received on August 12 is considered a counteroffer and not an acceptance.

  (A) I only
  (B) II only
  (C) both I and II
  (D) neither I nor II

324. Micki received an offer from Clark, Inc., that contained the following specific instructions: "We need to know soon whether you can agree to the terms of this proposal; you must accept by September 22 or we will assume you cannot meet our terms." If Micki's letter of acceptance is mailed by September 21 and arrives on September 25,

  (A) no contract exists since the acceptance was received after September 22
  (B) the attempted acceptance letter is a counteroffer
  (C) a contract is formed on September 21
  (D) a contract is formed on September 25

325. Rick promises to pay anyone in his office $150 if they pick his son Ricky up at school on April 8 and drive him home. Allison, a coworker, promises to be parked at the school waiting for little Ricky. Brad, another coworker, tells Rick that he may be available and will know more the day before. Which of the following is CORRECT?

  (A) The contract is bilateral because Rick promised to pay and Allison promised to perform.
  (B) The contract is unilateral because Rick's promise needs to be accepted by performance, not by promising to perform.
  (C) If Brad picks up Ricky and drives him home, he would not be entitled to the $150, because Allison promised to perform and Brad did not.
  (D) none of the above

326. To prevail in a common law action for fraud, a plaintiff must prove that the

  I. plaintiff is justified in relying on the misrepresentations

  II. defendant made the misrepresentations with knowledge of their falsity and with an intention to deceive

  (A) I only
  (B) II only
  (C) both I and II
  (D) neither I nor II

327. To prevail in a contract for a common law action for fraud, a plaintiff must prove that the
    I. misrepresentations were material
    II. defendant was an expert with regard to the misrepresentations

(A) I only
(B) II only
(C) both I and II
(D) neither I nor II

328. Dave negotiated the sale of his bagel store to Ed. Ed asked to see the prior year's financial statements. Using the store's checkbook, Dave prepared a balance sheet and profit and loss (P&L) statement as well as he could. Dave told Ed to go have an accountant examine it, as Dave is not an accountant. Ed later learned that the financial statements contained several errors that resulted in material overstatement of assets and net income. Dave was not aware of the errors. Ed sued Dave for fraud claiming that Ed relied on the financial statements in making the decision to buy the bagel store. Which is CORRECT?

(A) Ed will prevail, if the errors in the financial statements are material.
(B) Ed will not prevail because his reliance on the financial statements was not justifiable.
(C) Ed would be able to prove duress and cancel the contract.
(D) Ed would be able to cancel the contract even if the errors were not material.

329. If one party to a contract makes a material unilateral mistake,
    I. the contract could still exist unless the other party knows it's a mistake and is just trying to take advantage
    II. the contract is voidable by the party who made the mistake

(A) I only
(B) II only
(C) both I and II
(D) neither I nor II

330. Contracts made under which of the following conditions are voidable?
    I. duress
    II. undue influence

(A) I only
(B) II only
(C) both I and II
(D) neither I nor II

331. Which is CORRECT regarding consideration as an element of a contract?
  I. Consideration can involve money or goods but not services.
  II. Consideration is something that is bargained for and exchanged in a contract.

(A) I only
(B) II only
(C) both I and II
(D) neither I nor II

332. Mirro has almost completed the renovation of a building that he owns. Mirro urgently needs the plumbing inspector to inspect the property so that Mirro's new tenants can move in on time. Mirro promises a $125 bonus to the plumbing inspector if the plumbing inspector will come the following morning. Mirro's promise

(A) qualifies as consideration if the plumbing inspector conducts the inspection the following morning
(B) does not qualify as consideration, because the plumbing inspector already has a pre-existing legal duty to perform inspections
(C) does not qualify as consideration if the plumbing inspector conducts the inspection the following morning and Mirro fails the inspection
(D) qualifies as consideration if the plumbing inspector conducts the inspection the following morning and Mirro passes the inspection

333. Todd Winger, 15 years old, signs a contract to receive flying lessons at a local airport. It's legal in Todd's state for a minor to take flying lessons as early as age 14. Todd's parents drive him to the weekly lesson, the flight school gets paid each month, and Todd continues to show up for the weekly lessons for an entire year. Which of the following is CORRECT?

(A) Todd can cancel the contract at any time while still a minor, but not after reaching the age of majority.
(B) Todd can cancel the contract at any time while still a minor and even within a reasonable time after reaching the age of majority.
(C) The flight school, after learning it just did business with a minor, can cancel the contract at any time.
(D) Todd may cancel the contract at any time while still a minor but would have to pay for the flight lessons that he already received.

334. Darrel is a minor who attends college and lives 900 miles from his parents. Darrel entered into the following contracts and has already received some of the benefits of both contracts. Darrel must pay for what has already been received but can cancel the remainder of which of the following contracts?

   I. guitar lessons

  II. campus housing

(A) I only

(B) II only

(C) both I and II

(D) neither I nor II

335. Phil, who has not yet reached the age of majority, purchased a motorcycle from Whiting Cycles, Inc. Seven months later, the bike was stolen and never recovered. Which of the following statements is CORRECT?

   I. Phil may rescind the purchase because Phil is a minor.

  II. Phil effectively ratified the purchase because Phil used the bike for more than six months.

(A) I only

(B) II only

(C) both I and II

(D) neither I nor II

making it officially valid

336. Mona works as the secretary for Amazing Amusements for 13 years. Upon her retirement, Brian, the owner of Amazing Amusements, promises to pay Mona $500 per month for the next six years because of the wonderful job she has done for his company. Which of the following statements is CORRECT?

   I. Brian's promise is based on past consideration, and his promise is NOT a legal obligation.

  II. If Amazing Amusements pays Mona the $500 for more than six months, they would have to continue to pay her.

(A) I only

(B) II only

(C) both I and II

(D) neither I nor II

337. Black Bear, Inc., made a contract in writing to hire Ditka for five years for $150,000 per year. After two years, Ditka asked Black Bear, Inc., for a raise of $20,000 per year. Black Bear, Inc., at first refused but then agreed after Ditka put on some pressure. After the fifth year, Ditka left and Black Bear, Inc., sued to get back the extra $20,000 per year for the last three years. Who wins?

(A) Ditka, because Black Bear, Inc., agreed to the raise
(B) Ditka, if the raise was agreed to in writing
(C) Black Bear, Inc., even though Black Bear, Inc., agreed to the raise
(D) Black Bear, Inc., because Ditka had applied some pressure to get the raise

338. Which of the following is legally binding despite lack of consideration? *—without being affected by*

I. modification of a signed contract to purchase a parcel of land
II. a promise to donate money to a charity, which the charity relied on in incurring large expenditures

(A) I only
(B) II only
(C) both I and II
(D) neither I nor II

339. In contract law, which of the following correctly relates to the terms *valid, void,* and *voidable*?

(A) Once a party has been declared legally insane by a court with proper jurisdiction, all contracts entered into by that person would be voidable at the other party's option.
(B) Void contracts are otherwise valid, but one of the parties has the power to set the contract aside.
(C) Voidable contracts are agreements that are void from the start.
(D) Once a party has been declared legally insane by a court with proper jurisdiction, all contracts entered into by that person would be void.

340. Which of the following contracts are voidable?

I. contracts entered into by a minor
II. contracts entered into by an individual who is drunk every day

(A) I only
(B) II only
(C) both I and II
(D) neither I nor II

341. Under the law governing service contracts, if A hired B to kidnap C, which of the following is CORRECT?

    I. If A already paid B, the court would force B to refund A's money but would not force B to kidnap C.

    II. This would be an example of a voidable contract.

(A) I only
(B) II only
(C) both I and II
(D) neither I nor II

342. Which is CORRECT as it relates to licensing statutes?

    I. A revenue license is not required in order to collect for real estate services rendered in most states.

    II. A regulatory license is required in order to collect for legal services rendered in most states.

(A) I only
(B) II only
(C) both I and II
(D) neither I nor II

343. Which of the following contracts ordinarily needs to be in writing to be enforceable?

    I. contracts for the sale of real estate

    II. contracts for services that are impossible to complete within one year

    III. contracts for services with consideration of $500 or more

(A) I, II, and III
(B) I and II only
(C) I and III only
(D) II and III only

344. On September 18, Juan, a salesperson, orally contracted to service a piece of equipment owned by Genarro, Inc. The contract provided that for a period of 36 months, Juan would provide routine service for the equipment at a fixed price of $30,000 payable in three annual installments of $10,000 each. Which of the following is CORRECT?

    I. On October 29, Genarro, Inc.'s president could decide that Genarro does not have to honor the service agreement because there is no written contract between Juan and Genarro, Inc.

    II. This agreement need not be in writing if both parties have already fully performed their agreement.

(A) I only
(B) II only
(C) both I and II
(D) neither I nor II

345. Hayes agreed orally to repair Patterson's rare guitar for $389. Before the work was started, Patterson asked Hayes to perform additional repairs to the instrument and agreed to increase the contract price to $625. After Hayes completed the work, Patterson refused to pay and Hayes sued. Patterson's defense was based on the statute of frauds (the contract was oral). What total amount will Hayes recover?

(A) $389
(B) $625
(C) $0
(D) $500

346. Which of the following contracts if not fully performed must be in writing to be enforceable?

   I. sale of goods for a price of $1,500
  II. executor of a will
 III. a contract to co-sign the debts of another

(A) I and III only
(B) II and III only
(C) I and II only
(D) I, II, and III

347. Which of the following is CORRECT regarding the parol evidence rule?

   I. It allows for the admission of evidence of oral agreements that existed prior to the written contract if the oral agreements contradict the written contract.
  II. It does not apply if the contract did not have to be in writing.

(A) I only
(B) II only
(C) both I and II
(D) neither I nor II

348. Which of the following would NOT be prohibited by the parol evidence rule?

   I. oral evidence that existed prior to the writing that could prove fraud
  II. written evidence that existed prior to the writing that could prove fraud

(A) I only
(B) II only
(C) both I and II
(D) neither I nor II

349. Which of the following is CORRECT regarding assignment of rights in a contract?
   I. Assignment must be in writing and signed by the assignor.
   II. Most contract rights are NOT assignable as a matter of law.

(A) I only
(B) II only
(C) both I and II
(D) neither I nor II

350. Conisha contracted with White for Conisha to buy certain real property. If the contract is otherwise silent, Conisha's rights under the contract are

(A) assignable only with White's consent
(B) generally assignable
(C) not assignable, because they were meant only for Conisha; therefore, they would be considered highly personal contract rights
(D) not assignable as a matter of law

351. On December 19, Cutrone contracted in writing with Bonacorso Landscaping Corp. The contract provided Cutrone to deliver certain specified new equipment to Bonacorso by December 31. On December 23, Cutrone determined that he would not be able to deliver the equipment to Bonacorso by December 31 because of an inventory shortage. Therefore, Cutrone made a written assignment to Ricci Equipment, Inc. When Ricci attempted to deliver the equipment on December 31, Bonacorso refused to accept it, claiming that Cutrone could not properly delegate its duties under the December 19 contract to another party without the consent of Bonacorso. Which of the following statements is CORRECT?
   I. Since the contract is silent with regard to assignment, assignment is NOT allowed as the goods are considered inventory.
   II. The rights under this contract would be considered too "personal" to freely assign without permission.
   III. Assignment is generally allowed unless it is prohibited by the contract, would substantially increase someone's risk, or contains highly personal contract rights.

(A) I and II only
(B) III only
(C) I only
(D) II only

352. Fisk, Inc., is a creditor beneficiary of a contract between Larkin and Donner Industries, Inc. Donner is indebted to Fisk. The contract between Larkin and Donner provides that Larkin is to purchase goods from Donner and pay the purchase price directly to Fisk until Donner's obligation is satisfied. Without justification, Larkin failed to pay Fisk, and Fisk sued Larkin. Which is CORRECT?

    I. Fisk is an incidental beneficiary of the contract between Larkin and Donner.

    II. Fisk is a third-party donee beneficiary.

(A) I only
(B) II only
(C) both I and II
(D) neither I nor II

353. Which of the following third parties can sue to enforce a contract?

    I. incidental beneficiaries
    II. intended creditor beneficiaries
    III. intended donee beneficiaries

(A) I and III only
(B) II and III only
(C) I, II, and III
(D) II only

354. Which of the following describes an anticipatory repudiation?

    I. One party announces in advance that they will not perform a contractual obligation.

    II. One party reasonably demands an assurance of performance and does not receive one.

(A) I only
(B) II only
(C) both I and II
(D) neither I nor II

355. Which of the following represent actual dollar losses that when recovered would restore the parties to the position they would have been in had there been no breach?

    I. liquidated damages
    II. compensatory damages

(A) I only
(B) II only
(C) both I and II
(D) neither I nor II

356. In 1998 the American Institute of CPAs (AICPA) decided to computerize what had always been a paper-and-pencil CPA exam. After several vendors were interviewed, the AICPA contracted with Prometric, a technology company, to computerize the CPA exam and make it available on demand. The contract between the AICPA and Prometric contained a damages clause that said in the event that Prometric did not finish by a certain date, Prometric owed the AICPA a predetermined amount of money. This predetermined amount in the event of breach is referred to as

(A) liquidated damages
(B) specific performance
(C) compensatory damages
(D) punitive damages

357. Regarding breach of contracts and remedies, specific performance is an available remedy when which of the following contracts are breached?
 I. contract for services where one party refuses to perform
 II. sale of goods where the goods are unique
 III. sale of real estate

(A) II and III only
(B) I and III only
(C) I, II, and III
(D) III only

358. Murray and Rukke purchased a dog-grooming business from Eichmann. The agreement contained a covenant prohibiting Eichmann from competing with Murray and Rukke in the dog-grooming business. Which of the following is CORRECT regarding the covenant not to compete?
 I. For the covenant not to compete to be enforceable, the time period for which it is to be effective must be reasonable.
 II. For the covenant not to compete to be enforceable, the geographic area covered by the agreement must be reasonable.

(A) I only
(B) II only
(C) both I and II
(D) neither I nor II

359. Naomi contracted to sell May a building for $310,000. The contract required May to pay the entire amount at closing. Naomi refused to close the sale of the building. May sued Naomi. To what relief is May entitled?

(A) specific performance and compensatory damages
(B) compensatory damages or specific performance
(C) punitive damages and compensatory damages
(D) specific performance only

360. Which of the following is CORRECT regarding common law and the Uniform Commercial Code (UCC)?

   I. Whether the UCC sales article is applicable does not depend on the price of the goods involved.

   II. The common law rules apply to contracts for the sale of a business but NOT to contracts for real estate.

   (A) I only

   (B) II only

   (C) both I and II

   (D) neither I nor II

361. The Uniform Commercial Code (UCC) sales article applies

   (A) to a contract for personal services

   (B) to the sale of specially manufactured goods

   (C) to the sale of real estate

   (D) to the sale of goods only if the buyer and seller are merchants

362. Under the sales article of the Uinform Commercial Code (UCC), a firm offer will be created only if the

   I. offeree and offeror are both merchants

   II. offeree gives some form of consideration

   III. offer is made by a merchant in a signed writing

   (A) I, II, and III

   (B) I and III only

   (C) II and III only

   (D) III only

363. Carrabel Breads, Inc., offered to sell Shop and Cart Market's 20,000 pounds of Plantation Bread at $1.00 per pound, subject to certain specified terms for delivery. Shop and Cart replied in writing as follows: "We accept your offer for 20,000 pounds of Plantation Bread at $1.00 per pound, terms 2/10 net 30." In accordance with the sales article of the UCC,

   (A) a contract will be formed only if Carrabel Bread agrees to the 2% off

   (B) a contract was formed between the parties

   (C) no contract was formed, because Shop and Cart included the 2/10 net 30 in its reply

   (D) no contract was formed, because Shop and Cart's reply was a counteroffer

364. With regard to contract law, the price of the contract is sometimes considered too material to leave out and at other times can be left open. Which of the following contracts would fail if the price were left open?
   I.   sale of goods
   II. sale of real estate
   III. services

   (A) I only
   (B) II and III only
   (C) I, II, and III
   (D) II only

365. Which of the following would require additional consideration to both parties in the event that the original contract is modified?
   I.   contract for personal services
   II. contract for the sale of goods

   (A) I only
   (B) II only
   (C) both I and II
   (D) neither I nor II

366. Under the Uniform Commercial Code (UCC) sales article, which of the following statements is CORRECT concerning a contract for the sale of goods involving a merchant seller and a merchant buyer for a price of $10,000?
   I. If the contract is oral, and the seller sends the buyer a written confirmation, that confirmation could substitute for a signed contract.
   II. The contract would follow the common law rules rather than the UCC rules.

   (A) I only
   (B) II only
   (C) both I and II
   (D) neither I nor II

367. Collins, Inc., and Hackett Corp. agreed orally that Hackett would custom manufacture a piece of equipment for Collins at a price of $130,000. After Hackett completed the work at a cost of $95,000, Collins notified Hackett that the item was no longer needed. Hackett is holding the equipment and has requested payment from Collins. Hackett has been unable to resell the item for any price. Hackett incurred storage fees of $1,000. If Collins refuses to pay Hackett and Hackett sues Collins, the most Hackett will be entitled to recover is

   (A) $95,000
   (B) $96,000
   (C) $130,000
   (D) $131,000

368. In which of the following trial sales would title pass to the buyer before the expiration of the trial period?
   I. sale on approval
   II. sale or return

(A) I only
(B) II only
(C) both I and II
(D) neither I nor II

369. Under the sales article of the UCC, which of the following statements is CORRECT concerning a contract involving a merchant seller and a non-merchant buyer?

(A) The contract may not involve the sale of personal property with a price of more than $500.
(B) The contract will be either a sale or return or sale on approval contract.
(C) Only the seller is obligated to perform the contract in good faith.
(D) Whether the UCC sales article is applicable does not depend on the price of the goods involved.

370. Under the sales article of the Uniform Commercial Code (UCC), unless otherwise agreed to, the seller's obligation to the buyer is to

(A) deliver all the goods called for in the contract to a common carrier
(B) set aside conforming goods for inspection by the buyer before delivery
(C) hold conforming goods and give the buyer whatever notification is reasonably necessary to enable the buyer to take delivery
(D) deliver the goods to the buyer's place of business

371. Giant Retail Corp. agreed to purchase 20,000 phone systems from VoiceNext Telecom. VoiceNext is a wholesaler of phone systems, and Giant is a large technology retailer. The contract required VoiceNext to ship the phones by common carrier, free on board (FOB) VoiceNext, Inc., loading dock. Which of the parties bears the risk of loss during shipment?

(A) VoiceNext because the risk of loss passes only when Giant receives the goods
(B) VoiceNext because both parties are merchants
(C) Giant because the risk of loss passes when the goods are delivered to the carrier
(D) Giant because this is an example of a sale on approval

372. Under the Uniform Commercial Code (UCC), risk of loss passes to the buyer

(A) when the goods are delivered to the carrier if the terms are FOB destination

(B) when the goods are placed on the seller's loading dock if the terms are FOB destination

(C) when the goods are placed on the seller's loading dock if the terms are FOB shipping point

(D) when the goods are delivered to the carrier if the terms are FOB shipping point

373. If a seller ships **nonconforming** goods to a buyer in a sale of goods contract under the Uniform Commercial Code,

  I. risk of loss would remain with the seller even if the terms were FOB shipping point and the goods were already delivered to the carrier

 II. the buyer could reject the entire shipment and would NOT be able to accept a partial shipment and reject the rest

III. the seller has breached the contract, but the buyer must follow reasonable instructions from the seller as to what to do with the nonconforming goods

(A) I, II, and III

(B) I and III only

(C) I and II only

(D) III only

374. Your client buys a guitar from a seller. Rather than take the instrument home, your client leaves the instrument at the place he bought it for a few days. Thieves break in and steal the guitar. Your client would NOT bear the risk of loss if the guitar was sold by and ultimately stolen from a

  I. merchant seller

 II. non-merchant seller

(A) I only

(B) II only

(C) both I and II

(D) neither I nor II

375. Which of the following events will release the buyer from all its obligations under a sales contract?
    I. The goods are destroyed after the risk of loss had already passed to the buyer.
    II. The seller refuses to give written assurance of performance when reasonably demanded by the buyer.

    (A) I only
    (B) II only
    (C) both I and II
    (D) neither I nor II

376. Which of the following correctly describes a seller's right to cure?
    I. As long as the time for performance has not passed, the seller has the right to correct defects in shipments made.
    II. The seller must give timely notice of intent to cure before the buyer secures goods elsewhere.

    (A) I only
    (B) II only
    (C) both I and II
    (D) neither I nor II

377. Under the UCC sales article, which of the following legal remedies would a buyer NOT have when a seller fails to transfer and deliver unique goods identified to the contract?

    (A) recover the identified goods
    (B) suit for specific performance
    (C) purchase substitute goods (cover)
    (D) suit for punitive damages

378. Fessler contracted in writing to sell Fishman a portable generator for $600. The contract did not specifically address the time for payment, place of delivery, or Fishman's right to inspect the generator. Which of the following statements is CORRECT?
    I. Fessler is obligated to deliver the generator to Fishman's home.
    II. Fishman is entitled to inspect the generator before paying for it.

    (A) I only
    (B) II only
    (C) both I and II
    (D) neither I nor II

379. Which of the following warranties are given only by a **merchant** seller?
   I. express warranty
   II. implied warranty of title
   III. implied warranty of merchantability

   (A) I and III only
   (B) II and III only
   (C) III only
   (D) I, II, and III

380. Which of the following warranties would arise only by the buyer making known his needs to the seller and the seller selecting an item to fit the buyer's specific needs?
   I. implied warranty of fitness for a particular purpose
   II. implied warranty of merchantability

   (A) I only
   (B) II only
   (C) both I and II
   (D) neither I nor II

381. A merchant who attempts to disclaim "any and all warranties" has NOT adequately disclaimed the warranty of
   I. title
   II. merchantability
   III. fitness for a particular purpose

   (A) I only
   (B) I and II only
   (C) I and III only
   (D) I, II, and III

382. Which of the following must be proven by an injured party looking to recover damages from a seller of defective merchandise after being injured by the defective product?
   I. negligence on the part of the manufacturer
   II. the product was sold in a defective condition
   III. privity of contract with the seller

   (A) I, II, and III
   (B) II only
   (C) I only
   (D) II and III only

383. Traficante sues the manufacturer, wholesaler, and retailer for bodily injuries caused by a rechargeable battery system she purchased. Which of the following statements is CORRECT?

(A) The manufacturer will avoid liability if it can show it followed the custom of the industry.

(B) Traficante may recover even if she cannot show any negligence was involved.

(C) Privity will be a bar to recovery insofar as Traficante did not purchase from the wholesaler.

(D) Contributory negligence on Traficante's part will always be a bar to recovery.

384. Which of the following is CORRECT regarding a contract for the sale of goods?

  I. For the Uniform Commerical Code (UCC) rules to apply, the contract must be for a price of more than $500.

  II. Acceptance of the offer can be valid prior to receipt unless the offer requires the acceptance to be received by a particular date to be effective.

(A) I only

(B) II only

(C) both I and II

(D) neither I nor II

385. Which of the following is CORRECT regarding a written contract for the sale of goods in order for the agreement to be enforceable under the Uniform Commercial Code (UCC)?

  I. The written contract must contain the quantity of the goods to be sold.

  II. The written contract must contain the signature of the party seeking to enforce the contract.

(A) I only

(B) II only

(C) both I and II

(D) neither I nor II

386. Your client takes his guitar to Loria Music, a merchant seller, for repairs and is given a repair receipt. Your client leaves the instrument with Loria Music and is told to come back in a few weeks with the repair receipt. While the guitar was with Loria Music, Pete, a salesman at Loria Music, accidentally sells the instrument to Cace, a customer in the ordinary course of business. Pete and Loria Music know the identity of all parties but are refusing to reveal the identity of Cace to your client, who insists on getting the guitar back. What is the likely outcome?

(A) If Pete were the owner of the store rather than a salesman, Pete would have to get the guitar back from Cace at his own expense.

(B) Your client would have the option of Loria Music paying your client a sum of money in damages, or your client can choose to have Loria Music get the guitar back from Cace.

(C) The guitar now belongs to Cace; Loria Music owes money damages to your client.

(D) If the guitar were unique, Cace would have to return it to your client.

387. Which of the following is CORRECT regarding the sales article of the Uniform Commercial Code (UCC)?

(A) Merchants and non-merchants are treated alike.

(B) None of the contract terms may be omitted or the contract would fail.

(C) None of the provisions of the UCC may be disclaimed by agreement.

(D) The obligations of the parties to the contract must be performed in good faith.

388. Under the UCC, commercial paper can be described as a
  I. substitute for money
  II. means of providing credit

(A) I only

(B) II only

(C) both I and II

(D) neither I nor II

389. According to the Uniform Commerical Code (UCC), which of the following are commercial paper?
  I. note
  II. draft
  III. warehouse receipt

(A) I, II, and III

(B) I and III only

(C) I and II only

(D) II only

390. According to the commercial paper article of the Uniform Commercial Code (UCC), which of the following would be considered a promise to pay rather than an order to pay?
  I. certificate of deposit
  II. installment note
  III. check
  (A) I and II only
  (B) II and III only
  (C) I, II, and III
  (D) I and III only

391. Russell is the payee of a note and Diane is the maker. Which of the following, if found on the front of the instrument, would cause the note to be non-negotiable?
  (A) "Pay to the order of Russell"
  (B) "Pay to Russell or bearer"
  (C) "Pay to Russell or his order"
  (D) "Pay to Russell"

392. According to the commercial paper article of the Uniform Commercial Code (UCC), a note would be negotiable if the note was payable in
  (A) money only, payable in a foreign currency
  (B) money or goods
  (C) money or services
  (D) money, goods, or services

393. With regard to negotiability, what do you focus on to see whether or not the commercial paper is negotiable?
  (A) back of the instrument only
  (B) front and back of the instrument
  (C) front of the instrument only
  (D) commercial paper is always negotiable

394. Which of the following would destroy negotiability if found on the front of an otherwise negotiable instrument payable for $5,000?
  (A) an extension clause, extending out the time for payment to a date specified in the note
  (B) an acceleration clause, accelerating the time for payment in the event of default
  (C) a contingency that must occur before the note was payable
  (D) a different amount of interest, before and after default

395. Trixie holds a check that is written out to her. The check has the amount in words as "four hundred dollars." The amount in figures on this check states $450.

(A) The check is cashable for $400.
(B) The check is cashable for $450.
(C) The check is not cashable, because the amounts differ.
(D) The check is not cashable, because the amounts differ by more than 5%.

396. In order to negotiate **bearer** paper, one must:

(A) endorse the paper
(B) endorse and deliver the paper with consideration
(C) deliver the paper to the next party without the need for endorsement
(D) deliver and endorse the paper

397. To negotiate order paper, one must

(A) endorse the paper
(B) deliver the paper with consideration
(C) deliver the paper to the next party without the need for endorsement
(D) deliver and endorse the paper

398. Which of the following is a type of endorsement regarding negotiable instruments?
  I. qualified
 II. special
III. blank
IV. restrictive

(A) I, II, and IV only
(B) I, II, III, and IV
(C) I and IV only
(D) I, II, and III only

399. Advantage Telecom LLC received a check that was originally made payable to the order of one of its customers, Roy Hobbs. The following endorsement was written on the back of the check: Roy Hobbs, "for collection only." Which of the following describes the endorsement?
  I. blank
 II. restrictive
III. qualified

(A) II and III only
(B) I, II, and III
(C) I and III only
(D) I and II only

400. The front of an instrument is order paper and reads "Pay to the order of Mark Davis." Which type of endorsement on the back of that instrument would turn the order paper on the front into bearer paper on the back?

    I. blank endorsement

    II. special endorsement

(A) I only

(B) II only

(C) both I and II

(D) neither I nor II

401. Which of the following is CORRECT regarding commercial paper?

    I. If commercial paper is determined to be negotiable, it remains negotiable unless a blank endorsement appears on the back.

    II. If commercial paper is determined to be order paper, it remains order paper even if a blank endorsement appears on the back.

(A) I only

(B) II only

(C) both I and II

(D) neither I nor II

402. Corey is the holder of a note made payable to his order. He turns the instrument over and signs "without recourse," and then he signs his name and writes "pay to Stuart Sheldon." Which of the following describes the endorsement and the type of paper the instrument is after the endorsement?

(A) qualified and special endorsement, instrument becomes bearer paper

(B) qualified and special endorsement, instrument remains order paper

(C) qualified and blank endorsement, instrument becomes bearer paper

(D) qualified and blank endorsement, instrument remains order paper

403. Under the Uniform Commercial Code (UCC) commercial paper article, which of the following is a requirement to become a *holder in due course*?

    I. The instrument must be negotiable.

    II. The holder must give value for the instrument and in good faith.

    III. The holder must have knowledge that the instrument is past due or dishonored at the time the instrument is acquired.

(A) I, II, and III

(B) I and II only

(C) II and III only

(D) I and III only

404. Boyle is the purchaser of a negotiable note from Jordan. Boyle would still be a holder in due course even if, at the time of purchase,

    I. Boyle purchased the instrument at a 30% discount

    II. Boyle knew that the maker was three months behind on the payments

(A) I only

(B) II only

(C) both I and II

(D) neither I nor II

405. Capell, a holder in due course, is seeking to collect on a note where Sussman is the maker. Sussman would have a real defense and NOT have to pay Capell if

    I. Sussman was a minor

    II. Sussman's signature was a forgery

(A) I only

(B) II only

(C) both I and II

(D) neither I nor II

406. Rusty, a holder in due course of a $2,000 note, negotiates the note to your client Salas. At the time Salas acquires the instrument for value from Rusty, Salas notices that it was overdue by five weeks. Which of the following BEST describes Salas?

(A) Salas has the standing of a holder in due course.

(B) Salas has the standing of a holder through a holder in due course.

(C) Salas is unable to acquire the rights under the shelter provision since the instrument was overdue.

(D) none of the above

407. With regard to the commercial paper article of the Uniform Commercial Code (UCC) and the rights of a holder in due course, which of the following are real defenses?

    I. material alteration

    II. lack of consideration

    III. discharge in bankruptcy

(A) I and II only

(B) I and III only

(C) I, II, and III

(D) II and III only

408. Grace Gordon is a holder in due course of a promissory note. Therefore, she will take a note free of which of the following defenses?

(A) discharge of the maker in bankruptcy
(B) negligence of the maker
(C) extreme duress placed upon the maker at the time the maker signed the note
(D) the maker not yet having reached the age of majority

409. Which of the following parties has primary liability on a negotiable instrument?

I. maker of a note
II. drawer of a draft after the draft has been accepted
III. drawee of a draft before the draft has been accepted

(A) I and III only
(B) I and II only
(C) I only
(D) none of the above

410. Under the Uniform Commercial Code (UCC), which of the following are considered commercial paper?

I. bills of lading
II. warehouse receipts

(A) I only
(B) II only
(C) both I and II
(D) neither I nor II

411. According to the Uniform Commercial Code (UCC), documents of title and investment securities

(A) are NOT commercial paper unless they are negotiable
(B) are commercial paper if they are NOT negotiable
(C) are NOT commercial paper because they are not payable in money only
(D) are commercial paper because they are payable in money only

412. A document of title, like a warehouse receipt or bill of lading,

(A) can be negotiable if payable to "the order of Owen Michaels"
(B) cannot be negotiable if payable to "Owen Michaels or bearer"
(C) is NOT negotiable unless payable to bearer
(D) cannot be negotiable

413. According to the Uniform Commercial Code, warehouse receipts and bills of lading
- (A) are NOT commercial paper
- (B) cannot be negotiable unless they are payable to a named payee
- (C) can be negotiable only if they are considered commercial paper
- (D) cannot be negotiable unless they are payable to bearer

414. A bill of lading payable "to Billy Spence or bearer"
- (A) can be negotiated by delivery alone without the need for endorsement
- (B) is NOT negotiable because bills of lading are NOT commercial paper
- (C) can be negotiated but would require the endorsement of Billy Spence
- (D) is considered order paper rather than bearer paper since it's payable to a named payee

415. Under the Uniform Commercial Code (UCC) governing transactions involving debtor/creditor relationships, which of the following is CORRECT regarding the terms *attachment* and *perfection*?
  I. Attachment relates to the creditor's rights against the debtor.
  II. Perfection relates to the creditor's rights against third parties.
- (A) I only
- (B) II only
- (C) both I and II
- (D) neither I nor II

416. Under the Uniform Commercial Code (UCC) governing transactions involving debtor/creditor relationships, which of the following is CORRECT regarding the security agreement?
  I. It is an agreement to grant a security interest in certain personal property.
  II. It is an attempt to protect a creditor or lender.
- (A) I only
- (B) II only
- (C) both I and II
- (D) neither I nor II

417. Under the Uniform Commercial Code (UCC) governing transactions involving debtor/creditor relationships, which of the following is CORRECT regarding the attachment of the security interest?

    I. The security interest is enforceable once the security agreement has been signed.

    II. The security interest is intended to give the creditor rights against the debtor in the event of default.

(A) I only
(B) II only
(C) both I and II
(D) neither I nor II

418. Callahan goes to Lester-Glenn Motorcycle dealership late Saturday afternoon. Callahan takes test drives and talks financing with the salespeople. Callahan ultimately selects a special order bike that is not currently at the dealership. Callahan is promised by Lester-Glenn that they would deliver the bike in two days to Callahan's house if he signs the contract, the note, and security agreement while still at the Lester-Glenn dealership. Callahan agrees on Saturday and signs all the papers. The motorcycle is delivered to Callahan's house at 3 p.m. Monday just as promised by Lester-Glenn. According to the Uniform Commercial Code secured transactions article, when did attachment take place?

(A) Attachment took place Saturday night in the dealership when Callahan signed the security agreement.
(B) Attachment took place Saturday night in the dealership when Callahan signed the contract and promissory note.
(C) Attachment took place Monday afternoon when the motorcycle was delivered to Callahan's house.
(D) none of the above

419. Which of the following transactions would illustrate a secured party perfecting its security interest by taking possession of collateral?

    I. when the collateral is a stack of negotiable notes and the creditor takes possession of the negotiable instruments

    II. when a pawnbroker lends money

(A) I only
(B) II only
(C) both I and II
(D) neither I nor II

420. According to the Uniform Commercial Code secured transactions article, attachment and perfection will occur simultaneously when
  I. a pawnbroker lends money
  II. a financing statement is filed

(A) I only
(B) II only
(C) both I and II
(D) neither I nor II

421. Ivy is a former professional athlete. Retired, broke, and unable to qualify for a loan, Ivy decides to pawn a piece of valuable jewelry. Ivy pawns his League Championship Ring at the Tenderloin Pawn Shop, borrowing $15,000 from Tenderloin. Ivy takes the $15,000 from the Tenderloin Pawn Shop and purchases a used automobile outright for cash. Which of the following is CORRECT?
  I. Once Tenderloin Pawn Shop takes possession of Ivy's championship ring, Tenderloin Pawn Shop automatically receives a nonpossessory interest in the used automobile.
  II. Once Tenderloin Pawn Shop takes possession of Ivy's ring, Tenderloin Pawn Shop has a possessory interest in the piece of jewelry.
  III. Once Tenderloin Pawn Shop takes possession of Ivy's ring, Tenderloin does NOT need to file a financing statement to perfect its interest in the piece of jewelry.

(A) I only
(B) II and III only
(C) I and III only
(D) I, II, and III

422. Which of the following is CORRECT regarding a financing statement?
  I. A typical financing statement filing lasts for five years.
  II. If the debtor moves to a new state, the creditor need not file a financing statement in the new state because the original filing is good for five years.

(A) I only
(B) II only
(C) both I and II
(D) neither I nor II

423. Salika is a buyer in the ordinary course of business. If Salika purchases goods from a merchant seller,
   I. Salika purchases the goods free and clear of any security interest that she was NOT aware of at the time of purchase
   II. Salika purchases the goods free and clear of any security interest that she was aware of at the time of purchase
(A) I only
(B) II only
(C) both I and II
(D) neither I nor II

Use the following facts to answer Questions 424 and 425: Stacey is behind on the payments on her convertible, and the creditor has already attempted to repossess the car.

424. Which of the following rights does Stacey have after the convertible has been repossessed but before it has been sold?
   I. redemption
   II. right to be notified of the sale
(A) I only
(B) II only
(C) both I and II
(D) neither I nor II

425. Assume that Stacey's creditor has repossessed the convertible. Which of the following is CORRECT?
   I. If the car is repossessed and sold for less than the balance due, Stacey could not be sued for a deficiency, since she paid more than 60% of the purchase price.
   II. Once the car is repossessed by the creditor, Stacey could force the creditor to sell the car.
(A) I only
(B) II only
(C) both I and II
(D) neither I nor II

Use the following facts to answer Questions 426 and 427: Cliff bought a smart device for personal use from DC Appliance Corp. for $3,000. Cliff paid $2,000 in cash and signed a security agreement for the balance. DC Appliance properly filed the security agreement. Cliff defaulted in paying the balance of the purchase price. DC Appliance asked Cliff to pay the balance. When Cliff politely refused, DC Appliance peacefully repossessed the smart device.

426. As this transaction is covered by the Uniform Commercial Code (UCC) secured transactions article, which of the following is CORRECT?
    I. DC Appliance may retain the smart device over Cliff's objection.
    II. DC Appliance may sell the smart device without notifying Cliff.

    (A) I only
    (B) II only
    (C) both I and II
    (D) neither I nor II

427. Assume the smart device is sold at auction. Which of the following is CORRECT?
    I. If the smart device sells at auction for less than the amount owed, DC Appliance can obtain a judgment against Cliff for the deficiency.
    II. If the smart device sells at auction for more than the amount owed, DC Appliance could keep the surplus.

    (A) I only
    (B) II only
    (C) both I and II
    (D) neither I nor II

428. Which of the following is CORRECT regarding an agency relationship?
    I. An agency relationship must be in writing if the agent will earn more than $500.
    II. An agent owes a duty of loyalty to the principal, but no such duty of loyalty is owed from principal to agent.
    III. An agent for a disclosed principal would NOT be held liable to a third party if the principal backs out of the agreement.

    (A) I and II only
    (B) I, II, and III
    (C) I and III only
    (D) II and III only

429. Stump works as an agent for the New York Bombers, a major-league baseball team. Stump is paid to scout amateur baseball players and report information back to the Bombers' general manager. The Bombers send Stump from New York to Tokyo to follow a Japanese prospect named Hito whom the Bombers are interested in signing for the upcoming major-league season. It is not uncommon for Stump to travel to other countries to follow a player for the Bombers. Which of the following is CORRECT?

   I. Stump would be liable to the Bombers for disclosing information about Hito to other major-league baseball teams without the consent of the Bombers.

  II. The Bombers would be liable to Stump if they sent additional agents to Japan to follow Hito without the knowledge and consent of Stump.

(A) I only
(B) II only
(C) both I and II
(D) neither I nor II

430. If a principal wishes to no longer be obligated on any new contracts made by a recently dismissed agent, which of the following actions need be taken?

   I. Actual notice needs to be given to third parties with whom the agent had prior dealings.

  II. Constructive notice needs be given to potential third parties, even though it's not possible to ensure that all potential third parties would become aware of the agent's dismissal.

(A) I only
(B) II only
(C) both I and II
(D) neither I nor II

431. Which of the following is required for a surety contract?

   I. principal debtor, creditor, and surety

  II. written agreement between the surety and the principal debtor

 III. written agreement between the surety and the creditor

(A) I and III only
(B) I, II, and III
(C) I and II only
(D) II and III only

432. If a debtor defaults and one surety is left to pay the entire obligation, which of the following rights does that surety have after payment in full?

(A) contribution
(B) exoneration
(C) subrogation
(D) attachment

433. If a surety is asked by the creditor to pay for the default of a principal debtor's car loan, which of the following BEST describes a surety's rights?
    I. Exoneration refers to the surety's rights prior to payment.
   II. Subrogation refers to the surety's rights after payment in full.

(A) I only
(B) II only
(C) both I and II
(D) neither I nor II

434. Levon holds several credit cards from various banks. The federal Credit Card Fraud Act protects Levon from loss by

(A) restricting the interest rate charged by the credit card company
(B) requiring credit card companies to issue cards to qualified persons
(C) allowing the card holder to defer payment of the balance due on the card
(D) limiting the card holder's liability for unauthorized use

435. The Equal Credit Opportunity Act prohibits creditors from discriminating in consumer credit transactions on the basis of
    I. marital status
   II. race and gender

(A) I only
(B) II only
(C) both I and II
(D) neither I nor II

436. Liquidation is a key element in which of the following bankruptcy cases?
    I. Chapter 7
   II. Chapter 11
  III. Chapter 13

(A) I only
(B) II and III only
(C) III only
(D) I, II, and III

437. Green owes unsecured debts of $310,000 to nine creditors. Green owes each creditor more than $20,000. Which of the following is a requirement for these creditors to file involuntary bankruptcy against Green?
  I. Three or more creditors must file the petition.
  II. Green must be insolvent.
  III. Creditors must prove that Green is not paying her bona fide debts as they become due.
  (A) I and III only
  (B) III only
  (C) I, II, and III
  (D) II and III only

438. A debtor who declares bankruptcy is still entitled to which of the following assets if they are to be received by the debtor within 180 days of filing for relief?
  I. life insurance proceeds
  II. alimony
  III. inheritance
  (A) I and II only
  (B) II only
  (C) I, II, and III
  (D) neither I, II, nor III

439. Which of the following transfers could be set aside by the bankruptcy trustee and made property of the debtor's bankruptcy estate for the purposes of paying creditors?
  I. fraudulent conveyances
  II. preferential transfers in the course of the debtor's business
  (A) I only
  (B) II only
  (C) both I and II
  (D) neither I nor II

440. Based on the reorganization provisions of Chapter 11 of the Federal Bankruptcy Code, which of the following statements is CORRECT?
  I. A trustee always needs to be appointed.
  II. The commencement of a bankruptcy case may be voluntary or involuntary.
  (A) I only
  (B) II only
  (C) both I and II
  (D) neither I nor II

441. Based on the reorganization provisions of Chapter 11 of the Federal Bankruptcy Code, which of the following statements is CORRECT?
   I. Creditors could force a debtor into bankruptcy under Chapter 11, even if the debtor's total assets were greater than total liabilities.
  II. A reorganization plan may be filed by creditors.

(A) I only
(B) II only
(C) both I and II
(D) neither I nor II

442. In a bankruptcy estate, which of the following creditors would be paid FIRST?

(A) alimony and child support owed for seven months
(B) federal income taxes due no more than two years
(C) employees of the debtor who have not been paid in two months
(D) secured creditors who filed a financing statement on the debtor's inventory

443. Assuming a voluntary bankruptcy proceeding under the Federal Bankruptcy Code, which of the following claims incurred within 180 days prior to filing will be paid first?

(A) employee vacation and sick pay
(B) customer deposits
(C) secured creditors who were paid the value of their security but remain unsatisfied with a balance owed them
(D) unsecured federal taxes

444. Acts by a debtor could result in a bankruptcy court revoking the debtor's discharge. Which of the following acts will revoke the discharge?
   I. failure to list one creditor
  II. fraudulent conveyances

(A) I only
(B) II only
(C) both I and II
(D) neither I nor II

445. Which of the following events will follow the filing of a Chapter 7 involuntary petition?
   I. A stay against creditor collection proceedings goes into effect.
  II. A trustee is appointed.

(A) I only
(B) II only
(C) both I and II
(D) neither I nor II

446. Under the Federal Securities Act of 1933, which of the following relates to how the Securities and Exchange Commission (SEC) registration requirements affect an investor?
   I. The investor is NOT guaranteed by the SEC that the facts contained in the registration statement are accurate.
   II. The investor is provided with financial and nonfinancial information regarding the company seeking to raise capital.
   (A) I only
   (B) II only
   (C) both I and II
   (D) neither I nor II

447. If a Texas corporation were to issue securities for sale only to Texas residents, which of the following securities laws would the issuing corporation have to follow?
   I. Federal Securities Act of 1933
   II. State of Texas securities laws
   (A) I only
   (B) II only
   (C) both I and II
   (D) neither I nor II

448. Under the Federal Securities Act of 1933, which of the following is defined as a security and therefore would require registration with the Securities and Exchange Commission (SEC) prior to issuance unless an exemption applies?
   I. preferred stock
   II. corporate bonds
   (A) I only
   (B) II only
   (C) both I and II
   (D) neither I nor II

449. Certain exemptions from registration are allowed under the Federal Securities Act of 1933. Which of the following securities are allowed such an exemption?
   I. bonds issued by a not-for-profit charitable organization
   II. debenture bonds issued by a publicly traded company
   (A) I only
   (B) II only
   (C) both I and II
   (D) neither I nor II

450. Cramer, Inc., intends to make a $775,000 common stock offering under Rule 504 of Regulation D of the Federal Securities Act of 1933. Cramer, Inc.,

(A) may sell the stock to an unlimited number of investors
(B) may not make the offering through a general advertising
(C) must register the offering with the Securities and Exchange Commission (SEC)
(D) must provide all investors with a prospectus

451. In general, which of the following is part of Rule 505 of Regulation D of the 1933 act?

(A) No more than 35 investors and no advertising are allowed.
(B) No more than 35 accredited investors and advertising are allowed.
(C) No more than 35 nonaccredited investors and no advertising are allowed.
(D) The dollar limit is $1,000,000 and advertising is allowed.

452. Under Regulation D of the Securities Act of 1933, Rules 505 and 506 each require that

(A) the offering needs to be made without general advertising
(B) the dollar limit is $5,000,000
(C) immediate resale is unrestricted
(D) there will be a maximum of 35 total investors

453. Under Regulation D of the 1933 act, what do Rules 504, 505, and 506 all have in common?

(A) must report each sale to the Securities and Exchange Commission (SEC) within 15 days after each sale
(B) must report the first sale to the SEC within 15 days after the first sale
(C) must be totally sold out within 12 months
(D) no advertising or immediate resale to the general public

454. By itself, which of the following factors requires a corporation to comply with the reporting requirements of the Securities Exchange Act of 1934?

(A) 600 employees
(B) shares listed on a national securities exchange
(C) total assets of $2 million
(D) 200 holders of equity securities

455. Which of the following events must be reported to the Securities and Exchange Commission (SEC) under the reporting provisions of the Securities Exchange Act of 1934?

    I. unusual events not in the ordinary course of business

   II. unaudited quarterly earnings reports

  III. proxy solicitations

(A) I, II, and III

(B) I and II only

(C) I and III only

(D) II and III only

456. The annual report Form 10-K must be filed by a large reporting company within 60 days after the end of the fourth quarter of the fiscal year according to which of the following rules issued by the Securities and Exchange Commission (SEC)?

    I. Federal Securities Act of 1933

   II. Securities Exchange Act of 1934

(A) I only

(B) II only

(C) both I and II

(D) neither I nor II

457. Horizons, Inc., is a smaller reporting company under the Securities Exchange Act of 1934. The maximum number of days that Horizons, Inc., has to file its quarterly report Form 10-Q is

(A) 40

(B) 45

(C) 60

(D) 90

458. A party making a tender offer to purchase AT LEAST what amount of the shares of a class of securities registered under the 1934 act must file a report with the Securities and Exchange Commission (SEC)?

(A) 2% of the shares

(B) 5% of the shares

(C) 10% of the shares

(D) an amount considered material to the individual purchaser's net worth

459. Which of the following services would the Sarbanes-Oxley Act of 2002 permit a registered firm to perform for an audit client?
  I. tax services
  II. bookkeeping services

(A) I only
(B) II only
(C) both I and II
(D) neither I nor II

460. Two areas of the Sarbanes-Oxley Act of 2002 involve auditor *rotation* and auditor *retention*. Which of the following is CORRECT?
  I. The lead or coordinating partner and the reviewing partner must be *rotated* off an audit engagement for a publicly traded company every three years.
  II. *Retention* of the auditing firm is the responsibility of the audit committee.
  III. *Retention* of the audit documentation must be for a period of at least seven years.

(A) I and II only
(B) II and III only
(C) I, II, and III
(D) II only

461. According to the Sarbanes-Oxley Act, in order to enhance independence, the audit firm cannot have employed the issuer's CEO or CFO for how long a period preceding the audit?

(A) four years
(B) three years
(C) two years
(D) one year

462. Audit firms whose clients issue securities to the public must undergo routine periodic audits by the Public Company Accounting Oversight Board (PCAOB) based on how many audits of issuers they conduct annually. Which of the following is CORRECT?

(A) A firm that audits mostly privately held entities and audits just a few issuers annually would be inspected by the PCAOB every six years.
(B) A firm that regularly audits no issuers would still be inspected by the PCAOB every seven years.
(C) A firm that audits more than 25 issuers annually but less than 100 issuers annually would be inspected by the PCAOB every two years.
(D) A firm that audits more than 100 issuers annually would be inspected by the PCAOB every year.

463. If a CPA is found to have breached a duty of professional care and competence by lacking reasonable care in the conduct of the engagement, which of the following will the CPA most likely be sued for?

(A) gross negligence
(B) ordinary negligence
(C) constructive fraud
(D) actual or common law fraud

464. Which is CORRECT regarding accountants' liability under the federal securities laws?

  I. If a plaintiff is suing a CPA under the 1934 act, the plaintiff would have to prove that material misstatements were included in a filed document.
  II. If a plaintiff is suing a CPA under the 1934 act, the plaintiff would have to prove reliance on the financial statements.
  III. If a plaintiff is suing a CPA under the 1933 act, the plaintiff would have to prove reliance on the financial statements.

(A) I and II only
(B) II and III only
(C) I and III only
(D) I, II, and III

465. Which of the following statements is generally correct regarding the liability of a CPA who **negligently** gives an opinion on an audit of a client's financial statements?

(A) The CPA is liable only to the client.
(B) The CPA is liable only to those third parties who are in privity of contract with the CPA.
(C) The CPA is liable to anyone in a class of third parties whom the CPA knows will rely on the opinion.
(D) none of the above

466. Which of the following would support a finding of common law fraud (actual fraud) on the part of a CPA?

  I. material misrepresentation of fact
  II. intent to deceive
  III. justifiable reliance and damages

(A) I, II, and III
(B) I and II only
(C) I and III only
(D) I only

467. Under common law, which of the following statements most accurately reflects the liability of a CPA who fraudulently gives an opinion on an audit of a client's financial statements?

(A) The CPA probably is liable to the client even if the client was aware of the fraud and did not rely on the opinion.

(B) The CPA probably is liable to any person who suffered a loss as a result of the fraud.

(C) The CPA is liable only to known users of the financial statements.

(D) The CPA is liable only to third parties in privity of contract with the CPA.

468. Which of the following would support a finding of **constructive fraud** on the part of a CPA?

  I. CPA acting "recklessly"
 II. intent to deceive
III. justifiable reliance and damages

(A) I only

(B) I and II only

(C) I, II, and III

(D) I and III only

CHAPTER 5

Business Structures and Other Regulatory Areas

469. Under the Revised Model Business Corporation Act, which of the following statements regarding a corporation's bylaws is CORRECT?

I. A corporation's initial bylaws shall be adopted by either the incorporators or the board of directors.

II. A corporation's bylaws are contained in the articles of incorporation.

(A) I only
(B) II only
(C) both I and II
(D) neither I nor II

470. Noll is a promoter of a corporation to be known as Rotondo Corp. On January 1, Year 5, Noll signed a nine-month contract with Clark, a CPA, which provided that Clark would perform certain accounting services for Rotondo Corp. Noll did not disclose to Clark that Rotondo Corp. had not been formed.

Prior to the incorporation of Rotondo Corp. on February 1, Year 5, Clark rendered accounting services pursuant to the contract. After rendering accounting services for an additional period of six months pursuant to the contract, Clark was discharged without cause by the board of directors of Rotondo. In the absence of any agreements to the contrary, who will be liable to Clark for breach of contract?

(A) Noll only
(B) both Noll and Rotondo
(C) Rotondo only
(D) neither Noll nor Rotondo

471. Under the Revised Model Business Corporation Act, corporate directors are authorized to rely on information provided by the
  I. appropriate corporate officer
  II. independent auditor's report

(A) I only
(B) II only
(C) both I and II
(D) neither I nor II

472. Lucas owns 200 shares of Shea Corp. cumulative preferred stock. In the absence of any specific contrary provisions in Shea's articles of incorporation, which of the following statements is CORRECT?

(A) If Shea declares a dividend on its common stock, Lucas will be entitled to participate with the common stock shareholders in any dividend distribution made after preferred dividends are paid.
(B) Lucas will be entitled to vote if dividend payments are in arrears.
(C) Lucas is entitled to convert the 200 shares of preferred stock to a like number of shares of common stock.
(D) If Shea declares a cash dividend on its preferred stock, Lucas becomes an unsecured creditor of Shea.

473. Eco Environmental Services, Inc., is a C corporation. Which of the following is a characteristic of a C corporation?

(A) the business structure of choice for most privately held businesses
(B) is allowed to deduct dividends paid prior to paying taxes
(C) subject to double taxation on profits if dividends are paid
(D) must have only one class of stock

474. In the absence of fraud, the corporate veil is MOST LIKELY to be pierced and the shareholders held personally liable if
  I. a partnership incorporates its business solely to limit the liability of its partners
  II. the shareholders have commingled their personal funds with those of the corporation

(A) I only
(B) II only
(C) both I and II
(D) neither I nor II

475. Which of the following is a corporate equity security?

    I. a callable bond

    II. a share of convertible preferred stock

(A) I only

(B) II only

(C) both I and II

(D) neither I nor II

476. For what purpose will a stockholder of a publicly held corporation be permitted to file a shareholder's derivative lawsuit in the name of the corporation?

    I. to compel payment of a properly declared dividend

    II. to recover damages from corporate management for an ultra vires management act

(A) I only

(B) II only

(C) both I and II

(D) neither I nor II

477. In a corporation, which of the following rights does a shareholder typically have?

    I. right to vote on fundamental changes in corporate structure such as a merger

    II. right to reasonable inspection of corporate records

(A) I only

(B) II only

(C) both I and II

(D) neither I nor II

478. Which of the following is CORRECT regarding an agreement to form a general partnership?

    I. must be filed with the state government

    II. must be in writing

    III. may be oral, or implied by conduct

(A) I and II only

(B) I and III only

(C) II only

(D) III only

479. Under the Uniform Partnership Act, which of the following statements concerning the powers and duties of partners in a general partnership are CORRECT?
   I. Each partner is an agent of every other partner and acts as both a principal and an agent in any business transaction within the scope of the partnership agreement.
   II. Each partner is subject to joint and several liability on partnership debts and contracts.
   (A) I only
   (B) II only
   (C) both I and II
   (D) neither I nor II

480. When a new partner is admitted to an existing partnership to replace an outgoing partner, the liability of the newly admitted partner for *existing partnership* debts is
   (A) normally limited to the amount of his or her capital contribution to the partnership
   (B) normally unlimited, and the newly admitted partner's personal property may be seized to satisfy the existing debts
   (C) joint and several, as well as personal
   (D) limited to whatever liability the outgoing partner had

481. Which of the following actions of a partnership require unanimous consent of all partners?
   I. submitting a claim to arbitration
   II. admission of a new partner
   (A) I only
   (B) II only
   (C) both I and II
   (D) neither I nor II

482. A, B, C, and D are partners in the ABCD partnership. If Partner A retires from the partnership, then for Partner A to avoid liability for future debts of the partnership, actual notice needs to be given to existing creditors of Partner A's retirement and
   (A) Partner A needs to give actual notice to existing partnership creditors or Partner A will remain liable for existing firm debts
   (B) constructive notice needs to be given to existing creditors for Partner A to avoid liability on existing firm debts
   (C) actual notice needs to be given to potential creditors for Partner A to avoid liability for future partnership debts
   (D) constructive notice needs to be given to potential creditors for Partner A to avoid liability on future partnership debts

483. In which of the following respects do general partnerships and limited liability partnerships (LLPs) differ?
 I. in the level of personal liability for torts that partners themselves commit
 II. in the level of liability for torts committed by other partners of the same firm

(A) I only
(B) II only
(C) both I and II
(D) neither I nor II

484. A key advantage of the limited liability company (LLC) is that
 I. the entity is treated as a partnership for liability purposes
 II. the liability of members is limited to the amount of their investments

(A) I only
(B) II only
(C) both I and II
(D) neither I nor II

485. Harry, Ben, and Chico want to form a new business and be taxed as a partnership, yet have the same liability protection as shareholders in a corporation. If they carry on as co-owners of a business for profit but never file a limited liability partnership (LLP) application or articles of incorporation with their state government,
 I. they will be double taxed on all profits
 II. they will have unlimited personal liability for business debts

(A) I only
(B) II only
(C) both I and II
(D) neither I nor II

486. Which of the following characteristics apply to a limited liability partnership (LLP)?
 I. Profits and losses flow through to partners.
 II. Partners may agree to have the entity managed by one or more of the partners.
 III. A partner may be another entity.

(A) I, II, and III
(B) I and III only
(C) I and II only
(D) I only

487. Which of the following types of businesses may generally be formed without filing an organizational document with a state agency?
   I. proprietorship
   II. general partnership
   III. limited liability partnership (LLP)
   IV. limited liability company (LLC)

(A) I and II only
(B) I, II, and III
(C) I only
(D) I, II, and IV

488. Which of the following tax returns are due within three and a half months of the end of the business year?
   I. trusts
   II. individual tax returns
   III. partnership tax returns

(A) I, II, and III
(B) II and III only
(C) I and III only
(D) I and II only

489. Larry, an employee of Hanson Manufacturing, Inc., was injured in the course of employment while operating a forklift manufactured and sold to Hanson by Suzy Wong, Inc. Under the state's mandatory workers' compensation statute, Larry will be successful in obtaining
   I. workers' compensation even if Larry was negligent
   II. legal action against Hanson, Inc.
   III. legal action against Suzy Wong, Inc.

(A) I and III
(B) I, II, and III
(C) II and III
(D) I and II

490. Which of the following gets deducted from an employee's salary?
   I. federal unemployment tax
   II. social security tax
   III. workers' compensation insurance

(A) I and III only
(B) I and II only
(C) I, II, and III
(D) II only

491. Based on the Americans with Disabilities Act of 1990, which of the following is CORRECT?

    I. The act does NOT require companies to set up a specified plan to hire people with disabilities.

    II. The act requires companies to make reasonable accommodations for disabled persons unless this results in undue hardship.

    (A) I only

    (B) II only

    (C) both I and II

    (D) neither I nor II

492. Which of the following agencies is likely to enforce the law against an act of sexual discrimination in the workplace?

    (A) Occupational Safety and Health Administration (OSHA)

    (B) Federal Trade Commission (FTC)

    (C) Internal Revenue Service (IRS)

    (D) Equal Employment Opportunity Commission (EEOC)

493. According to the Employee Retirement Income Security Act (ERISA), which of the following agencies is empowered to regulate pension plans?

    I. Internal Revenue Service (IRS)

    II. US Department of Labor

    (A) I only

    (B) II only

    (C) both I and II

    (D) neither I nor II

494. According to the Bank Secrecy Act, financial institutions must file a currency transaction report (CTR) for each transaction in excess of

    (A) $2,500

    (B) $5,000

    (C) $7,500

    (D) $10,000

495. According to the Sherman Antitrust Act, which of the following would be considered evidence of a monopoly?

    I. a firm's ability to control prices

    II. a firm's ability to exclude competition

    III. a firm's market share of above 70%

    (A) I, II, and III

    (B) I and III only

    (C) I and II only

    (D) II and III only

496. Surett wrote a personal finance autobiography called *Million Dollars Later.* He wishes to copyright the book and protect his rights. Which of the following is CORRECT?

    I. A copyright would protect Surett's rights for Surett's natural life plus 70 years.

    II. The Fair Use Doctrine would allow for certain classroom uses of the book for educational purposes without Surett's permission.

(A) I only
(B) II only
(C) both I and II
(D) neither I nor II

497. Which of the following are rights included with the owner of a copyright?

    I. fair use

    II. license the copyright to others

(A) I only
(B) II only
(C) both I and II
(D) neither I nor II

498. The length of the creator's life is NOT a factor in determining the years of protection for a

    I. copyright

    II. patent

(A) I only
(B) II only
(C) both I and II
(D) neither I nor II

499. Which of the following are attributes that must be shown in order to obtain a patent for an invention?

    I. The invention is novel and useful.

    II. The invention is NOT obvious to others who work in the field.

    III. The invention is in a tangible medium of expression.

(A) I, II, and III
(B) I and II only
(C) I and III only
(D) II and III only

500. The Bank Secrecy Act requires
  I. the filing of a currency transaction report for any deposit, withdrawal, or exchange of currency of $5,000 or more
  II. a report to be filed within 30 days of a currency transaction in excess of $10,000

(A) I only
(B) II only
(C) both I and II
(D) neither I nor II

Bonus Questions

501. In connection with the Orderly Liquidation Authority established under Title II of the Dodd-Frank Act, which of the following is CORRECT before the FDIC can liquidate a banking institution?
  I. The banking institution must have more than $50 billion in assets.
  II. The banking institution must have paid into the Orderly Liquidation Fund for at least two years.

(A) I only
(B) II only
(C) both I and II
(D) neither I nor II

502. Nonqualified stock options are granted to employees on February 3, Year 1. Ordinary income is paid by the employees based on the options having a readily ascertainable value. Which of the following is CORRECT?
  I. If the options are exercised, the holding period for the shares begins with the date the options are granted.
  II. If the options expire without being exercised, the employees have a capital loss based on the ordinary income already recognized.

(A) I only
(B) II only
(C) both I and II
(D) neither I nor II

503. Assessment of the $100 preparer penalty for failure to employ due diligence in connection with the earned income credit applies to
  I. determining the client's eligibility for the earned income credit
  II. determining the amount of the client's earned income credit

(A) I only
(B) II only
(C) both I and II
(D) neither I nor II

ANSWERS

Chapter 1: Taxation of Individuals

1. (A) Filing status is determined on the last day of the year, not by a majority of days in the year. Although Theresa and John were both single for nearly the entire year, the only day that counts for filing status is the last day of the year.

2. (D) Usually, filing status is determined on the last day of the year, but in the case of death, filing status is determined on the date of death. For this reason, in the year a spouse dies (Year 1), the surviving spouse is permitted to file a joint return. In Years 2 and 3 following the spouse's death, the surviving spouse could qualify to file as a qualifying widower (or widow) and would therefore be able to use the same tax rates as those applied to a joint return. In this question, Gil Gallon had a qualifying child and could therefore file as a qualifying widower in Year 2 (and Year 3 as well, but the question only asked about Year 2). If the question had asked about Year 4, the answer would have been head of household because the qualifying widower (widow) filing status is available only for the two immediate years following a spouse's death, and Gil Gallon has met the requirements for head of household status.

3. (B) Normally, filing status is determined on the last day of the year, but in the case of death, filing status is determined at the date of death. Accordingly, in the year a spouse dies (Year 1), the surviving spouse is permitted to file a joint return. In Years 2 and 3 following the spouse's death, the surviving spouse could qualify to file as a qualifying widower (widow) and would therefore be able to use the same tax rates as those applied to a joint return. This status, however, is available only for the two years immediately following a spouse's death. Afterward, the surviving spouse would either file as head of household (if meeting the requirements for head of household filing status) or single. Since the question asks about Year 4, Bonnie would file as head of household as she otherwise meets the head of household requirements (i.e., she has a dependent child for whom she provides full support).

4. (C) Kathleen, as an abandoned spouse providing sole support for her four dependent children, would be permitted to file under the head of household filing status provided that she were truly abandoned for the last six months (or more) of Year 8.

5. (B) Normally, for a taxpayer to claim an exemption for a dependent, the dependent cannot earn more than the exemption amount ($3,900 for 2013). However, if the dependent is a full-time student under the age of 24, and the taxpayer furnishes more than 50% of the dependent's support, the taxpayer can claim an exemption for the dependent even though the dependent's earned income may exceed the exemption amount. If the taxpayer does not furnish more than 50% of the dependent's support, then the taxpayer cannot claim an exemption for the dependent. In this question, Shari earned more than the exemption amount, is under the age of 24, and is a full-time student, so her parents could still claim her as a dependent provided they furnished more than 50% of her support; otherwise, they would not be permitted to do so.

6. (C) Ben and Freeda furnished more than 50% of Harold's support, and since he is under the age of 24 and is a full-time student, they can claim him even though his income was more than the exemption amount ($3,900 for 2013). Ben and Freeda can also claim Susan, who is blind, is mostly deaf, and has no income, and for whom they provide full support. However, Susan's disabilities do not qualify the taxpayers for any additional exemption. If on the CPA examination, however, the *taxpayer* himself is blind (i.e., Ben, Freeda), a higher *standard deduction* is available. But nothing additional is available for having a blind *dependent.* Thus Ben and Freeda would claim four exemptions on their tax return: one for Ben, one for Freeda, one for Harold, and one for Susan.

7. (D) The tax laws provide a few tax benefits for the elderly. One of those is an increased standard deduction. If Walter does not itemize his deductions, he will take the standard deduction, which will be at an increased level because of his age.

8. (C) While interest income on obligations of a state or a possession of the United States (i.e., Puerto Rico, Guam, or Virgin Islands bonds or obligations) are tax-exempt, most other interest income is taxable. Thus the interest on both the federal and state income tax returns would be taxable, as well as the interest on US Treasury (federal government) obligations. Consequently, a total of $1,900 would be reported as taxable income on Erin and Mars's joint income tax return.

9. (B) The general rule is that most interest income is taxable with the exception of interest income on obligations of a state (i.e., municipal bonds) or a possession of the United States (i.e., Puerto Rico, Guam, or the Virgin Islands). Accordingly, from the items listed, only the municipal bond interest of $1,600 is tax free. The interest income received on the federal income tax refund, personal injury award, and US savings bonds would all be taxable. Griffin would therefore report $2,000 as interest income on his current year tax return.

10. (D) I is wrong. Accumulated interest on Series EE US savings bonds may be exempt from tax but *only if* certain conditions are met: (1) the bonds have been issued to the taxpayer after December 31, 1989, (2) the bonds must be purchased by the taxpayer or taxpayer's spouse and kept in the taxpayer's name (i.e., the taxpayer must be the sole owner of the bonds or joint owner with his or her spouse), (3) the taxpayer (owner) must be 24 years or older before the bond's issue date (i.e., the taxpayer or owner must be 24 years old when purchasing the bonds), and (4) redemption proceeds from the bonds must be used to pay for higher education costs (usually college costs) for the taxpayer, taxpayer's spouse, or taxpayer's dependents. II is wrong. Redemption proceeds from the bonds must be used to pay for higher education costs (usually college costs) for the taxpayer, taxpayer's spouse, or taxpayer's dependents. If proceeds are used for any other purpose, like home improvement, the interest would be taxable.

11. (A) Accumulated interest on Series EE US savings bonds may be exempt from tax but *only if* certain conditions are met: (1) the bonds have been issued to the taxpayer after December 31, 1989, (2) the bonds must be purchased by the taxpayer or taxpayer's spouse and kept in the taxpayer's name (i.e., the taxpayer must be the sole owner of the bonds or joint owner with his or her spouse), (3) the taxpayer (owner) must be 24 years or older before the bond's issue date (i.e., the taxpayer or owner must be 24 years old when purchasing the bonds), and (4) redemption proceeds from the bonds must be used to pay for higher education costs (usually college costs) for the taxpayer, taxpayer's spouse, or taxpayer's dependents.

12. (A) Most dividends are taxable. Sometimes the taxpayer reinvests the monies earned from the dividend receipt into additional shares. This in and of itself does not make the dividend tax exempt. Reinvested dividends are treated as if the cash received was used to immediately purchase new shares. If, however, an examination question stated that the dividend was paid in shares of the corporation's stock with no opportunity for the taxpayer to receive cash, then the dividend would be tax free. Dividends received on unmatured life insurance policies are generally tax exempt (provided those dividends do not exceed cumulative premiums paid). Dividends received on foreign corporations are taxable.

13. (A) Stock dividends issued on common stock are normally not taxable. Instead, the cost of the original shares must be spread over all shares owned (old and new) because that is the taxpayer's actual total cost. Tatum's original basis per share was $50 and is now:

$$\frac{\$50,000^*}{1,050 \text{ shares}^{**}} = \$47.62$$

Any gain or loss on the stock will be included on Tatum's tax return when the stock is eventually sold. Further, since there was no opportunity to receive cash, none of the stock dividend is taxable.

14. (D) Although interest income is taxed at ordinary income tax rates, and dividends (depending on how they are classified) may or may not be taxed at ordinary income tax rates, both interest and dividend income are reported on Schedule B. Schedule D is used to report capital gains and losses, and Schedule E is used to report supplemental income and loss (i.e., passive income and loss) such as rental real estate income or loss, income or loss derived from investments in partnerships or S corporations, and income or loss from estates and trusts.

15. (A) The question asked for the amount of net passive income or loss in Year 2. There were only two passive activities, a passive gain of $1,000 and a passive loss of $5,000. All passive activity gains and losses are netted to arrive at a single number. The two passive activities for Stegman net out to a $4,000 passive loss. Had the question then asked how much passive loss is deductible in the current year against nonpassive income, all $4,000 passive loss would be carried forward. A passive loss cannot be deducted in the current year against nonpassive income unless the passive loss is from a rental real estate activity. The deductibility of any potential rental real estate loss is further subject to an adjusted gross income threshold and active participation in the rental real estate activity. The salary of $50,000 earned from Stegman's employer does not qualify as a passive activity and therefore would not result in any passive gain or loss. The interest income of $100 is considered portfolio income, not passive income. Be careful on the CPA exam not to net passive and portfolio activities. If the question asks for passive income or loss, leave the portfolio income aside.

---

*1,000 original shares × $50 per share

**1,000 original shares + additional 50 shares issued in connection with the stock divided (i.e., 1,000 shares × 5%)

16. (A) Income or loss derived from a rental real estate activity is deemed passive income or loss. Passive losses up to $25,000 can be deducted against ordinary income if the taxpayer actively participates in the passive activity *and* does not have an adjusted gross income that exceeds $150,000 for the tax year. Because Adrian's adjusted gross income exceeded the $150,000 threshold, no deduction for the rental loss can be taken in Year 6. However, the entire $29,000 can be carried over to her Year 7 next tax year and beyond (indefinitely) until fully utilized. If Adrian's adjusted gross income had been $150,000 or less, she would have been able to deduct $25,000 of the loss and the remaining $4,000 would be carried over to her Year 7 tax return and beyond (indefinitely) until fully utilized.

17. (C) Income or loss derived from a rental real estate activity is deemed passive income or loss. Passive losses up to $25,000 can be deducted against ordinary income if the taxpayer actively participates in the passive activity *and* does not have an adjusted gross income that exceeds $150,000 for the tax year. In this case, since Cindy's Year 9 adjusted gross income is less than $150,000, and the $30,000 loss she incurred was derived from a passive activity in which she actively participated, she can deduct $25,000 of that loss against her ordinary income of $75,000 in Year 9 and the remaining $5,000 can be carried over to her Year 10 tax year and beyond (indefinitely) until fully utilized.

18. (B) All passive activity gains and losses are netted to arrive at a single number. If this net number is a gain, it is taxable; if it is a loss, that loss cannot be deducted unless it is from a rental real estate activity. Losses from such activities (up to $25,000) can be deducted against ordinary income if the taxpayer actively participates in the passive activity and does not have adjusted gross income that exceeds $150,000 for the tax year. In this case, Shan had two sources of passive income and loss: the S corporation investment and the rental real estate activity. Regardless of whether or not Shan had actively participated in the S corporate or rental real estate activity, he would net the income and loss from these activities, leaving him with a $20,000 net loss. Because Shan's adjusted gross income exceeded the $150,000 threshold, Shan would *not* be able to deduct the remaining $20,000 against his ordinary income in Year 10 and would have to carry over this amount to Year 11 and beyond (indefinitely) until the $20,000 loss was fully utilized. Thus Shan is able to deduct only $15,000 of the $35,000 loss against the $15,000 of passive income he earned from the S corporation investment. If Shan's adjusted gross income had been less than $150,000, Shan would have been able to deduct the entire remaining $20,000 loss against his ordinary income in Year 10, as this net loss was derived from a rental real estate activity.

19. (B) The answer is $4,200. The question expects you to be somewhat familiar with rental activities reported on Form 1040 Schedule E. Only the portion of expenses that applies to the tenant can be deducted on Schedule E. Skorecki can deduct on Schedule E half the mortgage interest, $1,500; half the real estate taxes, $2,500; and half the depreciation, $1,000. The rental apartment repairs, $800, can be 100% deducted because it was the tenant's apartment that was repaired. Skorecki did not perform repairs on the other apartment where he lives. Note: the other half of the real estate taxes and mortgage interest can be deducted on Schedule A if Skorecki itemizes.

Rent income	$10,000
Deductions:	
Mortgage interest	$1,500
Real estate taxes	$2,500
Depreciation	$1,000
Painting of rental	$800
	↓
Total deductions	$5,800
Net rental income	$4,200

20. (C) Rudnick's passive loss for Year 6 amounts to $2,500, or 5% of the partnership's operating loss. The $20,000 of interest earned on the US Treasury obligations is considered portfolio or investment income and does not qualify as passive income, so while Rudnick's share of this portfolio income is $1,000 (or 5% of $20,000), it would not be netted against Rudnick's passive loss of $2,500. Note: the passive loss of $2,500 would *not* be tax deductible, unless there was another source of passive income to offset it.

21. (C) All income items presented in this question comprise Benson's adjusted gross income. The passive loss can be netted against, and up to, the amount of any passive income. The only passive income included in her reported income items is the $7,000 of rental income. Thus the $9,000 passive loss from partnership B can be offset against this income, with a remaining $2,000 loss that cannot be offset or deducted in Year 7 (as it was derived from an equipment rental business, and not a rental real estate activity) and must be carried over to Year 8 and beyond (indefinitely) until fully utilized. Accordingly, Benson's adjusted gross income consists of:

$70,000	ordinary income from partnership A
+ $7,000	rental income
− $7,000	passive loss from partnership B (with $2,000 remaining loss carried over to Year 8)
+ 4,000	interest and dividends
$74,000	

22. (D) All $17,000 of the building rental loss is deductible by Shapiro in Year 9. That loss (a passive loss) is first offset against any passive income and gains. There is one passive gain presented in this question (i.e., the net gain from partnership B, a gain from a bike rental business without active participation). That passive gain amounted to $9,000, and therefore, $9,000 of the building rental loss (passive loss) is first used to offset against the $9,000 passive gain from bike rentals. The $8,000 passive loss remaining can be offset against Shapiro's ordinary income since the passive loss relates to a rental real estate activity and Shapiro's adjusted gross income (as can be derived from the data presented) is less than $150,000. Net passive losses are generally not deductible and are carried over indefinitely (until utilized), unless they are associated with a rental real estate activity and the taxpayer materially participates in the activity and his or her adjusted gross income does not exceed $150,000 for the tax year.

Passive loss from rental real estate	$17,000
Passive income	9,000
Passive loss from rental real estate in excess of passive income	8,000

The excess passive rental loss of $8,000 is deductible against ordinary income from the pinball arcade since adjusted gross income (AGI) is under $150,000 and the passive loss is from real estate rental. Therefore, the total passive loss deduction for Shapiro in Year 9 is $17,000.

23. **(D)** Unemployment compensation is taxable as are cash dividends on stocks, cash prizes awarded in a contest (unless the winner or recipient doesn't accept the check and has it sent directly to a charitable organization), and interest income on tax refunds. A college loan must be repaid and therefore would not be taxable. Neither a state scholarship awarded for tuition nor cash support received from parents is taxable. Therefore, his adjusted gross income for Year 9 amounts to $1,810 computed as follows:

$500	cash dividends on stocks
+ $300	cash prize awarded in contest
+ $1,000	unemployment compensation
+ $10	interest income on tax refund
= $1,810	adjusted gross income (AGI)

24. **(C)** The general rule for prizes is that prizes are taxable, except when the winner, recipient, or taxpayer doesn't accept the check but has it sent directly to a charity. If the taxpayer accepts the check and later donates it to a charity, the prize is taxable as other income on Form 1040. The taxpayer can then deduct the charitable contribution as an itemized deduction on Form 1040 Schedule A. The only way to avoid paying tax on the prize is to never take possession of the check.

25. **(D)** If an employer offers life insurance as part of a qualified plan, the premium paid (by the employer) on the first $50,000 of coverage is not included in the employee's gross income. That amount is viewed as a nontaxable fringe benefit. However, the employer must include (in the employee's taxable wages) the amount of premium paid for any life insurance coverage in excess of $50,000.

26. **(C)** If an employer offers life insurance (to its employees) as part of a qualified plan (i.e., group-term life insurance), the premium paid (by the employer) in excess of $50,000 of coverage, for an employee, is a taxable fringe benefit that must be included in the employee's taxable income. In this question, Cobbs is covered by a $90,000 policy, and therefore, the premium paid on the excess $40,000 of coverage ($90,000 − $50,000) would be taxable and computed as follows:

$$\frac{\$40,000 \text{ excess}}{\$1,000} = 40 \times \$8 = \$320$$

Although the $320 is taxable, it is not subject to social security tax.

27. **(B)** Even for an accrual basis taxpayer, all cash received is taxable when received. In this example, the only exception would be for the security deposits, since they are placed into a segregated account and will eventually be returned to the tenant. Thus these amounts do

not represent income to Olney. Olney will, therefore, include $55,000 in his current gross income computed as follows:

$30,000	current rents
+ $10,000	rents for next year—i.e., advance rents, which are taxable when received
+ $15,000	lease cancellation payments, which represent an additional source of rental income from the tenant
= $55,000	total to be included in Olney's current gross income

28. (C) In performing a service, if a taxpayer receives an asset other than cash, the fair market value of the asset received is taxable as ordinary income. In this case, Jay received $200 cash plus a catered party that had a fair market value of $350; thus Jay would report $550 as taxable income from this transaction. Note that the $250 that Lou earns as profit on these types of parties does not impact the taxable income attributable to Jay.

$200	cash
$350	fair value of the party
$550	total income

29. (B) I is wrong. Alimony must be paid in cash (it cannot be paid in property or any other form for that matter). II is correct. Alimony can be paid directly to a spouse or a third party on behalf of the spouse.

30. (B) Alimony can be paid directly to one's spouse or to a third party on behalf of one's spouse. Accordingly, the $6,000 cash paid directly to Karen, the $9,000 paid to her landlord, and the $5,000 paid to Wildwood College on behalf of Karen would all qualify as alimony. Payments that are deemed to be alimony are deductible by the paying party and taxable to the recipient. However, in this example, since the total $20,000 payment will be reduced by 30% (or $6,000) when Karen and Terry's child reaches 18 years of age, the $6,000 piece of the total $20,000 payment implicitly represents child support (since the required payment of child support ceases when a child reaches 18 years of age). Child support is not deductible to the paying party (i.e., Terry) and consequently, not taxable to the recipient (i.e., Karen). Thus the amount of payments that Karen should include in her Year 4 income includes:

$6,000	cash paid to spouse
$14,000	payments on behalf of spouse
($6,000)	30% of the total payment that represents child support
$14,000	taxable as alimony

31. (A) The plumbing supplies, web hosting, depreciation, and advertising ($4,900 total) are all expenses incurred that pertain to Buddy's business. Thus these expenses are deductible on Buddy's Schedule C. Buddy's salary of $5,200 is not deductible. The owner's salary is not a tax deduction for a sole proprietorship. Thus the $5,200 taken by Buddy is treated as drawings, not a deductible expense. The estimated federal tax of $4,000 is given the status of a tax credit on Buddy's return (tax credits are not included in Schedule C business deductions), and the charitable contribution to the Red Cross of $500 is an itemized deduction that gets reported on Schedule A.

Plumbing supplies	$2,500
Web page hosting	$300
Depreciation	$400
Advertising	$1,700
Total deductions	$4,900

32. (D) All cash is taxable when received. Thus the cash received from patients in Year 4 would be part of taxable net income for Year 4, as would the cash received from insurance companies for services provided in Year 3. Deductions in Year 4 would include salaries paid in Year 4 and other expenses paid in Year 4. The Year 4 bonuses of $4,000 that were paid to employees in Year 5 would be deductible in Year 5. Accordingly, Dr. Bernstein would report a taxable net income of $225,000 ($270,000 + $30,000 − $50,000 − $25,000).

33. (A) Alimony and interest are not subject to self-employment tax, as they are not derived from self-employment and providing consultative services. Thus only the consulting fees, the directors' fees, and the net profit Anita reported on her Form 1040 Schedule C would be subject to self-employment tax: $8,000 + $1,800 + $1,000 = $10,800.

34. (C) While all of the amounts Anita received in this question would be subject to federal income tax, only the consulting fees, directors' fees, and the net profit she reported on her Form 1040 Schedule C (collectively, her self-employment income) would be subject to self-employment tax. Thus Anita would pay both federal income tax and self-employment tax on her self-employment income.

35. (A) A portion of the self-employment tax Freedson must pay on her self-employment income is deductible from gross income in arriving at adjusted gross income (AGI). For 2013 and 2014, one-half of the self-employment tax is deductible to arrive at AGI. (B) is not correct, because a portion of the self-employment tax is deductible. Both (C) and (D) are not correct, because only a portion of the self-employment tax is deductible and it is deductible for AGI, not as an itemized deduction or in determining net income from self-employment.

36. (A) Income from net rental activities is subject to regular income tax but not self-employment tax. Rental income is passive, not active; consequently, it is not subject to self-employment tax.

37. (D) I is wrong. The land is being used as an outdoor marketplace; therefore, the land would be considered a Section 1231 asset, not a capital asset. Section 1231 assets include those assets held for more than one year and *used in the business* to generate revenue. Capital assets, on the other hand, are assets used for personal enjoyment or held for investment. The land cited in this question, for instance, could be classified as a capital asset if it was *not* being used in business and was instead being held for long-term appreciation (investment). It is the manner in which the asset is being used that determines its classification as a capital asset or a Section 1231 asset—not the asset itself.

  II is wrong. The large shed used for table storage is also being used in the business; therefore, the shed would be considered a Section 1231 asset.

38. (D) Section 1231 assets include "business assets," or *assets used in the business* to generate revenue, which are held for more than one year. Capital assets are those assets held for investment or used for personal enjoyment. In this question, neither the land nor the building is being used in the business, so both would be classified as capital assets. It is not the asset itself that determines its classification as a capital asset or Section 1231 asset; rather, it is the manner in which the asset is being used that determines its classification.

39. (A) Capital assets are assets used for personal enjoyment or held for investment. Section 1231 assets, on the other hand, include "business assets" used in the business to generate revenue, which are held for more than one year. In the question, the limousine is being used in the limousine service business to transport passengers to and from airports (i.e., it is being used in the business to generate revenues) and therefore would be classified as a Section 1231 asset, not a capital asset. The recreational skis are assets Rocky is using for personal enjoyment and consequently would be classified as a capital asset.

40. (B) The painting is considered a capital asset to Angie. Capital assets include investment property and property held for personal use. The question herein explicitly states that Angie had bought the painting for personal use. The gain from the sale should therefore be classified as a capital gain, which must be further classified as either long-term or short-term based on the asset's holding period. Long-term classification is required for assets held in excess of one year, while short-term classification is appropriate for holding periods of one year or less. Since Angie bought the painting in Year 1 and sold it in Year 6, the gain she experienced on the sale would be classified as a long-term capital gain.

41. (D) A married couple filing jointly, as well as an individual filing as single or head of household, can deduct capital losses to the extent of capital gains. Any excess capital loss deductions are limited to $3,000 of ordinary income, with any remainder carried forward to future periods indefinitely. For married couples filing separately, excess capital loss deductions are limited to $1,500 of ordinary income (for each taxpayer), with any remainder carried forward to future periods indefinitely.

42. (B) Individual taxpayers must report gains and losses on investment property (i.e., individual stock and bond investments), but only gains should be reported on personal property transactions. For example, if a taxpayer sells personal furniture at a gain, that gain must be reported (and would be reported as a capital gain). However, if the same personal property is sold at a loss, no deduction is allowed.

43. (C) *Accounting gain, economic gain,* or *realized gain* is synonymous terminology in the context of exchanges of like-kind property. Essentially a realized gain means the taxpayer has transacted (i.e., sold or exchanged) an asset (property) for a profit. Use of these terms does not necessarily mean that the gain is recognized for tax purposes.

44. (B) The general rule in a like-kind exchange is that no gain is recognized. However, when a taxpayer receives "boot" (cash or unlike property) in connection with a like-kind exchange, the boot results in a recognized gain to the extent of the lesser of the realized gain or the boot received. In this question, the realized gain is computed as follows:

Fair market value of new property	$450,000
Boot received	+ $50,000
Total amount realized	$500,000
Cost basis of property given up	− $300,000
Realized gain	$200,000

The gain recognized is limited to the lesser of the realized gain ($200,000) or the boot received ($50,000). The boot is the lesser amount, and therefore Saralee would recognize a $50,000 gain.

45. (D) Pollack would realize a gain in the amount of $175,000 computed as follows:

Fair market value of building received	$550,000
Mortgage on the apartment building given up	+ $100,000*
Cash/"boot" received	+ $25,000
Total amount realized	$675,000

From this amount subtract total cost basis:

Basis of old apartment building	$375,000
Mortgage on new apartment building assumed by Pollack	+ $125,000
Total basis	$500,000

Total amount realized: $675,000 Total basis $500,000 = $175,000 (realized gain).

46. (A) Pollack would recognize a gain on this exchange in the amount of $25,000. The general rule in a like-kind exchange is that no gain is recognized. However, when a taxpayer receives "boot" (cash or unlike property) in connection with a like-kind exchange, the boot results in a recognized gain to the extent of the lesser of the realized gain or the boot received. The realized gain on this transaction is $175,000 computed as follows:

Fair market value of building received	$550,000
Mortgage on the apartment building given up	+ $100,000
Cash received	+ $25,000
Basis of old apartment building	− $375,000
Mortgage on new apartment building assumed by Pollack	− $125,000

Since Pollack assumed a mortgage ($125,000), which is greater than that of which he was relieved ($100,000), the release of the mortgage is not considered boot. Thus the gain recognized in this transaction would be limited to the amount of cash boot received (i.e., $25,000), as that was less than the realized gain of $175,000.

47. (A) The general rule in a like-kind exchange is that no gain is recognized. However, when a taxpayer receives "boot" (cash or unlike property) in connection with a like-kind exchange, the boot results in a recognized gain to the extent of the lesser of the realized gain or the boot received. In this question, the total boot received is equal to the $30,000 cash received + the $70,000 of debt that Hymanson was relieved of, or $100,000. Hymanson's realized gain, on the other hand, is equal to $190,000:

Fair market value of real property received	$250,000
Cash received	+ $30,000
Debt relief	+ $70,000
Adjusted cost basis of investment real property given up	− $160,000

---

*This is considered a form of boot received since Pollack is being relieved of this mortgage.

Since the total boot received is less than the realized gain, Hymanson will recognize a $100,000 gain on the exchange transaction.

48. (C) I is correct. Losses are disallowed on the sale or exchange of property to a related party taxpayer. Examples of related party taxpayers include, but are not limited to, members of the family (i.e., spouse, brothers, sisters, ancestors, and lineal descendants), a corporation and a more than 50% shareholder, two corporations that are members of the same controlled group, and so on. In this question, Evan is Jerry's son (a related party taxpayer or transferee); thus Jerry is not permitted to deduct the $4,000 loss he incurs on the sale of ABC stock shares to Evan. II is correct. If the stock is later sold by the related party taxpayer (i.e., the transferee), any gain that may be recognized is reduced by the previously disallowed loss. However, when Evan resells the stock (and provided he does so at a gain), Evan can reduce his gain by Jerry's previously disallowed loss. Therefore, both statements presented in this question are correct statements.

49. (B) Losses are disallowed on the sale or exchange of property to a related party taxpayer. However, when the property is later sold by the related party taxpayer (i.e., the transferee), any gain that may be recognized is reduced by the previously disallowed loss. In this question, when Jerry initially sold the shares of ABC company stock to Evan, he experienced a loss of $4,000 (i.e., sell price: $11,000 – cost/basis: $15,000). Because Evan was his son (and therefore considered a related party taxpayer), Jerry was disallowed a deduction for the $4,000. However, because Evan resold the shares to an unrelated party at a $5,000 gain (sell price: $16,000 – cost/basis: $11,000), he is permitted to use the previously disallowed loss of $4,000 to reduce his gain. Evan would therefore report a $1,000 gain on his Year 9 income tax return ($5,000 gain – previous $4,000 disallowed loss).

50. (A) Losses are disallowed on the sale or exchange of property to a related party taxpayer. However, when the property is later sold by the related party taxpayer (i.e., the transferee) *any gain that may be recognized* is reduced by the previously disallowed loss. In this question, although Mitch and Glen are related parties, Glen is unable to use the $3,000 disallowed loss experienced by Mitch; therefore, Glen would report a short-term capital loss of $1,000. Note that the classification of the loss is short-term since Glen bought the stock from Mitch on July 1, Year 4, and resold it on November 1, Year 4. The two sales are illustrated as follows:

Related party sale from Mitch to Glen

Selling price	$7,000
Cost basis	– $10,000
Related party loss disallowed	– $3,000

Sale from Glen to unrelated party

Selling price	$6,000
Cost basis	– $7,000
Loss from sale to unrelated party	– $1,000

51. (B) The general rule for valuation of assets received through an inheritance is that those assets are valued at their fair market value on the date of death. An exception to this general rule occurs when the executor of the estate chooses to value all assets on the alternative valuation date (AVD), which is six months after the date of death or the date of conveyance of the estate assets, whichever comes first. In this case, because Jeff was distributed the stock prior to the AVD, the stock would be valued on the date of conveyance (i.e., March 31, Year 3); hence, Jeff's basis for the stock would be $240,000, the stock's value on March 31, Year 3.

52. (B) Normally, estate assets are valued as of the date of death. However, the executor does have the right to elect to value the assets at an alternative date. The alternative valuation date (AVD) is six months after the date of death or the date of conveyance of the estate assets, whichever comes first. Since no estate assets or property were conveyed until July 1, Year 2 (which was over a year from the date of Fanny's death), the assets should be valued at the AVD, or October 1, Year 1, six months after the date of Fanny's death.

53. (A) When assets are inherited, the beneficiary automatically inherits the assets under a long-term holding period. Even assets, which may only be held for a short-term period after the inheritance, can still qualify for long-term capital gain or loss treatment when sold.

54. (A) Denise must recognize a $10,000 gain on the sale of her personal residence in Year 15 computed as follows:

Proceeds from sale	$390,000
Cost basis of residence	– $105,000 (purchase price)
Patio addition	<u>– $25,000</u>
Realized gain	$260,000

Out of the $260,000 realized gain, the first $250,000 of gain from the sale of a primary residence is exempt from tax for a taxpayer filing as a single filer; $500,000 is exempt from tax for taxpayers filing as married filing jointly. Since Denise is single and would therefore be filing as such, she would be able to exclude $250,000 of the gain on her Year 15 tax return. Consequently, Denise would report a recognized gain of $10,000:

Realized gain	$260,000
Less gain exclusion	<u>– $250,000</u>
Taxable gain	$10,000

Note that a taxpayer can take advantage of this exclusion every two years. Several years had passed since Denise sold her last personal residence in Year 8.

55. (D) I is wrong. In order for a single taxpayer to exclude (from income) up to $250,000 of gain realized on the sale or exchange of a home or residence, the taxpayer must have owned and occupied the residence as a principal residence for an aggregate of at least two of the five years preceding the sale or exchange. A $500,000 exclusion is afforded married couples filing jointly provided they meet the same requirements. The home cannot be a vacation home; it must be a principal residence and used as such. II is wrong. There is no requirement that the taxpayer buy another residence in order to qualify for this gain exclusion.

56. (A) For married couples filing jointly, a gain realized on the sale of a personal (primary or principal) residence of up to $500,000 is excludable from income if the taxpayers jointly owned and used the property as a principal residence for an aggregate of at least two of the five years preceding the sale or exchange of the property. Taxpayers filing single may exclude up to $250,000 of realized gain provided they meet these same requirements. In this question, Barry and Saralee may exclude all of the gain realized on the home sale as they have met the requirements for gain exclusion and the gain does not exceed $500,000, computed as follows:

Net proceeds from sale of home

Selling price	$650,000
Real estate commissions paid on sale	− $36,000
Net proceeds from sale of home	$614,000
	↓
Less: Cost basis of home (Purchase price + improvements)	$340,000

Realized gain of $274,000 is less than $500,000, so none of the $274,000 of the realized gain would be recognized. The entire $274,000 realized gain is tax free.

57. (C) Koshefsky's taxable gain would be $60,000. The condemnation of the building by the state qualifies as an involuntary conversion. In such cases, the taxpayer must recognize the gain realized on the conversion or the amount of cash remaining after replacement of the condemned property, whichever is less.

Proceeds received from the state	$260,000
Less the building's tax basis	− $200,000
Realized gain	$60,000
Proceeds received from the state	$260,000
Less cost to replace	− $170,000
Excess proceeds received	$90,000

Since the realized gain was $60,000, and this amount was less than the $90,000 of excess proceeds received, Koshefsky would report a taxable gain on the involuntary conversion transaction in the amount of $60,000.

58. (B) Koshefsky would be required to recognize a $30,000 gain on this transaction, which qualifies as an involuntary conversion. When a transaction qualifies as an involuntary conversion, the taxpayer must report the gain realized on the conversion, or the proceeds remaining after replacement of the condemned property, whichever is less. In this case, the $30,000 excess proceeds received after replacement of the property is computed as follows:

Proceeds received from the state	$260,000
Less cost to replace	− $230,000
Excess proceeds received	$30,000

This was less than the $60,000 realized gain on the conversion:

Proceeds from the state	$260,000
Less building's tax basis	− $200,000
Realized gain	$60,000

59. (C) In order to qualify for nonrecognition of gain on a real property involuntary conversion transaction, the taxpayer must replace the property within three years from the date the cash proceeds are received from the condemnation. The taxpayer is given until *the end of the calendar year in which that three-year term falls.* For instance, in this case, the three-year term would technically elapse on March 1, Year 5, but a taxpayer is actually given until December 31 of Year 5. In the case of personal property (such as a car versus a building), the taxpayer is permitted a two-year period from the date the cash proceeds are received from the condemnation to replace the property (with extension to December 31 of that second year if that two-year period elapses within the second year). For any involuntary conversion question on the exam that asks when the last day to replace the property is, the correct answer is December 31. The correct answer of December 31 is either December 31 two years after proceeds are received (for personal property) or December 31 three years after proceeds are received (for real estate).

60. (C) Both I and II are correct. When property is received as a gift, the basis is not determinable until the property is sold, because the basis is dependent on the final selling price of the gifted property. When gifted property is sold for an amount above the prior owner's basis in the property, the prior owner's basis should be used as the gifted property's basis and a gain recognized in an amount equal to the difference between the final selling price and the prior owner's basis. On the other hand, when gifted property is sold for an amount below the prior owner's basis, then the basis in determining a loss is the lower of the prior owner's basis or the value of the gifted property at the date of the gift. In this case, the selling price of $360 is above the prior owner's basis of $200, so Stan would report a gain in the amount of $160.

61. (A) I is correct but II is wrong. When property is received as a gift, the basis is not determinable until the property is sold, because the basis is dependent on the final selling price of the gifted property. When gifted property is sold for an amount above the prior owner's basis in the property, the prior owner's basis should be used as the gifted property's basis and a gain recognized in an amount equal to the difference between the final selling price and the prior owner's basis. On the other hand, when gifted property is sold for an amount below the prior owner's basis, then the basis in determining a loss is the lower of the prior owner's basis or the value of the gifted property at the date of the gift. In this case, Barry would not be precluded from reporting a loss, since the final selling price ($144,000) was less than Harry's (the prior owner's) basis of $150,000. However, in determining the loss, Barry should use the value of the property at the date he received the gift from Harry ($147,000) as the basis in the property, since it is less than Harry's original basis of $150,000. Consequently, Barry would report a loss of $3,000 computed as follows:

Selling price to Larry:	$144,000
Basis in gifted property	− $147,000, which is lower than Harry's (prior owner's) basis of $150,000

62. (A) When property is received as a gift, the basis is not determinable until the property is sold, because the basis is dependent on the final selling price of the gifted property. When gifted property is sold for an amount above the prior owner's basis in the property, the prior owner's basis should be used as the gifted property's basis and a gain recognized in an amount equal to the difference between the final selling price and the prior owner's basis. On the other hand, when gifted property is sold for an amount below the prior owner's basis, then the basis in determining a loss is the lower of the prior owner's basis or the value of the gifted property at the date of the gift. In this question, the property is sold for $149,000, which is below the previous owner's basis, and would typically present a loss situation. When this type of situation occurs, the basis in determining the loss is the lower of the previous owner's basis (in this case, $150,000) or the value at the time of the gift ($147,000). Since the value at the time of the gift is lower, this amount would normally be used as the basis in determining the loss. However, when using $147,000 as the basis, a $2,000 gain (not a loss) results ($149,000 selling price − $147,000 basis). *Since this transaction should produce a loss, not a gain, NO taxable gain or loss is recognized on this transaction.*

63. (D) In this situation, the stock was initially bought by Debbie for $4,000. It then declined in value to $3,000 at the time it was gifted to Craig. Subsequent thereto and at the time Craig later sold the stock to an unrelated party, the stock's value had increased to $3,500, but did not increase to the amount of Debbie's (previous owner's) initial purchase price or basis. Thus in this type of situation, *there is neither a taxable gain nor taxable loss, and consequently, no defined basis.* This is so since computing a gain would arrive at a $500 loss (selling price: $3,500 − $4,000, which would be the basis used for computing a gain [the previous owner's basis]), and computing a loss would result in a $500 gain (selling price: $3,500 − $3,000, which would be the basis used for computing a loss [the lesser of the value of the stock at the time of the gift or the previous owner's basis]).

64. (A) When gifted property is sold for an amount above the prior owner's basis in the property, the prior owner's basis should be used as the gifted property's basis and a gain recognized in an amount equal to the difference between the final selling price and the prior owner's basis. In this question, Rochelle sold the diamond necklace that was gifted to her for $13,000, which exceeded the prior owner's basis of $10,000 by $3,000. Rochelle would therefore use the prior owner's (Grace's) basis of $10,000 when calculating her (Rochelle's) gain. Consequently, Rochelle's recognized gain would be $3,000, calculated as follows:

Proceeds from sale	$13,000
Cost basis (which is equal to prior owner's basis)	− $10,000
	$3,000 gain

65. (B) Capital assets are those assets held for investment or used for personal enjoyment. The diamond necklace would therefore qualify as a capital asset. (A) is not correct. Section 1231 assets include "business assets," or assets used in the business to generate revenue, which are held for more than one year. The diamond necklace is not being used for business purposes to generate revenue and therefore would not qualify as a Section 1231 asset. (C) is not correct. Rochelle sold the necklace. It was not involuntarily converted or lost due to theft or some other damage. (D) is not correct. A passive activity is either a rental activity or a trade or business in which the individual does not materially participate.

66. (D) Although no tax is paid by the recipient of a gift, the donor or taxpayer may have a gift tax to pay if the gift is greater than $14,000 (exemption limitation) to any one person. A taxpayer can gift up to $14,000 cash to any number of individuals without paying a gift tax. Married couples can gift up to $28,000 without a gift tax if both individuals consent to the gift. In this question, Lois gave a $5,000 cash gift to her child, which is below the $14,000 threshold, and she gave another gift of $25,000 to her grandchild for college tuition; however, that gift was paid directly to the university. An individual is permitted to gift more than the $14,000 exemption amount by paying another's medical bills or college tuition (not room and board) directly to the provider. Additionally, gifts between spouses are tax free, and the amounts between spouses are unlimited. Any other cash gifts given directly to the recipient that exceed the $14,000 exclusion limit will trigger a gift tax.

67. (B) Micki would be able to exclude an aggregate total of $34,000 on the three gifts. For 2013, a taxpayer or donor can exclude up to $14,000 for each cash gift given. Married couples can gift up to $28,000 without a gift tax if both individuals consent to the gift. In this question, Micki can exclude $14,000 on the cash gift to her grandson for the home down payment; $14,000 on the cash gift to her friend's son for his college tuition (note that the tuition was not paid directly to the college, which could have provided Micki with even more of an exclusion if the gift was in excess of $14,000); and the entire $6,000 cash gift to her cousin for the vacation trip because this gift was less than the $14,000 gift exclusion limitation. Thus Micki would only be subject to tax on $2,000 of the $16,000 cash gift she gave to her grandson.

68. (D) Alice can gift the entire $1,000,000 to Jeffrey without incurring any gift tax liability. There is no gift tax on gifts made between spouses. Gifts between spouses are unlimited, and no gift tax would ever apply.

69. (C) Luchentos can deduct an aggregate $320 of these gifts as follows:

4 gifts at $10 each = $40
4 gifts at $20 each = $80
4 gifts at $60 each = $100 ($25 limit for each individual gift)
4 gifts at $80 = $100 ($25 limit for each individual gift)
$\downarrow$
$40 + $80 + $100 + $100 = $320

The deduction for business gifts is limited to $25 per customer. When the exam indicates that the gift is "not of an advertising nature," this means that the amount paid or given is not to be considered an advertising expense, but rather a gift.

70. (A) I is correct. The sale of property received as a gift has no basis until it is sold. If the property is sold for an amount that exceeds the prior owner's (donor's) basis, the prior owner's (donor's) basis is used in computing and reporting a gain on the sale. If the property is sold for an amount below the prior owner's (donor's) basis, a loss could result. II is incorrect. Unlike gifted property, property received as an inheritance has a basis that is usually known to the taxpayer before the time of sale. The general rule for inherited property is that the basis of the property is equal to the property's fair value at the date of death, *or* its fair value six months after the date of death, or the date of conveyance of the property, whichever comes first, *if* the alternative valuation date is elected by the executor of the estate.

71. (C) I is correct. Moving expenses are deductible to arrive at AGI. II is correct. Student loan interest is deductible to arrive at AGI. Other expenses that are deductible for AGI include educator expenses, health savings account deductions, self-employment costs (i.e., portion of self-employment tax; self-employed retirement plan contributions—SEP

IRA, SIMPLE IRA, and other qualified plans; self-employed health insurance deduction), penalty on early withdrawal of savings, alimony paid, and tuition and fees.

72. (C) I is correct. Alimony is deductible to arrive at AGI by the spouse who pays the alimony and is includable in income by the spouse who receives it. III is correct. Contributions to a health savings account are deductible to arrive at AGI. Health savings accounts allow a taxpayer to pay for co-pays with pre-tax dollars. II is wrong. Child support is not deductible nor is it includable in income.

73. (A) I is correct. The only penalty deductible for AGI on a tax return is the penalty for early withdrawal of a savings account (i.e., certificate of deposit). If the savings account or CD was part of a retirement plan account, however, the penalty on the early withdrawal would *not* be deductible. II is wrong. Penalties assessed for late payment of income taxes are *not* deductible.

74. (B) Corey would be able to deduct $100 of the moving expenses. The only moving expenses (noted in this question) that would qualify for deductibility are the moving of Corey's household goods ($2,000) and the lodging costs he incurred on the way to Massachusetts ($100). Meals, temporary living expenses, and the penalty for breaking the New Jersey residence lease do not qualify as deductible moving expenses. However, since Corey is being reimbursed $2,000 from his employer, he would be permitted to deduct only $100 of the $2,100 total deductible moving costs.

Moving household goods	$2,000
Lodging while moving	+ $100
Reimbursement	− $2,000
Moving expense deduction	$100

75. (A) In order to qualify for the maximum 2014 IRA contribution of $5,500, a single taxpayer needs to have earned income of at least $5,500. Earned income for the purposes of an IRA includes wages, Schedule C business profits, and alimony. Alimony is not really earned income, but for purposes of qualifying for an IRA deduction, it counts toward the $5,500. (B) is wrong. The IRA deduction would be limited to the self-employment income of $2,000 and the alimony received of $1,000, since interest income is considered portfolio income. The $2,500 doesn't qualify. (C) is wrong. There would be no IRA deduction, since interest and dividends are portfolio income and do not qualify for IRA deduction. (D) is wrong. The IRA deduction would be limited to the wages earned of $4,500, since rental income is passive and does not qualify as earned income.

76. (B) The tax is $1,000. The 10% premature distribution tax will only be assessed on the $10,000 withdrawal used to pay off credit card balances. Withdrawals for qualified education expenses and qualified medical expenses are not subject to the 10% premature distribution tax.

77. (D) Whenever money is distributed to a taxpayer from a traditional IRA, there is an increase in taxable income unless the money is rolled over into another IRA. Regardless of the age of the taxpayer or what the money is spent on, distributions from traditional IRAs result in taxable income. This question did not ask about the penalty but about the increase in taxable income. Thus, all of the distributions presented, totaling $24,000, would increase Koslow's taxable income.

78. (C) I is correct. For tax years 2013 and 2014, the maximum IRA deduction is $5,500 for those under age 50. II is correct. For tax years 2013 and 2014, the maximum IRA deduction is $6,500 for those ages 50 or older.

79. (C) The advantage of Roth IRAs is that the qualifying distributions from Roth IRAs result in no tax. Distributions from Roth IRAs are tax free after five years as long as the taxpayer is 59½ years old. The disadvantage of a Roth IRA is that contributions to a Roth IRA are not tax deductible. CPA exam candidates need to understand the theory behind the traditional and Roth IRA as well as the advantages and disadvantages of each. The Roth IRA results in a tax-free distribution upon retirement but contributions are not tax deductible as they are made to the IRA. That can be contrasted to traditional IRAs that do not result in tax deductions as contributions are made but result in taxable distributions upon retirement.

80. (C) By age 70½, a taxpayer must begin to take at least minimum distributions from his or her traditional IRA. At 70½ an actuarial calculation is performed and minimum distribution from the IRA must be taken from that year on. (A) is wrong. When a taxpayer reaches age 59½, the taxpayer *may* begin to take distributions from a traditional IRA without penalty, but when a taxpayer reaches age 70½, he or she must begin taking minimum distributions. (B) is wrong. Age 65 is not the age that a taxpayer must begin to withdraw from an IRA. A taxpayer can actually wait until age 70½. (D) is wrong. The age that a taxpayer begins to collect social security is not related to the age that he or she must begin taking minimum distributions from a traditional IRA.

81. (C) Health savings accounts (HSAs) are used by taxpayers to help pay for deductibles and co-pays. If a taxpayer has a health insurance plan with high deductibles, a health savings account makes sense because deductibles and co-pays would be paid from pre-tax dollars. When taxpayers put money into a health savings account, they receive a *deduction in arriving at adjusted gross income.* Money is not taxable when removed from the HSA as long as it is used to cover medical expenses. If money is left over, it remains in the HSA into the following year. HSAs originally began for the self-employed taxpayer because the only health insurance that many self-employed taxpayers can afford is a high-deductible plan. Employees, on the other hand, originally did not require a high-deductible plan because their employer was paying most of the cost. Recently, employer health costs have become so expensive that employers have found that it's actually cheaper for an employer to drop the old employee health plan and instead get a high-deductible plan for each employee *and* put money in each employee's HSA to pay for deductibles. If the employer puts money into the HSA of an employee, that money is not taxed.

82. (D)

Gross income	$57,000
Health savings account contribution	− $4,000
Health insurance premiums	− $6,000
Alimony paid	− $5,000
Traditional IRA contributions	− $2,000
Adjusted gross income	$40,000

The child support of $3,000 and education IRA contribution of $1,000 are not deductible.

83. (A) Assuming their adjusted gross income (AGI) will exceed $43,000, their dependent care credit percentage is 20%. Qualifying expenditures cannot exceed $3,000 per dependent. With two or more dependents, a max of $6,000 is the base amount even though they spent $16,000. Multiplying the $6,000 base amount times the rate of 20% will produce a credit of $1,200. This credit is nonrefundable, and there is no AGI limit or threshold that might otherwise disallow the credit entirely: $6,000 base amount multiplied by 20% = $1,200 dependent care credit.

84. (C) The benefit of most credits cease if a taxpayer's income tax payable is reduced to zero. However, the earned income credit can further reduce a taxpayer's tax obligation, thereby creating a refund. For example, if a taxpayer's income taxes are reduced to zero even before factoring in an earned income credit of $490, the taxpayer will actually receive a $490 refund. Having more children in a low-income home would normally qualify for the maximum earned income credit, but a reduced earned income credit is also available even without having a child in the taxpayer's home.

85. (B) II is correct. While most credits are nonrefundable, the earned income credit is a refundable tax credit. I is wrong. Most credits are nonrefundable, like the dependent care credit. For example, if the tax was $800 but the dependent care credit was $1,200, total tax would be reduced to zero and there would be *no* refund of $400, because the dependent care credit is nonrefundable.

86. (B) I is wrong. In order to qualify for earned income credit, the taxpayer must have some earned income. Ziga had income but no earned income, so he would *not* qualify for the earned income credit. II is correct. The rental income is considered passive income; the interest and dividends are portfolio income. Neither the rental income nor the interest and dividends would qualify Ziga for the earned income credit.

87. (B) The American Opportunity Credit is limited to $2,500 per student and is available for the first *four* years of college. All equipment and related supplies required for courses qualify. Credit is taken by multiplying 100% of the first $2,000 and 25% of the next $2,000 spent. The maximum American Opportunity Credit is $2,500 per student which means that a family with twins who are seniors in college can claim a credit of $5,000 total.

88. (A) I is correct. The American Opportunity Credit can be taken for four years of college. II is wrong. Adjusted gross income (AGI) limits do apply to the American Opportunity Credit. Phaseouts begin with AGI of $80,000 single and $160,000 married filing jointly. The student doesn't have to be a full-time student to qualify, but "must be enrolled on a half-time basis" or more. Taking just "a few courses" will *not* qualify for the American Opportunity Credit. The CPA exam will say whether the student is enrolled at least "half time."

89. (C) The Lifetime Learning Credit is another credit that is meant to benefit students taking courses. Different from the American Opportunity Credit, the student does *not* need to be full time or even part time. The amount spent for courses (up to a maximum of $10,000) is multiplied by 20%. In this question, $8,000 spent × 20% = $1,600 Lifetime Learning Credit.

90. (A) I is correct. The American Opportunity Credit requires the student to be enrolled on a half-time status or more. II is wrong. The Lifetime Learning Credit can be used by a student who is enrolled only in a single course or even for an adult taking continuing education courses.

91. (A) For the 2013 tax year, a taxpayer is entitled to a tax credit of the 30% of the cost for amounts invested in property that uses solar, geothermal, or ocean thermal energy; the solar panel industry took off when this credit began. The solar credit is nonrefundable, but carries forward if not used up. There is no adjusted gross income (AGI) limit on the credit. $80,000 − $20,000 instant state rebate = $60,000 actual cost × 30% tax credit = $18,000.

92. (D) I is wrong. The Lifetime Learning Credit is nonrefundable as are most tax credits. The Lifetime Learning Credit, maximum $2,000, can reduce taxes to zero but would not create a refund should the credit exceed the tax. II is wrong. The foreign tax credit is nonrefundable as are most tax credits. The foreign tax credit can reduce the tax to zero but would *not* create a refund should the credit exceed the tax.

93. (A)

Legal expenses	$14,000
Agency fee	+ $15,000
Total qualifying expenses	$29,000

The medical expenses would *not* qualify for the adoption credit. Instead the medical expenses would be an itemized deduction. In 2013, costs expended in adopting a child could be taken as credit.

94. (B) II is correct. The retirement savings contribution credit is meant to help young newly working taxpayers save and contribute to an IRA. The taxpayer not only receives a deduction for contributing money to an IRA, but may also qualify to receive a credit for that contribution as well. One of the conditions for the credit is that the taxpayer *not* be a full-time student. I is wrong. A child who has special needs would not bring about an additional adoption credit. However, if the amount spent to adopt was less than the maximum credit, the taxpayer would still qualify for the maximum credit due to the child's special needs.

95. (A) I is correct. A taxpayer may claim a credit against US taxes due for foreign income taxes paid to a foreign country or a US possession. There is a limitation on the amount of the foreign tax credit an individual can obtain. II is wrong. Foreign taxes may be taken as a deduction rather than a credit but not as an adjustment to arrive at adjusted gross income (AGI). Instead, the deduction for foreign taxes paid would be a miscellaneous itemized deduction, not subject to 2% of AGI. Since the credit for foreign taxes paid is limited, an individual might find it better to deduct the taxes as an itemized deduction (*not* subject to the 2% floor) instead of taking the foreign tax paid as a credit.

96. (C) III is correct. Transportation to a physician's office for required medical care is a qualifying medical expense. II is wrong. Health club dues are *not* deductible for medical expenses. I is wrong. Vitamins are generally *not* deductible for medical expenses.

97. (D) Deductible expenses include

Physical therapy, net of reimbursement	$500
Insurance for prescription medicines	+ $600
Total deductible medical expenses	$1,100

The insurance policy that protects against the loss of earnings due to sickness or accident (i.e., a disability policy) of $1,000 provides income should the taxpayer become disabled. It does not pay for medical expenses; therefore, it does not qualify for a medical deduction.

98. (C) I is correct. You actually have to know the taxpayer's AGI before you can deduct medical expense. Medical expenses in excess of 10% of AGI can be deducted for taxpayers under age 65. II is correct. Medical expenses in excess of 7.5% of AGI can be deducted for taxpayers age 65 and older.

99. (D) I is wrong. With medical expenses, its common to swipe a credit card in December and pay the balance in the following year. Take the deduction in the year of the swipe for the taxpayer's or dependent's medical care. II is wrong. Taxpayers are allowed to deduct medical costs paid on behalf of elderly parents even if the elderly parent had a little too much income to qualify as the taxpayer's dependent.

100. (B)

Medicines prescribed	$300
Health insurance premiums	+ $500
Dental surgery	+ $4,000
Total	$4,800
Less insurance reimbursement	− 1,000
Medical expenses before adjusted gross income (AGI) limit	$3,800
	↓
Qualifying medical expenses before AGI limit	$3,800
7.5% of AGI	− $3,000
Deductible portion	$800

While Imhoff has qualifying medical expenses of $3,800, he gets only a $800 deduction because $3,800 net medical expenses exceed 7.5% of his AGI ($3,000) by $800.

Note: Taxpayers over 65 years old can deduct medical expenses in excess of 7.5% of AGI. Anyone under 65 can deduct medical costs only in excess of 10% of AGI.

101. (D) All three medical expenses are includable. The cosmetic surgery is not elective, since it was necessary to correct a congenital deformity. The AGI limit is 10% since the taxpayer is under age 65.

Doctor bills from fall	$3,500
Eyeglasses	+ $500
Surgery	+ $16,000
Total	$20,000
	↓
AGI limitation ($70,000 × 10%)	− $7,000 (threshold)
Deduction	$13,000

102. (D) $3,250 is deductible for medical expenses after the 7.5% adjusted gross income (AGI) limit. AGI is calculated as follows:

$95,000 W-2 − $5,000 IRA contribution = $90,000 AGI
$90,000 × 0.075 = $6,750 (AGI threshold is 7.5% since taxpayer is over 65)

Only the ear surgery is deductible, so $10,000 – $6,750 = $3,250. Hair transplant is considered cosmetic surgery and is not deductible.

103. (B) $1,700 is a Year 1 itemized deduction; $300 is a Year 2 itemized deduction. The amount paid during the tax year for state and local income taxes is deductible. Payments can be through employee withholding, through state estimated tax payments, or with the filing of a return. Since a return is always filed after the tax year, the $300 paid in April of Year 2 is a Year 2 itemized deduction for state taxes. Note: each year, the taxpayer has the option of taking a deduction for state and local sales taxes rather than state and local income taxes.

104. (A) Singer will deduct state and local income taxes of $1,500 and estimated state and local taxes of $400 as a Year 1 itemized deduction of $1,900. A deduction for sales tax expired in 2013, thus no deduction can be made for the sales and local taxes. Year 1 sales tax of $900 is ignored since the $1,900 state and local income tax is greater. The $100 paid in April (with the Year 1 state filing) is a Year 2 itemized deduction for state taxes.

105. (C) II is correct. Personal property taxes are deductible as an itemized deduction if they are based on the value of the personal property. Some states, for example, tax the value of an automobile every year. This tax would be deductible on Schedule A. I is correct. Real estate taxes paid on a vacation home are deductible as an itemized deduction; however, if the property was rented out, the deduction would likely appear on Schedule E versus Schedule A.

106. (A) I is correct. A taxpayer can deduct the medical expenses paid for someone who would be a qualifiable dependent but who may not be a dependent and is earning slightly more income than the exemption amount.

II is wrong. In order for the real estate taxes to be deductible, the property must belong to the individual who pays the real estate tax bill; otherwise the payment for real estate taxes is viewed as a gift and is not deductible by that individual who in this case, is Ben.

107. (D) Only the state income tax, real estate taxes in the Netherlands, and personal property taxes are deductible. Taxes paid on the mother's house would be considered a gift and would not be deductible by Simberg since Simberg is not the owner of the home. In some states like Connecticut, personal property taxes are paid every year on the value of a car. These personal property taxes are includable as an itemized deduction for state and local taxes on Schedule A. The $300 state unincorporated business tax is *not* deductible on Schedule A but is deductible on Schedule C for a small business owner. Notice that the real estate taxes are deductible even though the property is located outside of the United States.

State income tax	$2,000
Personal property tax	+ $10
Real estate tax	+ $900
Total	$2,910

108. (A) Real estate taxes are deductible on all the houses that a taxpayer owns. Since the question said the taxpayer is *not* renting any of the houses, the real estate tax would be deducted on Schedule A.

109. (C) When a taxpayer owns a home, it's common to have both real estate taxes and mortgage interest. Although both are deductible on Schedule A as an itemized deduction, real estate taxes deduction is different than mortgage interest deduction. Mortgage interest can be deducted on two of the taxpayer's homes; the real estate taxes however can be deducted on *all* the real estate the taxpayer owns. If a taxpayer owned three homes, the real estate taxes would be deductible on all three, but the mortgage interest would be deductible only on two of the three homes. The taxpayer would need to rent out the third home to get a mortgage interest deduction on the third home.

110. (C) I is correct. Interest is deductible in connection with a taxpayer's main home or second home. Even if the second home is a vacation home, the mortgage interest can be deducted on both homes. Taxpayers are allowed to deduct the mortgage interest on two homes, not just one. II is correct. With regard to a home equity loan, interest on a home equity loan is deductible regardless of what the taxpayer decides to do with the loan proceeds. Interest on home equity loans (proceeds of up to $100,000) can be deducted. A home equity loan is where the loan is secured by the residence, but the money does not have to be used to buy, build, or substantially improve the home. For example, proceeds from a home equity loan could be used to buy a car or send a son or daughter to college.

111. (A) Only the mortgage interest of $15,000 and the interest on the home equity loan of $1,500 qualifies as an interest deduction. The remaining interest is all considered personal interest and is *not* deductible. No deduction is allowed for credit card interest, interest on auto loans, or interest on late tax payments.

$15,000	mortgage interest
+ $1,500	home equity loan interest
$16,500	total interest deduction on Schedule A, itemized deductions

112. (B) If money was borrowed to finance investments, the interest expense can be deducted up to the amount reported as net investment income. Investment interest is deductible against net investment income.

Gross investment income	$120,000
Less investment expenses (unrelated to interest expense)	− $100,000
Net investment income	$20,000

The limit of $20,000 net investment income is deductible for investment interest on Schedule A itemized deductions.

113. (D) If money is borrowed to finance investments, the interest paid can be deducted up to the amount reported as net investment income. Since the net investment income of $4,300 exceeds the investment interest paid of $4,000, the $4,000 paid is deductible.

$5,000	mortgage interest
+ $4,000	net investment interest
$9,000	interest expense deductible on Schedule A as an itemized deduction

114. (C) If money is borrowed to finance investments, the interest paid can be deducted up to the amount reported as net investment income. Since the net investment income of $4,300 exceeds the investment interest paid of $4,000, the $4,000 investment interest paid is deductible. Interest on credit cards is not deductible. Points are deductible in full when paid in connection with obtaining a mortgage. Each point is 1% of the loan. For example, a $100,000 mortgage that costs 1 point means that the taxpayer must pay $1,000 up front to obtain a $100,000 mortgage. Points are normally deductible in the year paid unless the taxpayer is refinancing, in which case the points are amortized over the life of the new loan.

$2,500	points
+ $5,000	mortgage interest
+ $4,000	investment interest
$11,500	total interest deduction on Schedule A

115. (B) Home mortgage interest of $3,600 and $500 personal property tax paid are deductible as an itemized deduction. Late payment penalties are not deductible, and neither is the 10% penalty on premature IRA distribution.

116. (D) $4,000 cash to church + $600 car = $4,600. Cash contributions to individuals are gifts and *not* tax deductible; only contributions to recognized charitable organizations are tax deductible.

117. (A) There are two separate donations; The cash of $4,000 to the church nets Foltz a $3,800 deduction because of the tickets received with a fair value of $200. The jewelry purchased for $1,900 is above the fair value of $1,500, so the jewelry purchased at the church actually benefits the church by $400.

$400	jewelry
+ $3,800	cash
$4,200	total

118. (C) The cash contributed of $18,000 qualifies, plus the $10,000 carryover equals $28,000. However, the total contribution deduction is limited to 50% of adjusted gross income (AGI). AGI is $50,000, so the deduction is limited to $25,000. The other $3,000 carries over to next year.

Total contributions including carryover from prior year	$28,000
Limit	AGI of $50,000 × 50% = $25,000

119. (B) O'Keefe's deduction would be limited to cost basis, $1,400, since she did not own the asset for more than a year. If she had held the stock for more than one year, the fair market value of $3,000 would be deductible. Since she held the stock for only seven months, her deduction is limited to lower of fair value or cost basis, in this case, $1,400.

120. (C) Since Berman held the artwork for longer than one year, he is entitled to the full fair market value, $11,000, as a deduction. The built-in gain of $9,000 is not taxable. The next step is to compare the $11,000 deduction to 30% of AGI: $12,000. The deduction for any long-term capital gain property is limited to 30% of AGI each year. The deduction for property contributions is not allowed to exceed 30% of AGI.

$$\text{AGI } \$40,000 \times 30\% \text{ limit} = \$12,000$$

Therefore, the $11,000 charitable deduction is allowed in full.

121. (B) Since Brian held the artwork for longer than one year, he may be entitled to the full fair market value, $15,000, as a deduction. The built-in gain of $9,000 is not taxable. The first step is to compare the $15,000 potential deduction to 30% of AGI: $6,000. The deduction for any long-term capital gain property is limited to 30% of AGI each year. The deduction for property contributions is not allowed to exceed 30% of AGI.

Total potential charitable contribution before limit $15,000

$$AGI \$20,000 \times 30\% = \$6,000 \text{ limit}$$

The amount of property contribution that carries over to the next year is $9,000.

122. (B) Since Teri held the artwork for longer than one year, she may be entitled to the full fair market value, $11,000, as a deduction. The built-in gain of $9,000 is not taxable, since the art was donated to a charity. The first step is to compare the $11,000 potential deduction to 30% of AGI: $7,500. The deduction for any long-term capital gain property is limited to 30% of AGI each year. The deduction for property contributions is not allowed to exceed 30% of AGI. Since AGI is $25,000 and 30% = $7,500, only $7,500 of the $11,000 charitable contribution is allowed this year; the other $3,500 carries over to the next year. The next step is to add the cash contribution of $7,000 to the $7,500 property contribution deduction. The total of $14,500 is compared to 50% of her AGI: $12,500. $12,500 is the maximum deduction because charity is limited to an overall 50% of AGI maximum. The total charitable contribution deduction in the current year for Teri is $12,500.

Property contribution allowed this year	$7,500
Cash contribution allowed this year	$7,000
Total potential contribution before 50% of AGI limit	$14,500
50% of AGI limit	$12,500 (maximum deduction)
Amount that carries over to next year	$2,000

123. (C) The donation for the artwork is limited to 30% of AGI: $60,000 × 0.3 = $18,000. Although the artwork is worth $20,000 and was held for more than one year, $20,000 exceeds the AGI limit for property contributions of 30%. Harold's deduction for the artwork is limited to $18,000, and the other $2,000 carries over for a maximum of five years. The cash contribution of $5,000 is deductible in full, since the available total from long-term capital gain property plus all other contributions for the year is limited to 50% of AGI.

Property contribution limited to 30% of AGI	$18,000
Cash contribution	+ $5,000
Total potential contribution before AGI limit	$23,000

Harold would be allowed to deduct $23,000 since his AGI is $60,000 and his overall 50% limit is $30,000.

124. (C) A personal casualty loss deduction is allowed only where it exceeds a $100 floor for each separate loss and then 10% of a taxpayer's AGI.

125. (A) The personal casualty loss deduction is determined by taking the lesser of the decrease in the fair market value (FMV) of the property or its basis, less the insurance reimbursement, subject to a $100 floor, and then subject to 10% of the taxpayer's AGI. With the FMV and basis being identical, the computations are

$130,000 decline − $120,000 reimbursement = $10,000 potential loss
$10,000 potential loss − $100 floor = $9,900 loss
$9,900 loss − 10% of AGI ($7,000) = $2,900 deduction

126. (C) Gambling losses are miscellaneous itemized deductions *not* subject to the 2% AGI limitation. The deductions for gambling losses are, however, limited to gambling winnings. Unused gambling losses do *not* carry over.

127. (B) Unreimbursed expenses such as small tools and supplies, protective clothing, required uniforms not suitable for ordinary use, and business car expense are deductible subject to 2% of AGI. The separate amounts would be added and the amount in excess of 2% of the taxpayer's AGI would be deducted.

128. (B) Unreimbursed expenses such as small tools and supplies, protective clothing, required uniforms not suitable for ordinary use, and employee business car expense are deductible subject to 2% of AGI. Also included in the category of miscellaneous itemized deductions subject to the 2% of AGI floor are dues to professional organizations, subscriptions to professional journals, tax preparation fees, and union dues. The list is quite large and also includes rent on a safe-deposit box and certain investment expenses like the annual custodial fee for an IRA. Preparation of a will, funeral expenses, and credit card interest are not miscellaneous deductions but are often asked about on the exam.

129. (D) Preparation of a will and funeral expenses are not miscellaneous itemized deductions. Gambling losses are *not* subject to 2% of AGI, although gambling losses *are* considered miscellaneous itemized deductions. Safe-deposit box rental is the only one listed in the question that qualifies as a miscellaneous itemized deduction subject to 2% of AGI.

130. (C) I is correct. Among the items listed, only tax return preparation fees are miscellaneous itemized deductions subject to 2% of AGI. II is wrong. Foreign taxes paid may be taken as a credit or deduction. A credit is usually better than a deduction, but the foreign tax credit is limited so it's sometimes advantageous to take foreign taxes paid as a deduction. Foreign taxes paid taken as a deduction is a miscellaneous itemized deduction *not* subject to 2% of AGI. III is wrong. A penalty on early withdrawal of savings from a non-retirement account certificate of deposit (breaking a CD early) is deductible as an adjustment to arrive at AGI, *not* as an itemized deduction. IV is wrong. Penalty for late payment of mortgage is *not* deductible.

131. (C) Miscellaneous itemized deductions are deductible to the extent that they in total exceed 2% of AGI.

$85,500 − $5,500 IRA contribution	$80,000 AGI
Tax preparation	$500
Custodial fees	+ $100
Publications	+ $150
Union dues	+ $2,000
Total misc. deductions	$2,750
	↓
AGI $80,000 × 2%	− $1,600
Allowable deduction	$1,150

132. (D) Adjusted gross income (AGI) is gross income less adjustments or deductions. $6,000 in wages is part of gross income. Jury duty pay is taxable, so add $10 to gross income. Gross income is $6,010. The only adjustment listed is $400 in student loan interest, resulting in an AGI of $5,610. Charitable contributions and unreimbursed employee business expense are *not* deductions subtracted to arrive at AGI.

Wages	$6,000
Jury duty pay	+ $10
Less student loan interest	− $400
Total AGI	$5,610

133. (A) Federal income tax is *not* deductible. Penalties and interest related to federal income tax matters are not deductible.

134. (B) I is correct. Unique items of income that are taxable and sometimes tested on the CPA exam include damages awarded for a breach of contract. II is correct. Fees received for jury duty service are also sometimes tested on the CPA exam and are included in taxable income. IV is correct. Also sometimes tested on the CPA exam is the forgiveness of debt, which is an income-includable item and benefit received by a taxpayer. III is wrong. Workers' compensation awards are tax free.

135. (B) The calculation of AMT begins with taxable income, then adds back adjustments and preferences, and subtracts an AMT exemption. Common adjustments for the AMT include:

Personal exemption
State and local taxes
Miscellaneous itemized deductions *in excess of* 2% of AGI
Home mortgage interest where the loan proceeds are not used to buy, build, or
    improve a home

Private activity bond interest is considered a preference item (rather than an adjustment) for AMT and is added to taxable income to arrive at alternative minimum taxable income. Another preference item for AMT is percentage depletion. The excess of percentage depletion over cost depletion gets added back to arrive at the taxpayer's alternative minimum taxable income. An AMT exemption is then subtracted out to reduce the taxable income, but that exemption is lost by taxpayers with relatively high levels of income. What remains after adding back the adjustments and preference items and subtracting the exemption is alternative minimum taxable income. The alternative minimum taxable income is then multiplied by the AMT tax rate, and the additional amount must be paid in addition to the regular income tax.

136. (C) Alternative minimum taxable income starts with taxable income. Then certain items are added back to taxable income because they are not deductible for AMT. The items in this question that need to be added back include the state and local income taxes and the miscellaneous itemized deductions in excess of 2% of AGI. While these items are deductible to arrive at taxable income for normal tax rules, they are considered AMT adjustments and must be added back to arrive at alternative minimum taxable income. Gambling losses are not an AMT adjustment. Home mortgage interest on a loan to acquire a residence is *not* an AMT adjustment. Note: in a question about the AMT, watch out for a home equity loan. If the home equity loan proceeds are *not* used to fix up the house, the home equity loan interest cannot be deducted for AMT purposes. In this question, the calculation of reportable alternative minimum taxable income is as follows:

$70,000	taxable income
+ $5,000	state and local income taxes
+ $2,000	miscellaneous itemized deductions in excess of 2% of AGI
$77,000	alternative minimum taxable income

137. (A) Shirley's AMT adjustments include:

Personal exemption	$3,100
Home equity loan interest	$1,200
Total AMT adjustments	$4,300

Common adjustments for AMT include:

Personal exemption
State and local income taxes
Miscellaneous itemized deductions *in excess of* 2% of AGI
Home mortgage interest where the loan proceeds are not used to buy, build, or improve a home

138. (A) Only the $400 tax-exempt interest income on private activity bonds should be added back as a tax preference item. The personal exemption and state income taxes are not added back, because the question asked about preference items, not adjustments. The only preference item here is interest income from private activity bonds. Another common preference item is percentage depletion. The excess of percentage depletion over cost depletion is a preference item. While interest income from municipal bonds is exempt from regular income tax, for AMT purposes, municipal bond interest income is divided into two categories: general obligation bond interest and private activity bond interest. General obligation bonds are sold by the government, and the government can do whatever it wants with the money since the bonds are sold as "general obligation." Private activity bonds, on the other hand, are sold by the government, but the government must use the money for the specific private activity. If an investor buys private activity bonds, the interest income is taxable for AMT. If the investor buys general obligation bonds, the interest income is not a preference item and is *not* added to taxable income.

139. (C) I is correct. The standard deduction is an AMT adjustment for an individual taxpayer. The individual taxpayer begins with taxable income and then adds the impact of removing the standard deduction and other AMT adjustments. II is correct. The personal exemption is an AMT adjustment for an individual taxpayer. The individual taxpayer begins with taxable income and then adds the impact of removing the personal exemption and other AMT adjustments.

140. (A) I is correct. For an individual taxpayer, private activity bonds issued by a state or local government are a preference item for AMT and will result in the taxpayer paying additional AMT. While the interest from private activity bonds is not includable for regular tax purposes, for AMT purposes the amount is considered a preference item.

II is wrong. For an individual taxpayer, general obligation bonds issued by a state or local government are *not* taxable for regular tax or AMT.

Chapter 2: Taxation of Entities

141. (C) Steelman's share of the ordinary income is 75% of the $60,000 partnership ordinary income. To tax the $5,000 distribution would result in double taxation. Partners pay tax on the income, or the profits, from the partnership. Since tax is being paid by the partners based on the income earned by the business, profit *distributions* to the partners are normally tax free. A profit distribution is a payment of partnership profits to the partner. The profits are already being taxed at the partner level; therefore, the profit distribution would *not* be taxed to the partner—to tax it would result in double taxation.

142. (B) Ordinary income of a partnership is sales less ordinary business expenses (page 1 of Form 1065, partnership return). The dividend revenue, the charitable contributions, and the capital loss are pass-through items, which are separately allocated to the individual partners. Only the remaining $100,000 is the ordinary income of the partnership.

Sales	$450,000
Operating expenses	− $350,000
Partnership ordinary income	$100,000

143. (B) II is correct. Since a partnership is a pass-through entity, no tax is paid by the partnership. So all items of income and loss must eventually appear on the partner's tax returns. Schedule K-1 is the missing link between the partnership tax return and the 1040 tax return of each partner. Each partner receives the Schedule K-1, which lists the amounts of income and loss that need to be reported by each partner on their 1040. All items of income and loss, including ordinary income, capital gains and losses, charitable contributions, and interest and dividends, must be reported by each partner on Schedule K-1. The Schedule K-1 is filed with the 1065 partnership tax return so the Internal Revenue Service knows how much each partner should include on their Form 1040. I is wrong. A partnership tax return is due to be filed on April 15th, three and a half months after year end.

144. (C) I is correct. Partnership tax returns are informational only. No tax is due with the filing of a partnership tax return, because partnerships do not pay any tax. All tax is paid by the individual partners when they file their 1040. II is correct. Partnership tax returns are filed on Form 1065.

145. (B) II is correct. In a partnership, a fixed payment made to a partner for work that is done is known as a guaranteed payment. Payment is made regardless of whether the business is profitable. A guaranteed payment, sometimes known as guaranteed salary, is deductible by the partnership on Form 1065 as an ordinary business expense and then includable in taxable income by the recipient partner. It is quite common to see partnerships in the CPA exam where one partner receives a guaranteed payment but the other partners do not. I is wrong. A normal distribution is *not* the same as a guaranteed payment. A normal distribution is *not* deducted by the partnership *and* is *not* a normal distribution included in taxable income by the recipient partner. On the CPA exam it is quite common to see a partnership where one partner receives a normal distribution and the other partners do not. Candidates must be able to distinguish between a guaranteed payment and a normal distribution.

146. (A) I is correct. A salary that is "without regard to profits" is evidence that the payment to the partner is guaranteed. II is incorrect. A 17% interest in partnership profits is not guaranteed, because if there are no profits, there will be no payment to that partner.

147. (C) III is correct. Guaranteed payments to partners are an ordinary business deduction for a partnership. I is wrong. Charitable contributions made by a partnership are *not* deductible by the partnership but are deductible by the partners on their individual tax returns if they itemize. Each partner would receive Schedule K-1 from the partnership listing their share of the charitable contribution. II is wrong. Short-term capital losses are *not* deductible by the partnership but are deductible by the partners on their individual tax returns. On the K-1 form received from the partnership, the amount of short-term capital loss would be reported for each partner.

148. (B) Guaranteed payments are deducted to arrive at ordinary income of a partnership. Ordinary income before guaranteed payments: $100,000 less $40,000 guaranteed payment = $60,000 ordinary income.

149. (D) In determining the amount of ordinary income to allocate to the partners, guaranteed payments must first be subtracted and allocated to that partner. The balance is then allocated according to the partnership agreement. Disston gets 25% of all income and 100% of the guaranteed payment. Any distributions or withdrawals generally have no impact on the amount of taxable income recognized by the partner. Disston will be taxed on

100% of the guaranteed payment	$40,000
25% of $60,000 in partnership net income (after guaranteed payment)	+ $15,000
25% of 10,000 capital gain	+ $2,500
Total	$57,500

150. (A) The loss is limited to a basis of $36,000. Deductible loss is always limited to the amount at risk. Walter's basis balance prior to loss is $36,000.

151. (B)

Beginning basis is	$20,000
Income	+ $10,000
Distribution	− $8,000
Ending balance	$22,000

152. (C) First, tax basis must be updated for activity incurred during the year. Basis begins at $20,000 and is increased by $13,000 for Norris's 25% share of the municipal interest and ordinary income. Then basis is reduced by the $8,000 cash distribution, leaving a December 31 basis of $25,000. The municipal bond interest income increases basis even though it's not taxable. Note that the question did not ask how much is taxable to Norris.

Beginning basis	$20,000
25% of all income	+ $13,000
Distribution	− $8,000
Ending basis	$25,000

153. (D) Whether taxable or not, each partner's basis goes up for all income earned by the partnership. The tax-exempt interest income will *not* be taxed, but each partner's basis will increase by their proportionate share of the tax-exempt income.

154. (A) I is correct. Distributions are a decrease in basis. II is wrong. Loans made to a partnership from a partner are an increase in basis, not decrease. In the event of a total loss, the deductible loss for Krin would include the loan made to the partnership.

155. (C) Anytime the partnership borrows money from a third party, each partner's basis will increase by their share of the debt. If they were 50/50, the answer could have been (A), but there is no indication what their percentage of ownership is. (B) is wrong because all general partnership loans are considered recourse. Recourse means that the creditor can collect from the partner personally if the partnership fails to pay and the partnership has no funds of its own.

156. (B) Andy's tax basis starts with his beginning basis of $5,000 and includes his proportionate share of all items of income. Note that a partner's tax basis is affected by items that are nontaxable as well as taxable.

Beginning basis January 1, Year 2	$5,000
Ordinary income	+ $10,000
Tax exempt income	+ $4,000
Taxable interest	+ $2,000
Cash distribution	− $1,000
Ending basis December 31, Year 2	$20,000

157. (A) The basis rolls over from partner to partnership, so the land has a basis of $30,000 to the partnership and Luke has a $30,000 basis in the partnership as a result of his contribution of the asset.

158. (C) A partner's basis of an interest in the partnership is the basis of the property transferred less the debt relief. The basis is determined as follows: $30,000 original basis less debt transferred of $18,000 plus debt assumed of $6,000 by being 50% partner = $24,000.

159. (A) A partner's basis of an interest in the partnership is the basis of the property transferred plus any liabilities assumed. As a 50% partner, Mike assumes 50% of the mortgage transferred by Luke. The basis is determined as follows: $45,000 + $6,000 liability assumed by being a partner = $51,000.

160. (C) Klein's $24,000 basis is increased by Klein's share of the mortgage, which is 30% of $5,000, or $1,500. Klein's basis is equal to $24,000 + 1,500 = $25,500.

161. (D) $240,000 original basis less $150,000 cash distribution = $90,000 basis remaining for the real estate. When a partnership is liquidated, the partner removes his or her entire investment in partnership balance. Always distribute the cash to the partner *before* whatever other assets are received in liquidation. What remains after the cash is distributed will be the value of the real estate, because when the distribution is considered liquidating, the partner's basis must be reduced to zero.

162. (A) Since Anita received a liquidating cash distribution of $50,000 in exchange for her partnership $52,000 interest and no other assets were being distributed, the loss is $2,000. At the time of the cash distribution, Anita's adjusted basis of her interest was $52,000. Anita must zero out her entire basis since the distribution is considered liquidating. Since she held her interest longer than one year, she recognizes a $2,000 long-term capital loss determined as follows:

Basis prior to liquidation	$52,000
Cash received to zero out basis	− $50,000
Loss on liquidation	$2,000

163. (D) In liquidation, the partner's basis must be closed out. Cash received by the partner in liquidation is always recorded before any other assets. The first step is to use the cash received to reduce the partner's basis. If no other assets are distributed to the partner in liquidation, the remaining partner's basis is considered a loss from liquidation for tax purposes. A gain could result if more cash than basis is distributed. The partnership, on the other hand, doesn't pay tax, so the partnership itself would have no gain or loss from liquidation.

164. (B) $70,000 less $30,000 cash = $40,000. Always subtract the cash first. Since it's a liquidating distribution, all remaining basis must be closed out. Since Carol's basis stands at $40,000 after receiving the cash, to zero out her basis, Carol would need a basis of $40,000 for the car.

Basis prior to liquidation	$70,000
Cash received	− $30,000
Remaining basis	$40,000

165. (A) The general rule is that assets come out of a partnership at basis. Any partnership property distributed by the partnership to the partner decreases that partner's basis by the adjusted basis of that property, but only to the extent of the partner's remaining basis. Since this distribution is nonliquidating, Ryan's basis does *not* have to be zero after the distribution. Therefore, Ryan's basis in the capital assets is limited to $65,000, and Ryan would have a remaining basis in the Bruder Partnership of $5,000.

Basis prior to distribution	$70,000
Less assets distributed	− $65,000
Remaining basis	$5,000

166. (A) Any partnership property distributed by the partnership to the partner decreases that partner's basis by the adjusted basis of that property—but only to the extent of the partner's remaining basis. In this case, Ryan would value the capital assets at $40,000, and he would have a zero basis remaining in the Bruder partnership.

167. (C) The general rule is that no gain is recognized on a nonliquidating distribution, unless cash is being distributed in excess of basis. There is no possibility of loss on a nonliquidating distribution. In a *nonliquidating* distribution to a partner, any cash received is first used to reduce that partner's basis. Prior to the distribution, Tyler's basis was $80,000. There was no cash distributed. The capital assets received by Tyler would have the same basis of $75,000 that they had in the partnership, because Tyler had sufficient basis ($80,000) to allocate to the capital assets. The general rule is that assets come out of a partnership at basis and no gain or loss is recognized.

Basis prior to distribution	$80,000
Capital assets distributed	– $75,000
Tyler's remaining basis in the partnership	$5,000

168. (A) The general rule is that no gain is recognized on a nonliquidating distribution, unless cash is being distributed in excess of basis. In this problem, Yimeny's basis was $50,000 immediately before the distribution. Because the cash distributed of $20,000 was less than her basis, no gain is recognized.

169. (B) In a nonliquidating distribution to a partner, any cash received is first used to reduce that partner's basis. Then any in-kind property distributed by the partnership to the partner decreases that partner's basis by the adjusted basis of that property, but *only to the extent of the partner's remaining basis.* Yimeny's basis prior to the distribution was $50,000, as just described. After the $20,000 cash distribution, Yimeny's partnership basis was $30,000. Even though the basis and fair market value of the property in the partnership was $40,000 and $35,000 respectively, Yimeny's basis in the property will be limited to her remaining basis in the partnership of $30,000. No gain or loss is recognized on this transaction. Yimeny's eventual sale of the property in the future will trigger the gain due to the low basis allocated at this time.

Basis prior to distribution	$50,000
Less cash distributed	– $20,000
Remaining basis prior to receiving other assets	$30,000
Basis in other assets when received	$30,000

170. (C) In a nonliquidating distribution to a partner involving only in-kind property, the adjusted basis of the property distributed by the partnership to the partner decreases that partner's basis by the adjusted basis of that property, but only to the extent of the partner's remaining basis. Since Robyn's basis cannot go below zero, her basis in the land is limited to her basis remaining in the partnership, $5,000.

171. (A) Only cash received in excess of basis can cause a gain. Since no cash was received, there can be no gain. Robyn's basis prior to the distribution was $5,000. Even though the adjusted basis of the land was $6,000 and the fair market value of the land was $9,000, Robyn's basis in the land will be limited to the remaining basis in the partnership, or $5,000.

172. (B) The general rule is that assets come out of a partnership at basis. The exception is when the partner does *not* have enough basis. Here, Kelvin starts with a basis of $50,000, and after subtracting the cash of $25,000, he still has a basis remaining of $25,000. The land would then be transferred to Kelvin at its existing basis of $15,000. Note: had the distribution been liquidating, the basis in the land would have been $25,000, since Kelvin's basis would have needed to be zeroed out.

Basis	$50,000
Less cash distributed	– $25,000
Basis available prior to the distribution of other assets	$25,000
Basis of land distributed	$15,000

173. (D) The distribution is current because nothing in the question indicated that the partnership is being liquidated. The distribution seems rather proportionate since Lesnik is a 50% partner receiving 50% of the income as a distribution.

174. (B) II is correct. Guaranteed payments to partners are deductible by the partnership and includable in income by the recipient partners. I is wrong. Normal partnership distributions of cash are not includable in income by the recipient partners or it would result in double taxation. However, if the cash distribution ever exceeds basis, the excess would be taxable.

175. (D) Partnerships pay no tax! All tax is paid by the partners. Any answer choice that says a partnership pays tax is the wrong answer. If the question asked about basis, *both* taxable interest and tax-exempt interest would increase the partner basis.

176. (D) Distributions of cash that exceed basis are taxable, whether liquidating or non-liquidating. Distributions of cash that are *not* in excess of basis are *not* taxable.

177. (B) Corporations that wish to file as S corporations must make a timely election. Many small corporations file the S election (Form 2553) because S corporations get taxed like a partnership and thus avoid double taxation. All of the shareholders of the S corporation must consent to the election or it's not valid. If filed timely (two and a half months after incorporation date), the election reverts back to the first day of the year and there will be no double taxation for the entire year.

178. (B) If the S election is made after March 15, it takes effect January 1 of the following year. If a corporation is formed in Year 2 and doesn't file an S election, it is taxed as a corporation and is subject to double taxation each year until it files an S election. If the C corporation is formed in Year 2 and decides in Year 5 to become an S corporation, the S election would have to be filed before March 15th of Year 5. If it's filed late, the election for S status would be effective January 1, Year 6.

179. (B) All income, whether taxable or not, increases the basis of an S corporation stockholder.

$90,000 of income/2 stockholders = basis increase of $45,000 per stockholder

180. (D) Since municipal bond interest is tax exempt, each shareholder will report a basis increase of $25,000 of the $50,000, even though none of the interest will be taxable. This is because all income earned by an S corporation or partnership increases basis, even tax-exempt income.

181. (D) All income, even tax-exempt income, will increase basis:

Beginning basis	$60,000
Ordinary income	+ $30,000
Tax-exempt income	+ $5,000
Capital gains	+ $10,000
Cash distribution	− $20,000
Ending basis	$85,000

182. (D) An S corporation is allowed a maximum of 100 shareholders—minimum of 1 shareholder, max of 100. Having 101 shareholders would lose the eligibility. An S corporation is allowed to have only one class of stock: common stock. If an S corporation adds preferred stock, it loses its eligibility for S status. S corporations cannot have preferred stock. Note: an S corporation can have both common stock with voting rights and common stock with no voting rights, because that is still considered one class.

183. (D) In each of the three years, Bagel Bazaar, Inc., made distributions to the shareholders in excess of basis. Any distribution of cash in excess of basis would result in a capital gain to a shareholder.

184. (D) Wilson's basis is $5,000, so none of the $3,500 distribution is taxable to Wilson. Only when cash distributed exceeds basis does the partner have a taxable situation. For example, if the distribution was over $5,500, the capital gain would be $500.

185. (B) An S corporation shareholder's basis or amount "at risk" is reduced by distributions to the shareholders as well as loss or expense items. However, loss deductions are limited to a shareholder's adjusted basis in S corporation stock plus direct shareholder loans to the corporation. Any losses disallowed may be carried forward indefinitely and will be deductible as the shareholder's basis is increased. The total loss of $2,000 exceeds the amount "at risk," so only the amount "at risk" of $1,500 is deductible this year. The remaining $500 loss carries forward.

Beginning basis	$5,000
Less distribution of	− $3,500
Basis available	$1,500 (amount at risk)
	↓
Total loss	$2,000
Excess loss over amount at risk	$500

186. (A) Wolfson shareholders report $5,000 ordinary income and $2,000 long-term capital gain. The cash distribution is not taxable. Taxing the cash distribution of $4,000 would result in double taxation. The $4,000 distribution is considered a distribution of profits, and the profits are being taxed once already.

10% of $50,000 is $5,000 ordinary income.
10% of $20,000 is $2,000 long-term capital gain.

187. (C) An S corporation can take a tax deduction for ordinary business expenses, like compensation of officers. Charitable contributions and capital losses are not ordinary business deductions. Charitable contributions and capital losses pass through to the shareholders separately on the K-1 form the same way as for a partnership.

188. (C) Dauber's ordinary income is calculated as follows:

Revenue	$44,000
Operating expenses	− $20,000
Ordinary income	$24,000

Note: the long-term capital loss and charitable contributions are not considered "ordinary" and would *not* affect ordinary income of an S corporation (or partnership).

189. (D) Corporate tax returns are due March 15th or two and a half months after the close of the fiscal year. This is the case for all corporate tax returns, S corporations and C corporations. For partnerships and individuals, the answer would be April 15th or three and a half months after the close of the fiscal year. Note that S corporations must be on a calendar year.

190. (B) II is correct. An S corporation must adopt a calendar year. I is wrong. S corporations need only a minimum of one shareholder. Partnerships require a minimum of two owners; corporations require only one.

191. (B) An S corporation is a pass-through entity. The S corporation pays no federal income tax. The ordinary income and long-term capital gains flow through to its shareholders. Any answer choice on the exam that says an S corporation or partnership pays federal taxes is the wrong answer.

192. (C) I is correct. S corporations are considered pass-through entities. The advantage of a pass-through entity is that it avoids double taxation by allowing all income to pass through the entity and be picked up by the individual shareholders. II is correct. Partnerships are considered pass-through entities. The advantage of a pass-through entity is that it avoids double taxation by allowing all income to pass through the entity and be picked up by the individual partners.

193. (A) I is correct. For a corporation to elect S corporation status, unanimous consent of all shareholders is required. If all shareholders approve, the corporation would then file Form 2553 with the Internal Revenue Service in order to elect S corporation status and be treated as a pass-through entity for tax purposes. II is wrong. *Revocation* of an S election does *not* require unanimous consent of shareholders. A revocation of S election may be filed by shareholders owning more than 50% of an S corporation's outstanding stock. If the S corporation has both common voting and nonvoting shares, for this purpose both voting and nonvoting shares are counted. It's not important how many shareholders consent— more important is how many shares they own. A majority of total S corporation shares is needed to vote in favor of revoking an S election. Therefore unanimous consent is not required to revoke an S election.

194. (C) The basis of an S corporation for a shareholder is increased by all income items, including tax-exempt income, and decreased by all loss and deduction items, including nondeductible expenses and distributions.

Beginning basis	$60,000
Ordinary income	+ $39,500
Municipal bond interest income	+ $10,000
Capital loss	− $17,000
Distribution	− $20,000
Ending basis	$72,500

195. (D) If property is exchanged for voting stock and the owner winds up with 80% or more, the exchange is viewed for tax purposes in the same way as for a partnership. That is, the tax basis of the property is retained by both parties so that no taxable gain or loss is recognized.

196. (A) When an owner transfers property to a corporation and winds up with 80% or more of the outstanding stock, the transfer is handled like a partnership rather than a corporation. That is, the tax basis is retained by both parties, and no income effect results. Hametz gave up two assets with a tax basis of $220,000 ($100,000 + $120,000). He keeps that original basis amount as his tax basis for his investment. The business picks up the equipment at the same tax basis of $100,000.

197. (B) The general rule to incorporate is that property is transferred to the corporation at the same basis that previously existed, $40,000, if those who transferred the property came away with at least 80% of the new shares. Since Micki and Laura both transferred property in exchange for stock and together came away with more than 80% of the total shares, the incorporation is handled as a tax-free incorporation.

198. (C) If those who transferred the property came away with at least 80% of the new shares, the basis in the stock is equal to the basis of the transferred asset, and there is no gain or loss. Since Micki and Laura both transferred property in exchange for stock and together came away with more than 80% of the total shares, the incorporation is handled as a tax-free incorporation. That is, the tax basis of the property is retained by both parties so that no taxable gain or loss is recognized. The only difference here is that Laura had debt relief of $10,000, so her basis in the stock is $40,000 less $10,000 debt relief = $30,000 basis.

199. (A) If property is exchanged for voting stock and the owner winds up with 80% or more, the exchange is viewed for tax purposes as a tax-free incorporation. The tax basis of the property is retained by both parties so that no taxable gain or loss is recognized.

200. (B) The corporation's basis in the building is the greater of the debt assumed, $10,000, or the net book value of the asset contributed, $40,000.

201. (A) If property is exchanged for voting stock and the owner winds up with 80% or more, the tax basis of the property is retained by both parties so that no taxable gain or loss is recognized. The property is transferred to the corporation and retains the same basis that previously existed, $45,000. Micki's basis in the stock is $45,000.

202. (A) If property is exchanged for voting stock and the owner winds up with 80% or more, the exchange is viewed for tax purposes in the same way as for a partnership. That is, the tax basis of the property is retained by both parties so that no taxable gain or loss is recognized. Micki's basis of $45,000 for the equipment rolls over into the corporation.

203. (C) If property is exchanged for voting stock and the owner winds up with 80% or more, the exchange is viewed for tax purposes in the same way as for a partnership. That is, the tax basis of the property is retained by both parties so that no taxable gain or loss is recognized. Although Adrian did contribute property and so did Barry, *together they came* *home with only 70% of the stock of the new corporation.* As a result, the asset contributed by Adrian will be adjusted to the fair market value, $45,000.

204. (B) Adrian and Barry are the only transferors of *property* (Corey exchanged only services). Together, Adrian and Barry (who exchanged property) own less than 80% of the stock; therefore, Adrian is taxed on her built-in gain of $15,000. The transfer is treated as if Adrian sold the property to the corporation rather than transferred it. Adrian's gain is calculated as follows:

Fair value of $45,000 – basis of $30,000 = $15,000 gain to Adrian

205. (A) Although Parker contributed no property, Broussard and Monti, who did contribute property, end up with 80% or more of the stock. So no gain is recognized by Monti, because the assets do *not* get raised to fair market value.

206. (C) Although Parker contributed no property, Broussard and Monti, who did contribute property, end up with 80% or more of the stock. So the assets basis simply rolls over into the newly formed corporation, and there is no gain or loss. Since the asset had a basis to Broussard of $5,000, Kenpo Corp. picks up the asset at $5,000.

207. (B) For tax purposes, a company cannot anticipate its bad debts and can only recognize, for tax purposes, a bad debt expense when the account proves to be uncollectible. Ashbrook will recognize no bad expense for tax purposes in Year 1.

208. (C) For tax purposes, a company cannot anticipate its bad debts and can only recognize, for tax purposes, a bad debt expense when the account proves to be uncollectible. Ashbrook will recognize a bad expense for tax purposes in Year 2 of $23,000.

209. (A) Cash-basis taxpayers do not record bad debt expense. Since Fascination operates as a cash-basis taxpayer, it has not included any revenue for tax purposes, either for the original work that was done or the interest on the note. A bad debt can only be deducted to the extent that it was included in income. Bad debt expense is actually the removal of a previously recognized income that was never received. No income was recognized here, so no expense can be reported.

210. (C) Warranties arise when there is a sale of products and the manufacturer gives a promise to fix product defects for a period of time. The manufacturer knows that they will incur some cost to repair and ship the panels. The amount is unknown at the time of sale. For financial reporting, both bad debt and warranty expenses are accrued based on estimations. For tax purposes, warranties can only be deducted when an actual cost is incurred. Since no panels broke in Year 1, there is no warranty expense for tax purposes.

211. (B) For financial reporting, both bad debt and warranty expenses are accrued based on estimations. For tax purposes, warranties can only be deducted when an actual cost is incurred. Since no panels broke in Year 1, there is no warranty expense for tax purposes in Year 1. But in Year 2 the actual warranty cost incurred equals the deduction in the year the money is spent. The warranty expense for Year 2 is calculated as follows:

800 panels broke × $120 spent to fix each = $96,000

212. (A) I is correct. Life insurance premiums paid by a corporation on behalf of employees are expensed in full for financial reporting regardless of who the beneficiary of the policy is. II is wrong. If a company pays insurance premiums to cover the lives of its employees, the deductibility of those expenses depends on the identity of the beneficiary. If the company is *not* the beneficiary (the employee can name the beneficiary), the cost is tax deductible to the corporation. If the corporation were the beneficiary of the policy, no corporate tax deduction would have been allowed. Life insurance settlements are tax free; the Internal Revenue Service would not allow a deduction for something that will never be taxable.

213. (A) The starting point is book income of $200,000. The $5,000 for life insurance premiums was already expensed on the books and is also a tax deduction, also since the employee can name the beneficiary. Don't do anything with the $5,000. The warranty expense already deducted for book purposes of $4,000 needs to be added back, and $10,000 actual warranty costs paid should be deducted.

$$\$200,000 + \$4,000 - \$10,000 = \$194,000 \text{ taxable income}$$

214. (A) The net capital loss of $3,000 is not deducted from the $100,000 of ordinary income in the current year. The $3,000 capital loss carryover can either be carried back three years or forward five years to reduce capital gains in those years. For corporations, all capital gains and losses are netted to a single gain or loss. Stocks may be sold at a gain and bonds at a loss, and it all nets out to one final figure. If that net figure is a gain, it is taxed at *ordinary income rules*. If the figure is a loss, no deduction is allowed in the current year. A corporation is not permitted to take a tax deduction in the current year for capital losses. Unlike for an individual, there is no $3,000 deduction for a corporation.

215. (B) If a net capital loss results from all of the capital asset transactions of a corporation, that loss cannot be deducted in the current year. Instead, the net capital loss can be carried back for three years to reduce previous capital gains and then forward for five years.

216. (D) The net capital gains of $2,500 are added to taxable income from operations of $56,000 to determine total taxable income of $58,500. There is no difference in the tax rates for capital gains, unlike an individual. Drake Corporation must first net its capital transactions together as follows: the net capital gain simply gets added to the ordinary income of $56,000.

Total capital gains of $10,000 ($7,500 short-term capital gain + $2,500 long-term capital gain) − capital losses of $7,500 ($5,000 short-term capital loss + $2,500 long-term capital loss) = $2,500 net capital gain

217. (B) Taxable income remains at $66,000. Although there is a capital loss of $13,000 and a capital gain of $6,000 netting out to a loss of $7,000, that loss cannot be deducted in the current year. Instead, the $7,000 carries over as a short-term capital loss for a maximum of five years, which is available to reduce future capital gains.

218. (D) Book income is $227,000. The long-term capital loss of $5,000 gets added back since, for tax purposes, the capital loss is *not* deductible in the current year against ordinary income. The $3,000 premium for key-person life insurance is also added back since the company is the beneficiary. When the company is the beneficiary of a key-person life insurance policy, the company gets no deduction for the premium it pays for that insurance.

Utility expense is deductible for both tax and book purposes, therefore no reconciling adjustment needs to be made for it. Therefore, taxable income is computed as follows:

$$\$227,000 + \$5,000 + \$3,000 = \$235,000$$

219. (C)

Start with book income	$480,000
Subtract municipal bond interest income	− $50,000
Add municipal bond interest expense	+ $2,000
Add back federal income tax provision	+ $170,000
Taxable income	$602,000

The rent expense of $5,000 is handled the same way for books and tax purposes, so no reconciling adjustment needs to be made for rent expense.

220. (D) Start with book income of $240,000. Add back the $40,000 for federal income tax expense and the $25,000 for meals and entertainment since the tax code only allows a 50% deduction for meals and entertainment. The advertising expense is deductible for both book and tax purposes so no reconciling is adjustment needs to be made for the advertising expense. Therefore, Hampton Corporation's taxable income can be computed as follows: $240,000 + $40,000 + $25,000 = $305,000.

221. (C) I is correct. Interest incurred on loan to carry municipal bonds is included as a reconciling item on the M-1 Schedule because it's included in income on the books, but not on the corporate tax return. This is because municipal bond interest is tax free. II is correct. The provision for federal income tax is an expense for book purposes but is not deductible for tax purposes. An item is includable on the M-1 Schedule reconciliation only if it's handled differently for book and tax purposes.

222. (D) An item only makes the M-1 reconciliation if it's treated differently for tax purposes and book purposes. Interest on US savings bonds is considered income for both books and taxes. State income tax is an expense on the books *and* a deduction for taxes. State income tax expense on the books is a tax deduction, but federal income tax expense on the books is not a tax deduction.

223. (C) Legal and professional fees to file incorporation documents and state filing fees plus any other fees necessary to incorporate a business are deductible as organization costs. Stock issuance costs, printing of stock certificates, underwriter fees, and commissions to the broker are not deductible as organization costs.

224. (A) Deductible organizational costs include the accounting fees of $3,000, the state incorporation fees of $7,500, and the legal fees of $3,500, for a total of $14,000. Of that $14,000, the first $5,000 can be deducted immediately (without being amortized), which will reduce the remaining amount to $9,000. The $9,000 can then be amortized over 180 months, $50 per month. In Year 6, the company began doing business on July 1, so multiply $50 × 6 months = $300 and add that to the immediate deduction of $5,000. Therefore, the total deduction in Year 6 for organization costs is $5,300. Note that the $2,000 to print the stock certificates and the $5,000 to sell the initial shares cannot be expensed. Instead of a deduction, they are a reduction in the capital stock account.

Immediate deduction of	$5,000
$9,000/180 months = $50 per month for six months	+ $300
Total deduction for organization costs in Year 6	$5,300

225. (C) I is correct. The goodwill is referred to as a Section 197 cost. Even though not amortized for financial reporting purposes, goodwill should be written off over 15 years for tax purposes. When one company acquires another, some amount of the purchase price is usually assigned to goodwill (capital asset) or acquired intangible assets. Although goodwill is not expensed for financial statement purposes, for tax purposes these assets are amortized to expense over a 15-year period of time. II is correct. In Year 2, an expense of $20,000 can be deducted ($300,000/15 years).

226. (D) Acquisitions of goodwill, trademarks, trade names, and covenants not to compete are amortized on a straight line basis for tax purposes over a 15-year life, or 180 months.

227. (D) Business assets such as equipment, machinery, and buildings are known, in general, as Section 1231 assets. It is not the land itself that makes it a 1231 asset; it's what the land is being used for. Since the land is being used in the business right now, it's Section 1231. If the land was being held for long-term appreciation, then the land would be considered a capital asset. This is true for the shed as well. Classify assets as Section 1231 or capital assets based on what they are being used for.

228. (C) Goodwill is a capital asset and for tax purposes is amortized over 180 months. Treasury stock is not an asset, so it could not possibly be a capital asset. Assets used in the business, such as is the case hare in this question with the machinery and land, are Section 1231 assets, not capital assets.

229. (D) I is wrong. Although land does not depreciate, if the land is being used in business, the land qualifies as Section 1231 asset. Section 1231 assets tend to be fixed assets used in the production of ordinary income. II is wrong. Capital assets are *not* used in business to generate ordinary income. For a corporation, Capital assets are investments in stocks and bonds.

230. (A) A corporation will never recognize a gain or loss on the receipt of money or other property in exchange for its own stock.

231. (A) In the assets first year, begin depreciating real estate as of the 15th of the month of purchase. This is called the mid-month convention. This mid-month adjustment is only for Year 1 and only for real estate depreciation. Since the building was bought May 1, depreciation starts May 15th and only 7.5 months of depreciation will be taken for the first year. In Year 2 and beyond, depreciate all 12 months using the straight line method. Depreciation for Year 2 would be $6,000. Remember not to depreciate the land.

> $304,000 − $70,000 for the land = $234,000/39 years = $6,000 depreciation per year
>
> ($6,000 annual depreciation × 7.5 months)/12 months = $3,750

232. (A) In Year 2, a full year of depreciation is taken using the straight line method for real estate. Residential real estate is depreciated using a 27.5-year straight line. Only depreciate a partial year in the first year of real estate depreciation. Depreciation for Year 2 is equal to

$$\$225,000 - \$25,000 \text{ land} = \$200,000/27.5 \text{ years} = \$7,273$$

233. (B) While real estate is depreciated using the straight line method, personal property is depreciated using double declining balance. Five-year personal property such as computers would be depreciated 40% per year rather than 20% per year, since the double declining balance method is used rather than straight line. For personal property used for a partial year, the half-year convention is utilized in the first year. Do not subtract the salvage value. Two-fifths equals 200% of straight line, since straight line for a 5-year life would be one-fifth. Autos, light trucks, and computers have a 5-year life for tax purposes; furniture, fixtures, and equipment have a 7-year life. Notice that management's expected useful life of 8 years is *not* used for tax depreciation purposes. For personal property: Year 1 depreciation equals $8,000, calculated as follows:

$$(\$40,000 \times 2)/5 = \$16,000 \times \text{half year} = \$8,000$$

234. (B) The question asked about Year 2, but for personal property you have to calculate Year 1 depreciation first and then decline the balance. Remember to subtract the depreciation taken in the prior year from the carrying amount. Do *not* take half-year depreciation in the asset's second year.

Year 1 depreciation: ($40,000 × 2)/5 = $16,000 × half year = $8,000

Year 2 depreciation: $40,000 − $8,000 = $32,000; ($32,000 × 2)/5 = $12,800 in
    depreciation for Year 2

235. (A) For personal property used for a partial year, the half-year convention is utilized in the first year.

Year 1   equals $8,000 of depreciation
Year 2 $40,000 − $8,000 = $32,000; ($32,000 × 2)/5 = $12,800
Year 3 $32,000 − $12,800 = $19,200; ($19,200 × 2)/5 = $7,680

236. (D) According to the rules of MACRS, personal property is treated as placed in service or disposed of at the midpoint of the taxable year, resulting in a half year of depreciation for the year in which the property is placed in service or disposed of by the company.

237. (D) The allowable depreciation deduction taken in Year 3 for a commercial building that was placed in service in Year 1 is based on calculating the asset's depreciable basis over 39 years. (A) is wrong. A 27.5-year straight line is used to depreciate residential rental property. (B) and (C) are wrong. For real estate depreciation, the adjustment for midmonth depreciation is done only in the year of purchase, Year 1, and does *not* affect the amount of depreciation for future years.

238. (D) Real estate does *not* qualify for Section 179 deduction. To encourage the growth of smaller companies, the tax laws provide for the immediate expensing of the cost of tangible personal property used in a business as well as off-the-shelf computer software (as long as it has a life of more than one year). Real property (such as land and buildings) does not qualify. Because this deduction is for smaller companies, the amount of the expense is limited. That number has changed numerous times over the years. However, if the company buys a significant amount of such assets, the immediate expense deduction begins to be lost dollar for dollar after a limit is reached.

239. (C) Under the election to expense certain depreciable business assets (Section 179), the taxpayer may expense the cost of the depreciable asset up to the limitation, in this example, $108,000. Therefore, only the cost of the depreciable tangible business assets can be expensed ($100,000). (A) is incorrect. Land is not a depreciable asset. (B) is incorrect. Taxpayers can expense only up to the purchase price, not to exceed the limitation. (D) is incorrect. Land is not a depreciable asset.

240. (B) In an attempt to avoid triple taxation for corporations, there is a unique deduction that involves no outlay of expenditure. This is called the dividends received deduction (DRD). To determine the DRD, the first step is to determine the taxable income before the DRD, sometimes referred to as the base amount:

Gross business income	$160,000
Dividend income	+ $100,000
Total income	$260,000
	↓
Less operating expenses of	− $170,000
Taxable income before DRD	$90,000

The actual DRD is the lesser of 80% of the DRD: (1) dividends received of $100,000, or (2) taxable income of 90,000. Therefore the DRD is 80% of the $90,000, or $72,000, for Year 1. The DRD is 80% of the dividends if less than 80%, but at least 20% of the stock is owned. The DRD is 70% of the dividends if less than 20% of the stock is owned. The DRD is 100% if 80% or more of the stock is owned. When 80% or more is owned, the companies are viewed as an affiliated group.

241. (D) Prior to the dividends received deduction (DRD), the company has a tentative taxable income of $40,000. The DRD for a 17% ownership is 70%. The DRD is 70% of the dividends collected, unless the income before the deduction is lower than the dividends received. Here, the $40,000 tentative taxable income is less than the $50,000 in dividends. So the DRD is $28,000 (70% of $40,000), which reduces the income from $40,000 down to $12,000. The tentative taxable income and DRD are calculated as follows:

Sales revenue	$380,000
Add dividend income	+ $50,000
Less operating expenses	− $390,000
Taxable income before DRD	$40,000
	↓
70% of dividends received	− $28,000
Taxable income	$12,000

242. (B) Subchapter C corporations can deduct the amount donated up to 10% of the total of all revenues less all ordinary and necessary expenses. The dividends received deduction (DRD) is not an ordinary and necessary expense, so it gets added back before the charitable contribution is computed. To determine the allowable charitable deduction, the base amount must be determined. The base is taxable income, without regard to the charitable contribution itself and the DRD. The contributions available for use total $90,000. This comprises the current-year contribution of $80,000 plus the carryover of $10,000. Since $86,000 is the limit for contributions, $4,000 gets carried forward for five years. The $86,000 contribution limit is calculated as follows:

Taxable income	$820,000
Add dividend received deduction	+ 40,000
Base amount for charitable contribution deduction	$860,000
	↓
Multiply by 10% of the base amount ($860,000)	$86,000

243. (C) The contributions available for deduction total $45,000. This comprises the current year contribution of $40,000 plus the carryover contributions of $5,000. To determine the allowable portion, the base amount must be determined. The base is equal to taxable income, without regard to the charitable contributions, plus the DRD.

$$\$410,000 + \$20,000 = \$430,000 \text{ (Base amount)}$$

$$10\% \text{ of } \$430,000 = \$43,000$$

244. (B) In order for a gift to qualify for a deduction, the gift must be to a recognized charity. Thus, the $20,000 given to directly needy families (and not to a recognized charity) after a hurricane disaster, does not qualify. The $10,000 given to recognized charities does qualify as a charitable contribution.

Additionally, a contribution authorized to be paid to a recognized charity by a board of directors in one year, which will be paid within two and a half months subsequent there to and in the following year, is deductible in the year of authorization. Since Christie Corporation is an accrual-based taxpayer, and the authorization of the contribution payment was made by the board of directors within two and a half months of the payment date (i.e. authorization made on December 1, Year 4, payment made on February 1, Year 5), the $30,000 qualifies for deduction in Year 4. Christie can, therefore, take a $40,000 charitable contribution deduction in Year 4 ($10,000 + $30,000), since that amount falls below the 10% of taxable income limitation of $41,900 (i.e. $419,000 × 10% = $41,900).

245. (B) II is correct. A subsidiary may have one or more attractive tax attributes. Tax attributes refer to a company's ability to use a tax deduction simply because they are entitled to it from a previous year, such as a charitable contributions carryover or a capital loss carryover. These tax attributes make a company more attractive to a parent company looking to save taxes. A parent company can file a consolidated tax return with the subsidiary who has these tax attributes and save money. Operating losses of one subsidiary could reduce the profits of another subsidiary. I is wrong. A parent must own 80% or more of the subsidiary to file a consolidated tax return, but the decision to file consolidated is always optional.

246. (D) I is correct. The accumulated earnings tax is a penalty for not paying enough dividends. The Internal Revenue Service (IRS) assesses this tax because double taxation is avoided. An alternative to paying the accumulated earnings tax is for the corporation to pay the dividends late, by March 15th, the date the tax return is due for a calendar-year corporation. If a calendar-year C corporation pays the dividends to the shareholders but pays them after the end of the year, that would avoid the accumulated earnings tax. II is correct. The accumulated earnings tax is a penalty for not paying enough dividends. Once again, the IRS assesses this tax because double taxation is avoided. Another alternative to paying the accumulated earnings tax is "consent dividends." Consent dividends involve the corporation not actually paying the dividend but the stockholder consenting to paying the tax on the dividend. In a small C corporation, the individual taxpayers may consent to the dividends because the individual tax on the dividends is lower than the accumulated earnings tax. III is correct. The accumulated earnings tax is a penalty for not paying enough dividends. The IRS assesses this tax because double taxation is avoided. Accumulated earnings tax is based on the amount of the corporation's accumulated (retained) earnings that is in excess of the "reasonable needs" of the business. The primary way for a corporation to avoid the accumulated earnings tax is to pay enough dividends to shareholders. A corporation is allowed to argue that they reasonably need the earnings to grow; thus the term *reasonable needs argument*. The accumulated earnings tax can be imposed on C corporations regardless of the number of shareholders. An S corporation or partnership would never be subject to the accumulated earnings tax, since those entities pay no tax and there is no double taxation to worry about. Note that even a publicly traded company can be hit with the accumulated earnings tax. The IRS would send a letter.

247. (D) Small C corporations that do not pay sufficient dividends can be liable for the personal holding company tax. (A) is wrong. Personal holding companies are based on a stock ownership test. For example, if there are only a few owners, five or less owners hold half or more of the stock at any time in the last half of the year, this would be evidence of a personal holding company. (B) is wrong. If a company makes distributions in excess of earnings, no penalty (no personal holding company tax) will be paid. The whole idea of the personal holding company tax and the accumulated earnings tax is to compel C corporations to pay sufficient dividends to force double taxation upon the corporate entity and its shareholders. (C) is wrong. Corporations cannot get hit with both the accumulated earnings tax and the personal holding company tax in the same year.

248. (A) The accumulated earnings tax can be imposed on C corporations regardless of the number of shareholders. (B) is wrong. The personal holding company tax, like the accumulated earnings tax, is imposed on C corporations to compel them to pay sufficient dividends. If distributions are paid in excess of earnings, then it's clear that sufficient dividends have been paid so no personal holding company tax or accumulated earnings tax would be imposed. (C) is wrong. A company is not subject to both the personal holding company tax and the accumulated earnings tax, but it can be subject to one or the other. (D) is wrong, because partnerships do not pay tax.

249. (C) I is correct. Adjustments used in the corporate AMT computation include removing the benefit of using the installment sales method for inventory sales. II is correct. Adjustments used in the corporate AMT computation include removing the benefit of using the completed contract method for construction contracts. As with individual taxpayers, corporations have to compute their AMT and pay any amount in excess of the regular income tax. The AMT is designed to prevent taxpayers from receiving too much benefit from specific tax breaks. The computation is similar but not identical to that of an individual taxpayer.

250. (A) Municipal bond interest income from private activity bonds is an AMT preference item. (B) is wrong. The 80% dividends received deduction is not added back at all for AMT. (C) is wrong. Although the 70% dividends received deduction is added back for AMT, the 70% dividends received deduction is called an AMT adjusted current earnings (ACE) adjustment, not an AMT preference item. The ACE adjustments are a third round of add-backs that only corporations have to worry about for AMT. Individuals have to add back only adjustments and preference items, but corporations have to add back the ACE adjustment as well.

251. (B) II is correct. If a state or local government issues a bond for a "private activity" like an airport, a stadium, a bridge, or tunnel, the government must apply the proceeds to that activity. This is known as a *private activity bond.* The interest income from the bond is tax free to the investor for regular tax purposes. *But* for AMT, the interest income is a tax preference item and added back to arrive at alternative minimum taxable income, prior to another round of add-backs known as the ACE adjustment. I is wrong. If a state or local government issues a bond and the government can do whatever it chooses with the money raised, that bond is considered a *general obligation bond.* The interest income from general obligation municipal bonds is tax free to the investor for regular tax purposes and is *not* a tax preference item for corporate AMT.

252. (A) In computing the AMT for a corporation, municipal bond interest that is from private activity bonds is converted from tax exempt to taxable. Interest income from private activity bonds issued by a state or local government is considered a tax preference item for AMT. (B) and (D) are both wrong, since not all of municipal bond interest and not all of life insurance proceeds are added back in this same determination. There is a big difference between investing in private activity bonds and investing general obligation bonds. For AMT, 100% of the private activity bond interest income is an AMT preference item. Besides AMT adjustments and AMT preference items, there is another round of AMT add-backs for corporations, known as the ACE adjustment. If the municipal bond interest is from investing in general obligation bonds, only a percentage of the interest income, *not all,* of the general obligation bond interest is added back for the ACE adjustment. Note: general obligation bond interest income is *not* a tax preference item, although a percentage is added back for the ACE adjustment. (C) is wrong. Only relatively small companies receive an exemption for AMT because the AMT exemption phases out as income gets to a certain level.

253. (B) I is correct. Interest income from general obligation municipal bonds is part of the ACE adjustment for corporate AMT. 75% of the benefit of having general obligation bonds is removed. The net effect is that much of the interest income from general obligation bonds becomes taxable, not for regular tax but for AMT. II is correct. Life insurance proceeds received by a corporation upon the death of the officer are not taxable for regular corporate income tax. However, the ACE adjustment adds back 75% of the proceeds from the death benefit. The result of the ACE adjustment is that only 25% of the death benefit is tax free for AMT. III is correct. The 70% dividends received deduction (DRD) is part of the ACE adjustment. This means that 75% of the benefit of the DRD is lost due to the ACE adjustment. Only 25% of the DRD survives the AMT ACE adjustment. Note: although much of the benefit of the 70% DRD is lost to the ACE adjustment, the 80% DRD is not added back to the ACE adjustment. After the adjustments and preference items, the ACE adjustment is another series of add-backs designed to make corporations pay more tax. The ACE adjustment is not for individual taxpayers but for only corporations. The ACE adjustment removes 75% of the benefit of certain tax advantages, such as municipal bond interest on general obligation bonds, life insurance proceeds received by the corporation upon the death of an officer, and the 70% DRD.

254. (D) III is correct. If a corporation has five or fewer shareholders at any time during the last six months of the year, the corporation may be subject to the personal holding company tax. Therefore, the number of shareholders is a factor in determining whether the corporation is subject to the personal holding company tax. I is wrong. The number of shareholders in a corporation is *not* a factor in determining whether a corporation is subject to the AMT. While the number of shareholders is not a factor, a corporation would *not* be subject to the AMT in the first year of corporate existence. II is wrong. The number of shareholders in a corporation is *not* a factor in determining whether a corporation is subject to the accumulated earnings tax.

255. (D) I is correct. C corporations are subject to the AMT ACE adjustment. The ACE adjustment results in a C corporation having to pay additional tax through the loss of 75% of common tax breaks. II is wrong. S corporations are not subject to AMT at all, since S corporations are pass-through entities that do not pay any tax. S corporations are not subject to corporate tax rules. Any answer choice that says that S corporations pay income tax is the wrong answer choice. III is wrong. Individuals are subject to the AMT but not the ACE adjustment. The ACE adjustment is only for C corporations. IV is wrong. Partnerships are not subject to AMT at all, since partnerships are pass-through entities that do not pay any tax. Any answer choice that says partnerships pay tax is the wrong answer choice.

256. (B) Under Section 1244, a single taxpayer can deduct as an ordinary loss $50,000 per year and an additional $3,000 per year as a capital loss. The ordinary loss would go on other gains and losses, Form 4797. The excess would be reported on Schedule D capital gains and losses $3,000. Since Lemoi had no other capital gains, the limit for the capital loss deduction is $3,000 per year.

257. (C) The entire $60,000 would be claimed as an ordinary loss in Year 7. Although the limit for Section 1244 loss for a single individual is $50,000 ordinary loss plus $3,000 capital loss, the limit for a married couple is $100,000 ordinary loss plus $3,000 capital loss.

258. (B) If a stockholder sells Section 1244 stock over a two-year period, rather than all in one year, the deductible Section 1244 loss is $100,000 per year, not per security, which allows for far more than $100,000 total ordinary loss. Thus, sufficient stock can be sold in one year to obtain all ordinary loss, and then more can be sold the following year. In Year 5, $100,000 is the ordinary loss limit and then $3,000 capital loss—total of $103,000. The $7,000 carries over as a capital loss, not an ordinary loss.

259. (D) If a stockholder sells Section 1244 stock over a two-year period, rather than all in one year, the deductible Section 1244 ordinary loss is $100,000 per year, not per security, which allows for far more than $100,000 total ordinary loss. Thus, sufficient stock can be sold in one year to obtain all ordinary loss, and then more can be sold the following year. In this situation, $35,000 would qualify as an ordinary loss plus $3,000 capital loss.

260. (D) Since Aquilino did not sell any Section 1244 stock in Year 7, his total loss is limited to a $3,000 capital loss, which carried over from Years 5 and 6.

261. (A) Ordinary loss treatment is not available if the shareholder sustaining the loss was not the original holder of the stock. An individual who acquires by purchase, gift, or inheritance is not entitled to ordinary loss treatment; therefore, Junior cannot deduct any ordinary loss. The stock must have been issued in exchange for money or other property, and the stock must have been issued to the individual sustaining the loss.

262. (C) I is correct. C corporations can choose calendar year or fiscal year. III is correct. Partnerships are generally on a calendar year, but partnerships may choose a fiscal year. II is wrong. S corporations must operate on a calendar year.

263. (C) A trust must file Form 1041 by April 15th if it has any taxable income for the year or gross income of $600 or more for the year. A simple trust may report on the cash or accrual method. A trust may make estimated tax payments like individuals do. A trust must use the calendar year, and a trust is subject to the alternative minimum tax.

264. (C) The grantor creates the trust. A trust begins when a grantor conveys assets to a trustee to manage for the benefit of a third party, known as a beneficiary.

265. (A) I is correct. The trustee has the power to sell trust property. A trustee is a fiduciary who has the duty to manage the trust and carry out the trust purpose according to its terms. III is correct. The trustee has the power to pay trust expenses. The trustee must use his or her own skill, prudence, and judgment as a reasonable person would in making trust decisions and must abide by the trust instrument. II is wrong. The trustee does not have the implied power to borrow from the trust. Trustees may not profit personally from the role as trustee other than to receive whatever compensation is called for. Trustees cannot comingle personal assets with that of the trust.

266. (B) II is correct because stock dividends represent additional shares and would remain with the trust. The general rule is that proceeds from the sale of trust assets along with extraordinary expenses are charged to the trust itself. I is wrong. Cash dividends are generally allocated to the income beneficiaries. The question asked which would be charged to the trust principal, and cash dividends are ordinary income items and would be available for distribution to the income beneficiaries. Cash dividends, interest, and rents are generally given to the income beneficiaries to spend as they see fit.

267. (C) Stock dividends of $6,000 and proceeds from the sale of trust property of $7,000 for a total of $13,000 remain with the trust and are not distributed to the beneficiary. The rent income of $1,000 and the interest income of $3,000 are considered ordinary income and would be given to the income beneficiaries, unless the trust instrument specified otherwise.

268. (B) When the grantor of the trust retains the beneficial enjoyment or substantial control over the trust property or income, the grantor is taxed on the trust income. The trust is disregarded for income tax purposes. The grantor is taxed on the income if he or she retains (1) the beneficial enjoyment of the corpus or (2) the power to dispose of the trust income without the approval or consent of any adverse party.

269. (C) Someone making a will is known as a testator. Dying without a will is considered dying intestate (not interstate). State laws determine priority of someone who dies without a will after these general rules:

Priority	Family members
First	spouse
Second	children (if no living spouse)
Third	parents (if no living spouse or kids)
Fourth	siblings (if no living spouse, kids, or parents)

270. (C) I is correct. A trust that begins upon the creator's death is known as a testamentary trust. A trust that begins while the creator is still alive is known as an inter vivos trust. II is correct. Assets held in trust are known as trust corpus or trust res.

271. (A) I is correct. A complex trust is allowed to distribute less than its current earnings for the year, distribute more than its current earnings for the year, and make charitable contributions. II is wrong. A simple trust must distribute all of its current earnings to the beneficiary. A simple trust cannot distribute principal; therefore, a simple trust cannot distribute in excess of earnings or it would be effectively distributing principal. Complex trusts are subject to basically similar tax rules as simple trusts, except a complex trust is allowed only a $100 exemption, not $300 as in a simple trust. No personal exemption is allowed on a final return of a simple or complex trust, and both simple and complex trusts must use calendar years.

272. (C) A simple trust has an exemption of $300. Note: there is no standard deduction for a trust. Only an individual who does not qualify to itemize gets a standard deduction.

273. (A) I is correct. If a simple trust properly distributes all its income for a year, the simple trust will pay no tax for that year. II is correct. A simple trust receives an exemption of $300, but no exemption is allowed on the final return of a simple trust. III is wrong. A trust must use a calendar year.

274. (C) I is correct. For an estate tax return, a number of specific expenses and other costs can be deducted from the gross estate value. These deductions include administrative expenses of caring for an estate, legal and accounting fees, and executor fees. II is correct. For an estate tax return, a number of specific expenses and other costs can be deducted from the gross estate value. These deductions include debts and mortgages owed at the time of death. For an estate tax return, a number of specific expenses and other costs can be deducted from the gross estate value. These deductions include funeral expenses, administrative expenses, debts and mortgages, casualty losses, charitable bequests, and marital deduction. There is a big difference between the gross estate and taxable estate. The federal estate tax is imposed only on the taxable estate, computed as follows:

Gross estate
Less expenses and debts
Less charitable contributions in will
Less marital deduction
Equals the taxable estate

275. (C) If property is co-owned by husband and wife, one-half of its value is automatically included in the deceased spouse's estate regardless of whose funds were used to purchase the property.

276. (B) An unlimited marital deduction is permitted for gifts between spouses. The gift of the ring was prior to the marriage, so it does not qualify for the marital deduction. The $75,000 given after the wedding occurred between married persons and qualifies.

277. (A) Computing the taxable amount of Castellano's estate (when the tax-free exclusion is ignored) begins with its asset fair market value of $2 million:

$2,000,000	
− $400,000	liabilities
− $30,000	funeral expenses
− $290,000	charitable bequests
− $400,000	amount given to spouse
$880,000	taxable amount of Castellano's estate

278. (B) A gift to a child would not qualify as a deduction in arriving at the taxable estate. To determine the amount of a taxable estate, certain deductions are allowed for costs, such as funeral expenses, debts, administrative expenses, debts at death, and charitable bequests. Bequests to a spouse are deductible, but no other personal bequests (even to a son or daughter) can be used as a deduction.

279. (D) In determining the amount of a taxable estate, certain deductions are allowed for costs, such as funeral expenses, debts, administrative expenses, bequests to a spouse, and charitable bequests. There is no limitation to the amount that can be deducted because of a bequest to a spouse.

280. (A) Form 706 is due nine months after death if no extension is filed. An estate may use a calendar year or any fiscal year, and estimated taxes are not required for the first two years. After the first two years, estimated taxes are required.

281. (C) I is correct. Estates may adopt a fiscal year or calendar year.
II is correct. Estates are required to pay estimated income tax if any tax is due on income earned by estate assets. However, an estate is exempt from paying estimated taxes for the first two years.

282. (B) The threshold for filing a fiduciary return of an estate is the amount of the estate personal exemption of $600.

283. (B) II is correct. Unpaid income taxes would be a liability of the estate, so it would be deductible by the gross estate to arrive at the taxable estate. I is wrong. The federal estate tax is *not* a deduction from the gross estate to arrive at the taxable estate. State inheritance taxes are deductible from the gross estate, but federal inheritance taxes are not.

Chapter 3: Other Taxation Areas

284. (B) II is correct. This concept is known as backup withholding, and the purpose is to compel customers to provide their social security number to a financial institution when opening a new brokerage or bank account. The banks will withhold 31% of the portfolio income every year until Mac provides his social security number. Without the social security number, the Internal Revenue Service (IRS) is unable to tax the investment income. The bank or brokerage house is required to send the IRS a matching 1099 to report the income and is unable to do so without knowing the social security number of the investor. I is incorrect. Mac will *not* be limited to $500 of the portfolio income. Mac will be subject to backup withholding at the rate of 31%, until he furnishes a tax identification number or social security number to the brokerage firm.

285. (C) I is correct. Repackaging costs are among costs required to be capitalized for companies subject to uniform capitalization. For those companies, other costs that require capitalization include direct materials, direct labor, and applicable indirect costs. Applicable indirect costs required to be capitalized under uniform capitalization include utilities, warehousing costs, repairs, maintenance, indirect labor, rents, storage, depreciation and amortization, insurance, pension contributions, engineering and design, spoilage and scrap, and administrative supplies. Only when sold are the items allowed to be expensed. II is wrong. Although Stefano, Inc., is subject to uniform capitalization rules, research costs are expensed and are not part of uniform capitalization. III is wrong. Although Stefano Inc., is subject to uniform capitalization rules, advertising and marketing expenses are expensed and not capitalized. The uniform capitalization rules do not apply to inventory acquired for resale if the taxpayer's average gross receipts for the preceding three tax years are less than $10,000,000. Even for a company that must comply with uniform capitalization rules, costs that are not required to be capitalized include selling, advertising and marketing expenses, certain general and administrative expenses, research, and officer compensation not attributed to production services.

286. (C) I is correct. A company subject to uniform capitalization rules would still be able to expense officers' compensation that is *not* attributed to production. II is correct. Service companies, like accounting and law firms, are *not* subject to uniform capitalization rules. Companies would be subject to uniform capitalization if their average sales of inventory exceed $10,000,000 over a three-year period.

287. (B) To avoid penalties, if a taxpayer owes $1,000 or more in tax payments beyond withholdings, that taxpayer will need to have paid in taxes the lesser of the following: 90% of the current year's tax ($50,000 × 90%) = $45,000, or 100% of the previous year's tax ($40,000 × 100%) = $40,000. However, if the taxpayer had an adjusted gross income in excess of $150,000 in the prior year, 110% of the prior year's tax liability is used to compute the safe harbor for estimated payments. (Previous year's tax $40,000 × 110% = $44,000.) (A) is wrong. $40,000 is 100% of last year's tax. This would be sufficient if the previous year's income were $150,000 or less. (C) is wrong. $45,000 is 90% of this year's tax, which is sufficient, but the question is looking for the minimum amount. (D) is wrong. $50,000 is 100% of the current year's tax, which is sufficient, but more than required. The question asked for the minimum that would *not* result in a penalty: $44,000 is the minimum.

288. (C) Because taxable income is in excess of $1,000,000, Selzer cannot use its tax for the preceding year as a safe estimate. To avoid a penalty, a corporation must pay estimated tax payments each quarter. If a company will have a taxable income of over $1 million, estimated tax payments must be based on estimated income for the *current year*; if taxable income is less than $1 million, then estimates can be based on the prior year. Note: the prior year cannot serve as the basis if the company had no tax liability in the prior year.

289. (C) I is correct. C corporations must pay estimated tax each quarter. For Year 4, the payments due for a C corporation's estimated taxes are due April 15, June 15th, September 15th, and December 15th. The fourth installment for a corporation in Year 4 is due December 15, Year 4. II is wrong. Individuals get the holidays off; their final estimated tax payment for Year 4 is not due until January 15 of Year 5. For individuals, the first three estimated payments for Year 4 are due April 15th, June 15th, and September 15th. The final installment for Year 4 is due January 15th of Year 5. In this way, the Internal Revenue Service (IRS) expects a self-employed taxpayer to have all Year 4 taxes paid by January 15th of Year 5. So when the taxpayer files his Year 4 1040 return, the taxes should have already been paid. Employee taxpayers don't pay estimated taxes, because most of their tax gets paid through a withholding each pay period. III is wrong. S corporations do not pay federal income taxes; therefore, they do not pay estimated taxes.

290. (B) The general rule is that the statute of limitations runs for three years from the time the statute begins. The question is, when does the statute begin? The statute of limitations for individual tax returns begins to run from the due date of the return, if it is filed on or before the due date, April 15th. Since Quirk filed before the due date (March 12, Year 2), the statute of limitations begins on April 15th, Year 2, and expires on April 15th, Year 5. If the taxpayer files one or more extensions and files the return after the due date, the statute of limitations begins on the filing date.

291. (A) The three-year statute of limitations is extended to six years if there is a substantial understatement of gross income. If *gross* income is underreported by 25% or more, the three-year rule is extended to six years. Gross income represents $436,000 × 0.25 = $109,000.

292. (A) Since there was no fraud or substantial underpayment of gross income in excess of 25%, the three-year statute applies. Statute of limitations would begin April 15th if you file early or by the due date. Only if you file after April 15th does the statute begin on the date you file.

293. (B) According to IRS Circular 230, a tax preparer is charged a $50 penalty for failing to keep a copy of prepared returns for three years. The penalty is $50 for each tax return copy not maintained, up to a maximum of $25,000. Keeping a listing of just the name and ID number of each taxpayer for whom the preparer prepared a return is an adequate substitute for keeping a completed copy of the return. Other tax preparer penalties tested on the CPA exam include:

$50 preparer penalty for failure to sign the client's tax return
$50 preparer penalty for failure to report the tax preparer's identification number (PTIN) on the return
$50 preparer penalty for failure to give the taxpayer a completed copy of the return

294. (D) I is correct. A practitioner must return all client records at the request of the client; a dispute over fees does *not* relieve the practitioner of the responsibility to return the client's records. II is correct. A contingent fee is allowed in connection with the filing of a client's *amended* tax return but not when filing an original tax return. III is correct. A paid preparer is required to sign a tax return and include his or her PTIN on the client's return. A PTIN is a number that identifies the preparer, much like a social security number. In the past, paid preparers were allowed to include either their PTIN or social security number on the client's return. With Circular 230, only the PTIN is allowed.

295. (B) II is correct. If new legislation will have an impact on tax advice previously given, a practitioner has no obligation to advise the client of the new legislation even if the original advice was given in writing. III is correct. According to Circular 230, a tax return preparer is *not* permitted to endorse a taxpayer's refund check. I is incorrect because the statement is not entirely correct. When considering whether to give oral or written advice to a client, a CPA should consider the tax sophistication of the client but *not* whether the client will seek a second opinion.

296. (A) I is correct. According to Circular 230, registered tax return preparers may represent taxpayers before the IRS. II is correct. According to Circular 230, attorneys may represent taxpayers before the IRS. III is correct. According to Circular 230, CPAs as well as enrolled agents may represent taxpayers before the IRS.

297. (C) I is correct. The tax court hears a case before any assessed tax is paid. If the amount of the case is no more than $50,000, the tax court may handle the case under the "small tax case procedures." Small tax case procedures are special informal procedures that result in faster and easier court decisions. II is correct. If the assessed tax has already been paid and a claim for refund has been filed, a suit may generally be filed in the district court or the claims court. This would be the case if the tax was paid in error and the IRS refused to refund the money—then the case would be brought not to tax court but to district court or claims court.

298. (A) I is correct. The State Board of Accountancy is the party that ultimately grants a successful CPA candidate a license to practice public accounting. II is wrong. The State Board of Accountancy is also the party with the power to suspend and revoke a CPA's license to practice. The state board must provide due process of law before revoking a license. The state board may conduct a formal hearing regarding the licensee. If the state board determines, by preponderance of the evidence, that the CPA's actions constituted professional misconduct, the license may be suspended. The decisions made by the State Board of Accountancy may be reviewed by the courts. Notice that the state board doesn't have to prove guilt beyond a reasonable doubt to revoke or suspend a license. It only needs to establish guilt by preponderance of the evidence.

299. (D) I is wrong. The CPA has no right or obligation to contact the prior CPA without client permission. II is wrong. The CPA should notify the client concerning the noncompliance and recommend the proper course of action to the client. The CPA is not allowed to contact the IRS without the client's permission. Upon discovery of an error in a previously filed return involving the client's failure to file a required return, the CPA should promptly notify the client (either orally or in writing) of the error, noncompliance, or omission and advise the client of the appropriate measures to be taken. In this case the CPA should advise the client to correct the error in the previously filed return. If the client does *not* correct the error, the CPA should consider withdrawing from the engagement.

300. **(D)** When a tax preparer signs a taxpayer's return, the tax preparer's declaration on the tax return indicates that the information contained therein is true, correct, and complete to the best of the preparer's knowledge and belief. In this case, the tax preparer knowingly deducted non-business expenses on a business return and will be subject to a penalty possibly as high as $1,000.

301. **(A)** I is correct. If the tax preparer relied on the advice of an advisory preparer to calculate the taxpayer's tax liability and the tax preparer believed that the advisory preparer was competent and that the advice was reasonable, the IRS would examine the facts further to determine if a penalty applies, since the result was an understated income tax liability. II is wrong. Under Circular 230, there is an automatic penalty assessed if a tax preparer endorses and negotiates the client's refund check. The IRS would *not* have to examine the facts further, because the penalty automatically applies. There is no good faith exception to this rule. III is wrong. There is no penalty for revealing confidential client information during a peer review by the state society quality control team. While it's likely that confidential client information would be exposed, the IRS would *not* have to examine the facts further to see whether the good faith exception applies, because revealing client information is expected and appropriate in order to comply with peer review regulations. Tax preparer penalties may be assessed for improper use or disclosure of confidential client information. Acceptable circumstances for disclosure include peer review and also in response to a court order.

302. **(A)** The installment method is used rather than the accrual method when collection is in doubt. Under the installment sales method, the profit from the sale must be recognized proportionally as the cash is collected. The key to applying the installment sales method correctly is the determination of the gross profit and the gross profit percentage. Using the installment method, the first step is to calculate the dollar amount of gross profit from the sale. The sale price of $20,000 less the $15,000 cost equals the gross profit of $5,000. The second step is to determine the gross profit percentage from the sale. The gross profit percentage is the gross profit on the sale divided by the sales price. The third step is to multiply the cash collection times the gross profit percentage.

Step 1: gross profit from sale: $20,000 − $15,000 = $5,000 gross profit
Step 2: gross profit percentage from sale: $5,000/$20,000 sales price = 25%
Step 3: realized gross profit: cash collected $8,000 × 25% = $2,000

303. **(D)** The gross profit is $480,000 ($1,200,000 − $720,000). Thus the gross profit percentage is 40% ($480,000/$1,200,000). The company still has $700,000 in receivables from the installment sales ($1,200,000 − collections of $500,000). Of that amount, 40% represents the gross profit that will not be recognized until the cash is collected. Deferred gross profit is $280,000 ($700,000 × 40%). Note: at any point in time, the deferred gross profit is the accounts receivable balance multiplied by the gross profit percentage. Deferred gross profit equals the amount not yet collected times the gross profit percentage. The first two steps to determine the deferred gross profit are the same as to calculate the realized gross profit.

Step 1: gross profit from sale is $1,200,000 − $720,000 = $480,000
Step 2: gross profit percentage: $480,000/$1,200,000 = 40% gross profit
Step 3: deferred gross profit: $700,000 × 40% = $280,000

304. (A) The cost recovery method does not recognize profit until the entire cost of goods sold has been collected. In Year 1, $500 of cost of goods sold is yet to be collected, so no profit is recognized until Year 2. The cost recovery method is used if there is significant uncertainty about collection. When the cost recovery method is used, all profit is initially recorded as a deferred gross profit. Under the cost recovery method, no profit at all is recognized until *cash equal to the cost of the asset sold is collected.* After that point, each dollar collected is viewed as being equal to a dollar of profit. In Year 1 only $2,000 was collected, and that is not enough to equal the cost of goods sold amount of $2,500. Therefore, in Year 2 when $3,000 more is collected, the first $500 from Year 2 is still recovering cost. At that point enough cash has been collected to equal the cost of goods sold. Therefore, the remainder of cash collected in Year 2, $2,500, is recognized as profit.

305. (B) The percentage of completion method involves three steps in order to determine profit recognition on a long-term contract. Step 1 involves estimating costs. For Year 1, dividing the $240,000 costs incurred to date by $600,000 total estimated costs means 40% of the project is estimated to be completed at the end of Year 1. Step 2 involves using that estimate of completion percentage to determine profit recognized to date. Since 40% of the project is estimated to be complete at the end of Year 1, 40% is multiplied by the $400,000 estimated total profit. Therefore, estimated total profit at the end of Year 1 equals $160,000. Step 3 involves subtracting any profit recognized in prior years under this contract. Since this is the first year, there is nothing to subtract and only the first two steps are relevant for Year 1. Notice that although no cash was received, profit is still recognized. The percentage of completion method is based on accrual accounting.

> Step 1: costs incurred to date $240,000/$600,000 total estimated costs = 40% complete
> Step 2: 40% × $400,000 expected profit equals $160,000 profit recognized to date
> Step 3: subtract any profit recognized in the previous year; none, since this is the contract's first year

306. (D) The percentage of completion method involves estimating costs in order to recognize revenue and profit. For Year 2, $1,800,000 cost incurred to date divided by $2,400,000 total estimated costs means that the job is 75% completed as of December 31, Year 2. Total estimated profit of $600,000 × 75% means $450,000 profit should be recognized to date. Since $450,000 profit should be recognized to date and $300,000 profit was recognized in Year 1, $150,000 profit should be recognized in Year 2. Total estimated profit for Year 2 of $600,000 is calculated by subtracting the total estimated costs as of December 31, Year 2 of $2,400,000 and subtracting that from the $3,000,000 contract price. Total estimated costs of $2,400,000 is calculated by adding the costs incurred through Year 2 of $1,800,000 and adding the estimated costs remaining at December 31, Year 2, of $600,000.

> Step 1: costs incurred to date: $1,800,000/$2,400,000 = 75% complete after Year 2
> Step 2: 75% times the expected profit of $600,000 = $450,000 profit to date
> Step 3: Subtract $300,000 profit already recognized in Year 1 from the $450,000 profit to date = $150,000 profit to recognize in Year 2

307. (B) II is correct. Cash received is the critical event for income recognition in the installment method because under the installment, the cash collected is multiplied by the gross profit percentage to equal the realized gross profit from the installment sale. III is correct. Cash received is the critical event for income recognition in the cost recovery method since the amount of cash collected must exceed the cost of the item sold in order to recognize any profit from the sale. I is wrong. Billings and cash collections have no impact on profit recognized in either the percentage of completion method or the completed contract method of accounting for long-term construction contracts. Under the percentage of completion method, the profit earned over a long-term construction contract is based on costs incurred already in proportion to total estimated costs remaining. Under the completed contract method, no revenue is recognized until the job is substantially complete.

308. (D) I is wrong. Under the percentage of completion method, profit recognition is not based on cash received, but rather on costs incurred. The fact that no costs have yet been incurred by Everlast means that no profit will be recognized in Year 4. II is wrong. Under the completed contract method, profit recognition is delayed until the job is substantially complete. The completed contract method is *not* based upon cash received.

309. (B) If a tax-exempt organization has gross receipts of $50,000 or more, it must file an informational return each year, Form 990, listing major contributors and highest employee salaries. If the not-for-profit (NFP) has gross receipts of under $50,000, the filing requirement is much simpler: only Form 990-N would be filed, which does not include listing major contributors or employee salaries. Form 990-N includes only the basic information, NFP name, federal ID number, website address, and name and address of one principal officer of the NFP. Churches do not have to file 990 information returns; private foundations do.

310. (C) A not-for-profit (NFP) files Form 990-N if its gross revenues are less than $50,000 per year. This would be considered a small NFP, and the filing requirements are simple compared to larger NFPs. The filing requirements for a small NFP, that files a Form 990-N would include the name and mailing address of the NFP; the federal employer identification; the number, name, and address of a principal officer; website address; and confirmation of the fact that the revenues are less than $50,000. Information on major contributors and employee salaries are only included in a filing for larger NFPs with gross income exceeding $50,000.

311. (C) Most organizations exempt from income tax must file an annual information return (Form 990 or 990-EZ) or submit an annual electronic notice (Form 990-N), depending upon the organization's gross receipts for the year and total assets at year end. The simple Form 990-N electronic notice is permitted if the organization's average gross receipts are less than $50,000 per year. Form 990-EZ is permitted if average gross receipts are between $50,000 and $200,000 and total assets are less than $500,000.

Form 990, the long form, is the most sophisticated form of the three and applies to the larger not-for-profits. It is required if average gross receipts are greater than or equal to $200,000 or total assets are greater than or equal to $500,000 at the end of the tax year. Gross receipts include the total amounts the organization received from all sources during its three most recent tax years, without subtracting any costs or expenses for those years.

312. (C) Since Olney's gross receipts are greater than $200,000 for the three most recent years, the long-form 990 must be filed. This is the case even though Olney's total assets were below $500,000. If total assets are above $500,000 or if average revenues are greater than or equal to $200,000, Form 990, the long form, must be filed. (A) is wrong. For a not-for-profit organization, if average gross revenues (for the past three years) are below $50,000, only Form 990-N needs to be filed. Form 990-N is sometimes called an E-postcard in that it contains only the entity name, employer ID number, name and address of a principal officer, and website address of the organization. (B) is wrong. Olney's gross receipts are too high to file 990-EZ. If average gross receipts were between $50,000 and $200,000, Form 990- EZ could have been filed as long as total assets were less than $500,000. (D) is wrong. Filing Form 990 is required of a not-for-profit, unless the entity is a church. Churches are exempt from filing Form 990.

313. (A) A tax-exempt organization must pay income taxes on any unrelated business income in excess of $1,000. Some income activities are not taxable even though they are unrelated to the charitable purpose: sale of donations, operations run by volunteers or patients of the not-for-profit (NFP), and legal bingo at the church. Although the preceding represent unrelated business from the charitable purpose, income from these activities is exempt from tax.

314. (B) Since the museum's mission involves the education of the public about art, the proceeds from such courses are tax exempt because they are related business income, which is tax exempt for a not-for-profit.

315. (C) I is correct. Unrelated business income is taxable to the not-for-profit (NFP) after a $1,000 exemption. The tax is paid at the corporate tax rate. If this income were not taxed, then NFPs would directly compete with for-profit business and not have to pay tax, which would give the NFP a lower cost structure and an unfair advantage in the marketplace. II is correct. If an NFP carries advertising for business that has nothing to do with its mission, then the income from advertising on its website is considered unrelated business income.

316. (C) The deadline for filing the Form 990-N is four and a half months after the close of the year. For a calendar year NFP, the E-filed postcard would be due May 15th of the following year.

Chapter 4: Business Law, Ethics, and Professional Responsibilities

317. (B) II is correct. A contract can be for any legal purpose. A contract made for an illegal purpose is considered void. I is wrong. An offer would have to be accepted in order for a legally enforceable agreement to take effect. A contract (agreement) starts when one party makes an offer, but the other party would need to accept the offer to have an agreement. Silence does *not* normally act as acceptance.

318. (B) Advertisements are *not* considered offers. Instead, advertisements are considered invitations for the customer to come in and make an offer. Therefore, no offer existed here at all. Exam hint: this question could have been answered without even reading the facts. Knowing the rule that advertisements are not offers would have made (B) the correct choice regardless of the facts.

319. (C) I is correct. Counteroffers must be received to be effective. Once received, the counteroffer destroys the original offer. II is correct. Rejections must be received to be effective. Once received, rejections destroy the original offer. Other communications in contracts that must be received to be effective include offers and revocations of offers. Both must be received to be effective. Only acceptances can be valid prior to receipt. Although the general rule is that acceptance of an offer is valid upon dispatch (the mailbox rule), an offeror could require acceptance to be received by a certain date in order to be effective. Therefore it's essential to look to the offer to see if there are any specific instructions with regard to acceptance.

320. (A) I is correct. An option or option contract is an offer that is irrevocable for an agreed time period and is supported by consideration. II is wrong. Option contracts are very common in real estate where the price is high and financing may need to be secured. The buyer may need time to qualify for a loan, and maybe the buyer wants some time to decide whether or not to proceed.

321. (A) I is correct. An option is used when the dollar value of the deal is high and the financing may need to be secured, but the buyer isn't sure that he or she could even get the financing or whether he or she is 100% dedicated. Options give buyers time to think. II is incorrect. Generally a counteroffer like this would destroy the original offer, but not when there is an option contract in place. An option contract is when an offer is made in writing and supported by consideration (payment is made to keep the offer open). The option keeps the offer open and the offer cannot be terminated before the agreed-upon date, even by what looks like a counteroffer.

322. (B) The general rule is that acceptances only have to be sent (they do not have to be received) to form a contract. This is known as the *mailbox rule* or the early acceptance rule. However, the mailbox rule *can be eliminated* by the parties. The offeror can state in the offer that acceptance must be received to be effective.

323. (B) II is correct. A late-arriving acceptance is considered a counteroffer.

I is incorrect. While the general rule is that acceptance can be valid when mailed, the offer here requires acceptance to be received to be effective; therefore, acceptance is valid on August 6 not August 3.

324. (C) The general rule for acceptance is that acceptance only has to be sent; it does not have to be received to be effective. Since the offer stated only that Micki must accept by a certain date, and not that Clark, Inc., must receive the acceptance by any particular date, then the mailing on September 21 is a valid date for acceptance.

325. (B) This is an example of a unilateral contract, an offer for a reward. In a unilateral contract, one party (Rick) promises and the other party needs to perform in order to accept the contract. When deciding whether a contract is bilateral or unilateral, look at the offer. Rick's offer stated that whoever picks up Ricky gets paid, not whoever promises to pick him up.

326. (C) To prove common law fraud, the injured party must prove *all* of the following:

Material misrepresentation
Intent to deceive, scienter, bad faith
Justifiable reliance
Damages, usually money damages

327. (A) I is correct. In order to prove fraud, the misrepresentations must be material. II is wrong. The defendant need not be an expert to commit fraud; experts and nonexperts can both potentially commit fraud. For example, a seller lying about an appraised value of a diamond ring is committing fraud. Although the appraiser was the expert, the one who lied about the appraised value committed fraud even though he himself was not an expert.

328. (B) Just as you have to know what fraud is, sometimes you have to know what fraud is not. This is not an example of fraud, because all the elements of fraud cannot be proven. There is no intent to deceive and therefore no fraud. There is also no justifiable reliance. No one is justified in relying on accounting work done by a nonaccountant. Notice that all the elements of fraud need to be proven, not just one or two elements.

329. (C) I is correct. For example, suppose I offer to sell you my accounting firm for $500,000, but you accept for $5,000,000! I am eager to close that deal, but you discover your mistake just before closing. Result: although you made the mistake, it's clear that I know it's a mistake and am just trying to take advantage. You will have a defense called a unilateral mistake and not have to pay me $5,000,000 for my $500,000 firm unless you want to. The contract would be voidable if you don't want to pay me $5,000,000. II is correct. The term *voidable* refers to an otherwise valid contract, but one party has the right to cancel—in this case because of the unilateral mistake. In the event of a unilateral mistake, the contract could still exist if both parties agree. On the CPA exam, the party who made the mistake will discover the mistake prior to performance. The mistake would be a defense, and the contract would be voidable since the other party knows it's a mistake and is simply trying to take advantage.

330. (C) I is correct. Duress involves threatening someone and physically forcing that person to enter a contract against his or her will. Duress would result in a voidable agreement. II is correct. Undue influence involves using one's position to take unfair advantage of a person in a close personal relationship. Lawyers and accountants could easily influence an individual into making a contract that they would otherwise not make.

In addition to fraud and unilateral mistake, duress and undue influence are two additional situations where someone would have a defense and could back out of a contract.

331. (B) II is correct. Consideration is something that is bargained for and exchanged in a contract. For example, if a person pays $50,000 for a used car, the $50,000 is consideration to one party and the car is consideration to the other. I is incorrect. Consideration can involve money, goods, or services.

332. (B) Although Mirro promised the $125, if the plumbing inspector shows up the following morning, Mirro does *not* have to pay the plumbing inspector. This is because the plumbing inspector is *not* offering any additional consideration by showing up earlier than scheduled. The plumbing inspector already gets paid and is obligated to perform inspections. Mirro's promise is a moral obligation rather than a legal obligation.

333. (B) As a minor, Todd can cancel the contract at any time while still a minor and even for a reasonable time after becoming an adult, thus, answer choice (A) is incorrect. (C) is incorrect. The flight school after learning it just did business with a minor cannot cancel the contract. Only the party who lacks capacity may cancel; the party with capacity cannot back out. A minor's contract is voidable at the minor's election. (D) is incorrect. If the contract was for necessaries, the minor must pay reasonable value for what has been already received, even though the minor is still allowed to void the remaining contract. This would be the case if the minor's parents were not able to provide the food and shelter, and so on. Necessaries include food, clothing, shelter, and medical attention.

334. (B) II is correct. If the contract was for campus housing or other necessaries, the minor must pay reasonable value for what has been already received, even though the minor is still allowed to void the remaining contract. This would be the case if the minor's parents were not able to provide the campus housing. Necessaries include food, clothing, shelter, and medical attention. I is wrong. Guitar lessons are not considered necessaries, so the minor could skip out on those services already received and could certainly cancel the remaining lessons while still a minor and even within a reasonable time after becoming an adult.

335. (A) I is correct. Phil may rescind (cancel) while still a minor and even within a reasonable time after becoming an adult. Minors are allowed to cancel contracts even if the other contracting party (adult) suffers a financial loss. II is wrong. Ratification means acceptance. Ratification has nothing to do with how long the minor kept or used the item. A minor cannot ratify (accept) a contract while still a minor. Notice that even an item stolen from a minor can be the subject of a cancelled contract.

336. (A) I is correct. Brian's promise is based on past consideration and is a moral obligation rather than a legal obligation. Mona would have to work or do something for Amazing Amusements to be entitled to the $500 per month, or there is no consideration to the company. Brian's promise is based on past consideration. Past consideration is not viewed as consideration. II is wrong. Even if Amazing Amusements began paying Mona each month, neither Amazing Amusements nor Brian would be required to continue the payments unless Mona came back to work or did something in return.

337. (C) Modification of an existing services contract requires consideration. Since Black Bear, Inc., did not receive any consideration when they agreed to modify and give Ditka the raise, Black Bear, Inc., does not have to pay Ditka the increase and can sue him to recover it. It is important to know for the CPA exam that with regard to service contracts, modification requires consideration be given to both sides, not just one side.

338. (B) II is correct. The general rule is that a promise needs to be supported by consideration for the promise to be legally enforceable. An exception is when a person makes a promise to donate money to a charity. This promise to the charity can be enforced by the charity even though the charity never promises anything in return to the donor. On the exam, look to see whether the charity already spent the money or incurred debt based on the expectations of the large donation. If the charity spent the money already or incurred debt with anticipation of the large donation, the donor's promise is enforceable. I is wrong. Modification of a real estate or services contract requires additional consideration be given (to both sides, not just one side). If the contract to purchase the land is signed, both sides would need additional consideration for modification to take place. The question asked which of the given statements would be valid without consideration. Modification of a real estate agreement would need consideration to be valid.

339. (D) The question asked which answer choice correctly relates to the terms *valid*, *void*, and *voidable*. Once a party has been declared legally insane by a court with proper jurisdiction, all contracts entered into by that person would be void. *Void* means without legal effect. Contracts require a party to have mental capacity and be competent in order for a contract to be valid and enforceable. A person having been declared mentally incompetent lacks such capacity, and all contracts would then be void, without legal effect. This is done to protect the mentally incompetent from being taken advantage of. (A) is wrong because once a party has been declared legally insane, all contracts entered into by that individual are *void*, not *voidable*. Voidable contracts are otherwise valid and enforceable, but if a contract is voidable then one party would have the power to set the contract aside. (B) is wrong because if a contract is otherwise valid, but one party has the power to set the contract aside, the contract would be *voidable*, not *void*. (C) is wrong because voidable contracts are not void from the start. *Void* means without legal effect. Voidable contracts are otherwise valid and enforceable, but if the contract is voidable, one party has the right to set the contract aside. An example of a voidable contract is a contract entered into by a minor (under age 18) is valid but may be set aside by the minor.

340. (A) I is correct. A minor may cancel a contract anytime while still a minor and even within a reasonable time after becoming an adult. Therefore, a contract entered into by a minor is voidable by the minor. II is wrong. Contracts entered into by a person who is drunk every day are not voidable. Being drunk at the time of entering into a contract can sometimes be a defense to a contract but sometimes not. If a person who doesn't normally abuse alcohol had too much to drink and then enters into a contract, that person can avoid the contract because that person could say that they were "accidentally drunk." The court would likely have sympathy and release the "accidentally drunk" individual from the terms of the contract. However, if alcohol is part of that person's daily diet, if that same person drinks alcohol every day, then that person would *not* be able to say that he or she was "accidentally drunk." Therefore contracts entered into by a person who is drunk every day are not voidable. Notice that with alcohol as a defense, it's not how much an individual had to drink, but how often he or she drinks.

341. (D) I is wrong. In an illegal contract, the court will not help either party. The court would leave the parties where they stand. II is wrong. This would be an example of a void contract, not a voidable contract. Contracts that are illegal are void from the start. Voidable contracts, on the other hand, are valid contracts, but one or more parties have the power to set the contract aside, like a minor. Other examples of voidable contracts include where there is a mistake, fraud, duress, or undue influence.

342. (C) I is correct. A revenue license is not required in order to collect for professional services rendered in most states. A revenue license is just a tax ID number. Someone can still get paid for services rendered if they are missing a tax ID number or what is sometimes known as a revenue license. Make sure you know the difference between a revenue license and a regulatory license. II is correct. A regulatory license is a competency license. A regulatory license is required in order to collect for professional services rendered in most states. If someone performs a service on the exam, look to see if they have the required competency (regulatory) license. If they don't have the required regulatory license, they are not entitled to getting paid even if they performed the services flawlessly.

343. (B) I is correct. Contracts for the sale of real estate need to be in writing. II is correct. Contracts for services that are impossible to complete within one year need to be in writing. III is wrong. Sales of *goods* of $500 or more need to be in writing, but *not* all contracts over $500. Service contracts over $500 do not need to be in writing unless they are impossible to complete within one year.

344. (C) I is correct. The statute of frauds applies to contracts that cannot be fully performed within one year. This means that the contract between Juan and Genarro should have been in writing and signed. The fact that Genarro, Inc., did not sign the contract means that Genarro, Inc., is not obligated to perform. II is correct. The statute of frauds applies to contracts that have not yet been fully performed and provides a defense—a reason to cancel. A fully performed contract is not subject to any writing requirement.

345. (B) Hayes will recover $625 because a contract for services does not have to be in writing unless it is impossible to complete within one year. So even though the price is above $500, an oral contract for services is enforceable. The fact that this contract was not in writing is irrelevant since goods were not being sold.

346. (D) I is correct. While most oral contracts are valid, certain contracts are required to be in writing, and if they are not signed, the party who did not sign is allowed to back out. An example of this would be a contract for the sale of goods with a price greater than $500. II is correct. If a contract that is required to be in writing is not signed, the party who did not sign the written agreement has the right to back out. An example of this would be an executor of a will. The party agreeing to be the executor must sign the will agreeing to the role of executor. III is correct. If a contract that is required to be in writing is not signed, the party who did not sign the written agreement has the right to back out. An example of this would be a co-signor. An oral promise to pay the debts of another would *not* be enforceable.

347. (D) I is wrong. If a contract is in writing, the parol evidence rule states that the terms of the contract must be determined from the writing itself. Any evidence that existed prior to the written contract is not allowed to dispute the final written contract. II is wrong. If a contract is in writing, regardless of whether it needs to be in writing, the parol evidence rule states that the terms of the contract must be determined from the writing itself. The moral of the story of the parol evidence rule is to read and understand the contract before you sign it. If you don't like the contract after you sign it, it's often too late.

348. **(C)** I and II are correct. While most evidence that exists prior to a written contract would be excluded by the parol evidence rule, both oral and written evidence that could prove fraud would not be prohibited by the parol evidence rule.

349. **(D)** I is wrong. An assignment of rights in a contract to another party need not be in writing. The parties to the contract could agree orally on the rights to be assigned. Note that consideration is *not* required for assignment to be valid. II is wrong. Most contract rights are assignable, and the assignor is generally permitted to transfer the contract rights to a third party provided the assignment of those contract rights are not prohibited by the contract itself. If a contract is silent with regard to assignment, assignment is usually permitted unless assignment would increase the other party's risk. An example of a contract that cannot be freely assignable would be the following: a doctor cannot assign his or her malpractice insurance policy to another doctor without the consent of the insurance company because it may increase the insurance company's risk.

350. **(B)** The rule for assignment is that most contract rights are generally assignable. The only contract rights that are not assignable are when the contract prohibits assignment, if it increases the other party's risk, or if highly personal services are involved. Nothing in this question indicates that assignment would be prohibited.

351. **(B)** III is correct. Most contract rights are assignable. Assignment is generally allowed, unless it is prohibited by the contract, would substantially increase someone's risk, or contains highly personal contract rights. I is wrong. Since the contract is silent with regard to the rights of assignment, assignment is allowed. II is wrong. The right to receive delivery of landscaping equipment would *not* be considered highly personal contract rights. An example of highly personal contract rights would be the right to receive an operation scheduled for surgery with the chief of staff. This would be an example of a highly personal contract and cannot be assigned without permission in advance.

352. **(D)** I is wrong. Fisk is a third-party intended beneficiary, not an incidental beneficiary. As a third-party intended beneficiary, Fisk is able to sue to enforce the contract made to benefit him. II is wrong. While Fisk is a third-party intended beneficiary, Fisk is a creditor beneficiary rather than a donee beneficiary. As a creditor beneficiary, money is owed to Fisk and this contract was made to benefit Fisk—to help him get paid. Therefore, as an intended creditor beneficiary, Fisk has the rights to sue to enforce the contract. Had Fisk been a *donee* beneficiary rather than a creditor beneficiary, he would still have been able to sue. An example of a donee beneficiary would be a child in a life insurance policy contract. The child is a third party who is intended to benefit from the contract and has the rights to enforce the agreement as a third-party intended beneficiary. Note: had Fisk been only an *incidental* beneficiary, Fisk would *not* have been able to sue.

353. **(B)** II is correct. When two parties make a contract intending to benefit a third-party beneficiary, the third-party beneficiary may have the right to sue to enforce the contract if the third party is an intended creditor beneficiary. Creditor beneficiaries are owed money from one of the parties in the contract, and the contract is entered into to facilitate the payment. The third-party creditor beneficiary has the right to sue to enforce the agreement because the creditor beneficiary is intended to benefit from the agreement. III is correct.

When two parties make a contract intending to benefit a third-party beneficiary, the third-party beneficiary may have the right to sue to enforce the contract if the third party is an intended donee beneficiary. An example of an intended donee beneficiary would be a child in a life insurance contract. The contract is between the parents and the life insurance company, but the contract is intended to benefit the child. The contract gets donated to the child; thus the term *donee beneficiary*. I is wrong. Incidental beneficiaries cannot sue, as they were never named in the contract or intended to benefit from the original contract between the parties. An example of an incidental beneficiary is a party who buys land where a casino development contract is under way. The buyer of the land stands to benefit from the increased property values when the casino is developed. But if the casino never gets built, the buyer would have no rights to sue anyone, as he was never intended to benefit from the casino development contract.

354. (C) I is correct. Anticipatory repudiation occurs if one party announces in advance that they will not perform as required. II is correct. Anticipatory repudiation occurs if one party reasonably demands an assurance of performance from the other and does not receive one. In either case, the threatened party may sue immediately and does not have to wait until performance is due.

355. (B) II is correct. Compensatory damages represent actual dollar losses that when recovered would restore the parties to the position they would have been in had there been no breach. *Compensatory* means designed to compensate. I is wrong. Liquidated damages are an amount of general damages agreed to in advance when actual damages are difficult to determine. Liquidated damages are designed to alleviate litigation delays in seeking damage awards to contract breaches. Note that liquidated damages are not automatically awarded in contract breaches. If the court determines that the liquidated damage clause is too severe, it would be thrown out even though both parties agreed to it. Therefore, any answer choice to a multiple-choice question on the CPA exam that says a liquidated damage clause is automatically enforceable is the wrong answer. For the liquidated damages clause to survive a court challenge, the amount of predetermined damages must bear a reasonable relationship to the probable loss.

356. (A) Liquidated damages are damages that are agreed to (in amount) at the time the parties enter the contract. Liquidated damages will be enforced as long as they are not punitive. (D) is wrong. Punitive damages are designed to punish and are not granted in breach of contract cases. (B) is wrong. Specific performance does not involve money damages; rather, it is where the court orders the party to do what they agreed to do in the contract. (C) is wrong. Compensatory damages are actual dollar losses, and in the case of the AICPA contract with Prometric, actual damages were almost impossible to determine. So for that reason, the liquidated damages clause was inserted into the contract. It should be known that Prometric finished on time, but if they had not, Prometric would have paid the AICPA the liquidated damages, agreed to in advance, or would have gone to court in order to establish that the liquidated damages were too severe. Therefore, any answer choice to a multiple-choice question that says "liquidated damages are automatically awarded in a contract" is never the right answer because liquidated damages are not awarded by the court if the court determines that the previously agreed to amount is nothing but a penalty.

357. (A) II is correct. Specific performance is available where the contract calls for the sale of unique goods. Contracts that call for ordinary goods are not entitled to specific performance. III is correct. Specific performance is available where the contract calls for the sale of unique items like real estate. All real estate is considered unique; therefore, specific performance is available in real estate contracts. I is wrong. Specific performance is not a remedy when the subject matter is personal services. In the case of services when a party refuses to perform as contractually obligated, you can't force them. Instead, if you have to hire another at a higher price, you can sue for the difference. Specific performance is where there has been a breach and the injured party tells the court she would rather have the court enforce the contract rather than collect any money damages.

358. (C) I is correct. With respect to a covenant not to compete, the agreement not to compete must be reasonable in time. The restraint must be no more extensive than is necessary to protect the goodwill purchased by Murray and Rukke. II is correct. With respect to a covenant not to compete, the agreement not to compete must be reasonable in geographical area. A covenant not to compete is very common where there is a sale of a business. Without a covenant not to compete, there is nothing to stop a seller of a business from opening a competing business across the street from the buyer. These restrictions on the seller must be reasonable to be enforceable. An example of a reasonable covenant not to compete that could be expected to go along with this sale would include that the seller cannot open a competing business for a term of five years within a radius of 20 miles.

359. (B) In a real estate contract breach, both specific performance and compensatory damages are available, but the injured, non-breaching party, is only entitled to receive one or the other, not both. Specific performance would involve the non-breaching party asking the court to force the breaching party to perform as contractually obligated.

360. (A) I is correct. The UCC rules apply to contracts that involve the sale of goods. The minute goods are being sold, the UCC rules apply, regardless of the price of the goods and whether the seller is a merchant seller or non-merchant seller. II is wrong. The common law rules apply to real estate contracts, contracts for the sale of a business, and personal services contracts.

361. (B) The UCC rules apply to contracts that involve the sale of goods. The minute goods are being sold, the UCC rules apply, regardless of whether the goods are ordinary goods or custom made.

362. (D) III is correct. A firm offer must be in writing, for the sale of goods, and signed by a merchant. The firm offer must contain some assurance that the offer will be held open. I is wrong. Under the sales article of the UCC, a firm offer will be created only if the offeror is a merchant. The offeree need not be a merchant for the offeror to create a firm offer. II is wrong. Under the sales article of the UCC, a firm offer does *not* require consideration to be given in exchange for the irrevocable offer. Note that this is different than the option contract under the common law that did require consideration to be exchanged. The option contract requires consideration; the firm offer does not.

363. (B) In the sale of goods under the UCC, the acceptance need not always be a mirror image of the offer. Under the UCC, acceptance with additional terms acts as acceptance of the original offer. This is often tested on the CPA exam because it represents a difference between the common law rules and the UCC rules. Under common law rules, if the subject matter was real estate, services, or the sale of a business, adding additional terms would be a counteroffer and *not* a valid acceptance. Under the UCC, when goods are sold, the acceptance of the offer will likely include additional terms on the CPA exam. The additional terms become part of the contract.

364. (B) II is correct. If the contract were for real estate, the price would be considered material and the contract would fail if the price of a real estate contract were left open. III is correct. If the contract were for personal services, the price would be considered material and the contract would fail if the price of a services contract were left open. I is wrong. Under the Uniform Commercial Code (UCC) for the sale of goods, price can be left open and the contract would still exist. The buyer would simply pay the reasonable value for the goods. Under the UCC, terms may be left open, changed, deleted, or added by the acceptance and it will still create a valid agreement. While the *price* of a contract under the UCC is not considered material, quantity would be considered material and cannot be left open.

365. (A) I is correct. Contracts under the common law rules, including services or sale of a business and real estate, require additional consideration to both sides for modification to be valid. II is incorrect. If a contract is for the sale of goods, consideration is not necessary for modifications to be valid. The only requirement for modification of a contract for the sale of goods is that the modification must be in good faith.

366. (A) I is correct. Between merchants, a written confirmation of an oral agreement for the sale of goods can substitute for a signed contract if the confirmation is received and *not* disputed within 10 days. II is wrong. A contract for the sale of goods would follow the Uniform Commercial Code rules rather than the common law rules regardless of whether the parties are merchants or non-merchants.

367. (D) The general rule is that contracts for sale of goods of $500 or more must be in writing and signed, setting forth the terms to be enforceable according to the statute of frauds. There is an important exception to that rule being tested in this question. With specially manufactured goods, if the goods are custom made to the buyer's specifications, the seller can recover full contract price plus storage fees if the buyer backs out, even if the contract is oral. Recoverable damages include the full contract price plus storage fees.

368. (B) II is correct. In a trial sale known as a sale or return, the seller ships goods to a buyer to use or test for 10 days. In a sale or return, title and risk of loss pass to the buyer immediately. The buyer has the right to return the goods. In a sale or return, the buyer is not the ultimate consumer but instead is buying for resale. The buyer would have risk of loss during the trial period since the buyer is also a merchant. I is wrong. If the buyer is *not* a merchant buying for resale but rather the ultimate consumer, then the trial sale is considered a sale on approval rather than a sale or return. In a sale on approval, title and risk of loss will *not* pass during the trial period.

369. (D) When goods are involved, the UCC rules apply. If a merchant is the seller, the UCC rules apply. If a non-merchant is the seller, the UCC rules apply. The UCC rules apply regardless of the price of the goods. (A) is wrong because the price can be greater than $500 and the UCC would still apply regardless if the buyer and seller were merchants. (B) is wrong because there is no evidence that the contract is a trial sale.(C) is wrong. Both parties must always perform in good faith.

370. (C) Unless the contract calls for delivery, the seller only has to set aside the goods called for in the contract, conforming goods, and hold those goods and give the buyer notification to take his or her own delivery.

371. (C) The contract between VoiceNext and Giant is FOB shipping point. In FOB shipping point, the seller has no risk during shipment. In FOB shipping point the buyer bears all risk during shipment. Another term for FOB shipping point is FOB seller's loading dock, or a "shipping contract." Conversely, with FOB destination, the seller would bear all risk during shipment. When it's FOB buyer's loading dock, risk passes only upon tender of delivery at destination.

372. (D) Under the UCC, risk of loss passes to the buyer when the goods are delivered to the carrier if the terms are FOB shipping point. In FOB shipping point, the seller is responsible only until the goods are delivered to the carrier.

373. (B) I is correct. If a seller ships nonconforming goods, no title and no risk of loss passes to the buyer even if the shipping terms were FOB shipping point. In the event of nonconforming goods, the seller has breached the contract by shipping the wrong goods. III is correct. Although the seller has breached the contract by shipping nonconforming goods, the buyer must follow reasonable instructions from the seller as to what to do with the nonconforming goods that have been rejected. The buyer must act in good faith as to what to do with the nonconforming goods. II is wrong. Example: If a seller ships *nonconforming* goods to a buyer, the buyer could reject the entire shipment or could accept a partial shipment. For example, if a seller ships 90 cases of bottled water and 10 cases of iced tea to a buyer, but the contract called for 100 bottles of water, the entire shipment is nonconforming. The buyer could accept or reject all or part. If partially accepted, the buyer must pay for what has been accepted but can send back the rest.

374. (A) I is correct. If the item was purchased and ultimately stolen from a merchant seller, the store bears risk of loss because the risk of loss passes from a merchant seller to a buyer only when the buyer takes goods out of the store. II is wrong. If the item was purchased and ultimately stolen from a non-merchant seller, your client bears risk of loss because risk of loss passes from a non-merchant seller to a buyer upon tender. The word *tender* means to make available. Once the non-merchant seller tenders the guitar, title and risk of loss pass.

375. (B) II is correct. If the seller refuses the buyer's reasonable request for a written assurance of performance, that would result in a breach of contract known as an anticipatory repudiation, or breach in advance. I is wrong. If the risk of loss had already passed to the buyer, that would not release the buyer. Rather, that would be bad news for the buyer, because the buyer would have to pay for goods that were already destroyed.

376. (C) I is correct. If the seller ships nonconforming goods, the seller may be able to cure and ship conforming goods and mitigate any losses suffered by the buyer. II is correct. As long as the time for performance has not passed, the seller has the right to correct defects in shipments made. The seller must give timely notice of intent to cure.

377. (D) Regardless of the question, punitive damages are NOT available in contract breaches. The buyer's right to cover relates to the buyer's right to go into the market and purchase substitute goods. If the buyer has to pay more, the buyer could sue the seller for compensatory damages.

378. (B) II is correct. A buyer has the right to inspect goods prior to payment unless the contract is COD (cash on delivery). There is no indication that this contract is COD. I is wrong. The seller has no obligation to deliver the goods to the buyer. Unless otherwise agreed to, the seller's obligation to the buyer is to hold conforming goods and give the buyer whatever notification is necessary for the buyer to take his or her own delivery. Unless you see that delivery is called for in the contract (FOB shipping point or FOB destination), no delivery is required.

379. (C) III is correct. The implied warranty of merchantability warrants that the item must be fit and safe for normal use. Only a merchant seller gives this warranty. I is wrong. An express warranty is a statement of fact made by the seller that the buyer relies upon when making the purchase. An example of an express warranty would be the seller explaining to the buyer the high price on the used baseball glove is because it "used to belong to Derek Jeter." Any seller, merchant or non-merchant, would be liable for such an express warranty. II is wrong. Title means ownership: all sellers warrant good title and rightful transfer. Merchant and non-merchants are responsible if they breach the warranty of title. If a neighbor sells a stolen baseball glove to your client, the client would have to surrender the glove to the rightful owner because the warranty of title has been breached. Even a merchant seller cannot pass stolen goods to a buyer in the ordinary course of business.

380. (A) I is correct. Implied warranty of fitness for particular purpose arises where the seller knows the particular purpose for which goods are to be used and that the buyer is relying on the seller's skill or judgment—there is an implied warranty that the goods will be fit for such purpose. II is wrong. The implied warranty of merchantability would arise anytime goods are being sold by a merchant seller.

381. (A) I is correct. The warranty of title can only be disclaimed with use of the word *title* in the disclaimer. For example, to properly disclaim the warranty of title, the seller should say, "There is no warranty of title for this sale." II is wrong. A merchant who attempts to disclaim "any and all warranties" has adequately disclaimed the warranty of merchantability. III is wrong. A merchant who attempts to disclaim "any and all warranties" has adequately disclaimed the warranty of fitness for a particular purpose.

382. (B) II is correct. The following four items must be proven to collect damages for product liability injury:

1. The defendant was in the business of selling the defective product.
2. They sold the product in a defective condition.
3. The product was unreasonably dangerous.
4. Use of the product caused the injury (must be physical injury not mental).

I is wrong. Historically, a person who is injured because of a product defect could successfully sue the seller only if the injured party was the purchaser. This is because only these two parties were in privity of contract. Today, privity rules vary from state to state, but generally privity is not required if injury occurs. III is wrong. Negligence on the part of the seller or manufacturer need not be proven in order to collect damages in product liability cases.

383. (B) Product liability lawsuits are difficult to defend since no negligence needs to be proven on the part of the seller or manufacturer, and the manufacturer is not allowed to hide behind the "we have been building it this way for 150 years" and no one has ever gotten hurt before defense. To collect on a product liability lawsuit, the injured party must prove all four of the following:

1. The defendant was in the business of selling the defective product.
2. They sold the product in a defective condition.
3. The product was unreasonably dangerous.
4. Use of the product caused the injury (must be physical injury not mental).

384. (B) II is correct. The mailbox rule applies to the UCC contracts for the sale of goods just as it does to the common law contracts for services and sale of a business and real estate. I is wrong. The UCC rules apply to *all* contracts for the sale of goods, regardless of price. Note that the UCC applies to contracts for the sale of goods whether the contracts are oral or written.

385. (A) I is correct. In a written contract under the UCC, the quantity is considered material to the contract and cannot be left open. Price would be allowed open but not quantity. II is wrong. To enforce a written contract against another party, the written contract must contain the signature of the party against whom enforcement is sought. If A wanted to hold B liable on a written contract, A would need to show the court B's signature. If A signed the contract but B didn't, that would not help A seeking to enforce the contract.

386. (C) Under the entrustment rule, if a merchant seller sells goods entrusted to its care to a customer in the ordinary course of business, that customer gets good title. The store would have to pay your client a sum of money in damages, but that guitar, even if unique, would belong to the good faith purchaser. A customer who buys in the ordinary course of business from a merchant seller automatically gets good title. Otherwise, you would have to ask every time you bought something from a merchant seller whether the item actually belonged to the store or to someone else!

387. (D) Regardless of the question, any answer that says, "the obligations of the parties to the contract must be performed in good faith" has to be the correct answer; no one is allowed to perform in bad faith.

388. (C) I is correct. Commercial paper is a substitute for money and includes notes and drafts. II is correct. Commercial paper is a means of providing credit. The purpose of commercial paper, both notes and drafts, is to provide credit and facilitate commerce.

389. (C) I is correct. A note is a type of commercial paper. Notes have two parties, maker and payee. The maker of the note is the debtor, and the payee is the party to whom the note is made payable. Notes are a substitute for money and a means of providing credit. II is correct. A draft is a type of commercial paper. A draft has three parties: drawer, drawee, and payee. An example of a draft is a check. In a check, a drawer orders a drawee bank to pay a payee. Drafts are substitutes for money and a means of providing credit. III is wrong. A warehouse receipt is not commercial paper, because commercial paper is payable in money and a warehouse receipt is payable in goods.

390. (A) I is correct. A certificate of deposit is an example of a promise to pay made by a bank to pay its customer an amount borrowed plus interest on a specific date. II is correct. Installment notes are an example of a promise to pay often made by a customer in a consumer purchase where the note will be satisfied in installments (of principal and interest) rather than just a single payment. III is wrong. A draft is considered an order to pay rather than a promise to pay. In a check, the drawer *orders* a drawee bank to pay a payee. A check is the most common type of draft.

391. (D) For an instrument to be negotiable, it must be payable to order or bearer. "Pay to Russell" on the front would make the instrument non-negotiable, since in order to be negotiable, the instrument must show a willingness to pay more than just one party. If the note were payable only to Russell, it would not be a substitute for money, because Diane would only be agreeing to pay Russell. (A) is wrong. "Pay to the order of Russell" is negotiable because Diane is willing to pay Russell or anyone Russell orders her to pay. (B) is wrong. "Pay to Russell or bearer" is negotiable because Diane is willing to pay Russell or a bearer. *Bearer* means anyone in possession of the note. (C) is wrong. "Pay to Russell or his order" is negotiable because Diane is willing to pay Russell or anyone Russell orders her to pay. To be negotiable, the front of the note must show willingness to pay more than just one party.

392. (A) According to the UCC, to be negotiable the instrument must be payable in money only. A note payable in a foreign currency satisfies the requirement for negotiability. (B), (C), and (D) are wrong. An instrument that allows for the payment of money or goods or the payment of money or services is non-negotiable.

393. (C) To determine whether an instrument is negotiable, look only at the front of the instrument. The back of the instrument is only for the endorsements. By the time you get to the back of the instrument, you already know whether or not it's negotiable. The front determines negotiability. Only if an instrument is negotiable can it be a true substitute for money, or a means of providing credit. If it's negotiable on the front, then it's negotiable on the back. Remember this phrase, "once negotiable, always negotiable." Remember this phrase, "once non-negotiable, always non-negotiable."

394. (C) is correct. If an instrument is conditional, it's non-negotiable. To be negotiable, the instrument must be unconditional. (B) is wrong. An acceleration clause would accelerate the time for payment in the event of default—making it so the lender would not have to sue the debtor separately over every missed payment. The acceleration clause allows the entire note to be due immediately upon default. Acceleration clauses are very common with installment notes and do *not* destroy negotiability. (A) is wrong. An extension clause is common also and allows the debtor an opportunity, for example, to renegotiate a five-year note to six years. Extension clauses are common with installment notes and do *not* destroy negotiability. (D) is wrong. Remember, commercial paper is a substitute for money and a means of providing credit. If the debtor defaults, it's common to have the interest rate rise, and if specified in the note, the note would still be negotiable.

395. (A) In case of a discrepancy, the words control figures but the instrument is still negotiable, in this case for $400.

396. (C) Bearer paper is payable to no one in particular, possibly even payable to cash. The instrument can be negotiated without endorsement by delivery alone, simply by handing it off to the next person. Delivery is always required to negotiate commercial paper. Delivery refers to handing the paper to the new owner.

397. (D) Order paper is made payable to someone in particular, and that special someone must sign his or her name on the back to further negotiate the instrument. For this reason, order paper requires endorsement and delivery.

398. (B) I is correct. A qualified endorsement is "without recourse," which attempts to remove the liability to pay if the primary party defaults. II is correct. A special endorsement names the next party to receive the instrument, so as a result the instrument would need to be endorsed to be negotiated. If the instrument were order paper on the front, the special endorsement would allow the instrument to remain order paper on the back. III is correct. A blank endorsement does not name the next party, so the instrument could then be negotiated by delivery alone. If the instrument were order paper on the front, the blank endorsement on the back would convert the order paper on the front to bearer paper on the back. IV is correct. A restrictive endorsement would be "For Deposit Only," which locks the instrument into the banking system. Only a bank can become a holder, but the instrument would still be negotiable. Remember the phrase, "once negotiable, always negotiable."

399. (D) I is correct. The endorsement is blank since Hobbs signed his name but failed to indicate the next party to whom the instrument is payable. As a result, the instrument becomes bearer paper. II is correct. The endorsement became restrictive when Hobbs added "for deposit only." A restrictive endorsement restricts what can be done with the instrument, although the instrument remains negotiable. III is wrong. Roy would need to endorse the instrument "without recourse" for the endorsement to be qualified. The general rule is that endorsers are at least secondarily liable for payment except for the party who endorses "without recourse."

400. (A) I is correct. While the instrument is order paper on the front, it would become bearer paper after a blank endorsement. An example of a blank endorsement would be if Mark Davis turns the instrument over and signs his name "Mark Davis" and leaves the rest blank without naming the party he is about to negotiate the instrument to. Since a blank endorsement does not name the next party, the instrument could then be negotiated by delivery alone. II is wrong. A special endorsement on the back of an instrument names the next party to receive the instrument. As a result, the instrument would need to be endorsed again to be further negotiated; therefore, the instrument would remain order paper.

401. (D) I is wrong. Once an instrument is negotiable on the front, no endorsement on the back could render the instrument non-negotiable. II is wrong. An instrument can start out as order paper on the front, but then become bearer paper on the back as a result of a blank endorsement. The instrument may remain bearer paper at that point or could flip back to order paper again with the use of a special endorsement.

402. (B) The endorsement is both qualified and special. The endorsement is qualified because by Corey signing "without recourse," he is not obligated to pay if the primary party defaults. The endorsement is a special endorsement because by naming Stuart Sheldon, the instrument remains order paper. Since the instrument remains order paper, Stuart Sheldon would need to sign the instrument to further negotiate it.

403. (B) I is correct. For the third party to qualify as a holder in due course, the instrument must be negotiable. There cannot be a holder in due course of a non-negotiable instrument. II is correct. For the third party to be a holder in due course, that party must give value for the instrument in good faith. The advantage of being a holder in due course, or sheltered party, is that these parties have greater rights to collect from the maker than the original payee had. III is wrong. For the third party to be a holder in due course, that party must have *no knowledge* of the instrument being dishonored or any payments being overdue. Note that the original payee is *not* a holder in due course. On the CPA exam, the original payee usually transfers the instrument to a third party who will probably qualify as a holder in due course. The next thing that will happen is that the holder in due course will negotiate the instrument to a fourth party who will *not* qualify (for whatever reason) to be a holder in due course. But it is important to know that the fourth party receives the same rights as a holder in due course under the "shelter rule."

404. (A) I is correct. Boyle can purchase the note at a discount and still acquire the status of a holder in due course. Most instruments are acquired at a discount. The advantage of being a holder in due course, or sheltered party, is that these parties have greater rights to collect from the maker than the original payee had. II is wrong. Whether or not Boyle obtains the status of a holder in due course is determined at the time Boyle acquires the instrument. For a holder to receive the status of a holder in due course, he or she cannot be aware of the fact that the maker was behind on the payments. Since Boyle was aware of that fact, Boyle would *not* qualify as a holder in due course.

405. (C) I is correct. If Sussman were a minor, he would *not* have to pay the holder in due course, Capell or anyone else. A minor can avoid any contract while still a minor and even within a reasonable time of becoming an adult. II is correct. If Sussman's signature on the note were a forgery, that would mean that someone else signed Sussman's name pretending to be Sussman. In the event of a forgery, Sussman would have a real defense to payment and *not* have to pay the holder in due course, Capell or anyone else.

The advantage of being a holder in due course, or sheltered party, is that these parties have greater rights to collect from the maker than the original payee had. The only ways that a holder in due course would not collect from the maker is if the maker, Sussman, has a real defense. Both forgery and infancy (minor) are real defenses. It would seem in both I and II that Sussman would avoid liability to the holder in due course. Other real defenses include discharge in bankruptcy of the maker, extreme duress, material alteration of the note, and fraud in the execution.

406. (B) Rusty provides shelter to Salas, and Salas will have the same rights as a holder in due course. But Salas does not qualify as a holder in due course, since Salas knew that the instrument was overdue at the time Salas acquired the instrument. If Salas knows something is wrong, he cannot be a holder in due course. But he will have the same rights as a holder in due course under the shelter rule, which means Salas can collect from the primary party unless the maker has a real defense.

407. (B) I is correct. A material alteration is an example of a real defense. If a $30,000 note is materially altered to read $300,000, the primary party does *not* have to pay the holder in due course (or sheltered party) the altered amount of $300,000. Rather the primary party pays *just* the original amount of $30,000, because material alteration is a real defense. III is correct. A discharge in bankruptcy is an example of a real defense. If the maker of a note declares bankruptcy, that will excuse the maker from having to pay a holder in due course (or sheltered party) any amount. II is wrong. Lack of consideration is a personal defense rather than a real defense. If the maker of a note has a personal defense, that personal defense is only good against the original payee, not good against a holder in due course or sheltered party. For example, if the maker was buying a car and the payee was a car dealer, once the car dealer negotiates the note to a holder in due course, a dispute between the maker of the note and car dealer would *not* affect the rights of a holder in due course to get paid from the maker. This is because the holder in due course gave value to the payee, in good faith and without knowledge of the dispute. The court would force the maker to pay the holder in due course (or sheltered party) the monthly payments.

408. (B) As a holder in due course Grace would take the note free of all personal defenses. Personal defenses, such as negligence, would *not* stop Grace from collecting from the maker. The most popular personal defenses on the CPA exam include negligence. With negligence, the maker will have lacked reasonable care and left blank spaces so the amount was easily able to be altered. Rather than be considered a real defense, negligence is just a personal defense, good only against the party who raised the amount of the note. Negligence is *not* a valid defense against a holder in due course or sheltered party. The primary party would need a real defense (rather than a personal defense) to prevent a holder in due course or sheltered party from collecting. (A) is wrong, because discharge in bankruptcy is a real defense and the question is looking for a personal defense. (C) is wrong, because extreme duress is a real defense and the question is looking for a personal defense. (D) is wrong. Infancy is a real defense and the question is looking for a personal defense. If the primary party were a minor (infancy), the primary party would *not* have to pay.

409. (C) I is correct. The maker of a note has primary liability. The maker of a note promises to pay the original payee or anyone that the original payee orders them to pay. II is wrong. The drawer of a draft has secondary liability, not primary liability. In the case of a check, the drawer draws up a check and has secondary liability in case the bank does *not* honor the check. III is wrong. The drawee of a draft has primary liability only after the drawee accepts the draft. In the case of a check, the drawer draws up the check and has secondary liability. The drawee bank has primary liability only after determining that the drawer has money in his or her bank account. Prior to accepting the draft, the drawee has no liability.

410. (D) I is wrong. Bills of lading are shipping documents. Shipping documents are payable in goods. Commercial paper must be payable in money only. Therefore, shipping documents like bills of lading are *not* commercial paper. II is wrong. Warehouse receipts are payable in goods. Commercial paper must be payable in money only; therefore, warehouse receipts are not commercial paper. Note: although bills of lading and warehouse receipts are *not* commercial paper, they follow the same rules with regard to negotiability.

411. (C) Documents of title are *not* commercial paper because they are *not* payable in money only. While documents of title like bills of lading and warehouse receipts may be negotiable, they are payable in goods rather than in money. Investment securities are *not* commercial paper under the UCC definition, because investment securities are payable in shares of stock.

412. (A) Documents of title and investment securities are *not* commercial paper, but they follow similar rules as commercial paper when it comes to negotiability. If a document of title is payable "to the order of Owen Michaels," the document of title is negotiable (order paper). A document of title that is considered order paper requires a signature and delivery to further negotiate the document of title. (B) is wrong. If the same document of title were payable "to Owen Michaels or bearer," then the document of title would be negotiable (bearer paper). Bearer paper requires delivery alone to negotiate the document of title to the next party. It is important to remember for the CPA exam that documents of title and investment securities are not commercial paper, because they are not payable in money. But they follow similar rules regarding negotiability. (C) is wrong. If a document of title were made payable to bearer, then it would be negotiable by delivery alone without the need for endorsement. (D) is wrong. Documents of title and investment securities are *not* commercial paper, but they follow similar rules as commercial paper when it comes to negotiability.

413. (A) Documents of title include warehouse receipts and bills of lading. Documents of title are *not* commercial paper but follow similar rules regarding negotiability. A document of title payable to bearer (bearer paper) can be negotiated by delivery alone. A document of title payable to the order of a named individual (order paper) can be negotiated by endorsement and delivery.

414. (A) A bill of lading payable "to Billy Spence or bearer" is bearer paper and can be negotiated by delivery alone without the need for endorsement. (B) is wrong. Although documents of title are not commercial paper, they can still be negotiable if they are payable to a named payee or if they are payable to bearer. (C) is wrong. The bill of lading is bearer paper, and bearer paper does not require a signature to negotiate it. (D) is wrong. The instrument is bearer paper, rather than order paper. To be considered order paper, the bill of lading would have had to read, "pay to the order of Billy Spence." Documents of title are not commercial paper, but generally follow the same rules with regard to negotiability.

415. (C) I is correct. With regard to debtor/creditor relationships governed by the UCC, attachment relates to the creditor's rights against the debtor. II is correct. With regard to debtor/creditor relationships governed by the UCC, perfection relates to the creditor's rights against third parties.

416. (C) I is correct. A security agreement gives the creditor a security interest in the debtor's property. For example, without a security agreement, when a consumer buys a new car, the debtor would have to make all the payments first prior to being able to drive the car out of the showroom. The UCC refers to this security interest as either possessory or nonpossessory, depending on whether the creditor is in possession of the collateral while the payments are being made. In the case of a consumer buying a car, the creditor allows the consumer to drive off with a car that has not been fully paid for because of the security agreement that is in place. For this reason, the UCC considers the creditor's security interest to be nonpossessory. II is correct. While the security interest allows the debtor to drive off in a car while money is still owed, the security agreement is in place to protect the lender. In the event of default, the creditor having a security agreement signed by the debtor will allow the creditor to repossess the car from the debtor should the debtor fail to make the payments. The creditor's right to repossession is written into the security agreement.

417. (B) I is wrong. A security interest is *not* enforceable until the debtor has rights in the collateral. For a security interest to attach and be enforceable, there is often a written security agreement between the debtor and creditor. In the case of a consumer purchasing a car, the written security agreement is signed by the debtor at the dealership but is not enforceable until the debtor has the keys to the car. For example, if the security agreement is signed Saturday night at the dealership but the car is not delivered to the debtor until Monday morning, the security interest is not enforceable until Monday morning when the debtor gets behind the wheel. In this example, the CPA exam will ask which day attachment took place: Saturday night at the dealership when the security agreement was signed or Monday when the debtor had the rights to the car. The answer is that attachment took place Monday when the debtor got the car—the creditor would then have attachment of a nonpossessory security interest. The UCC considers the creditor's security interest to be nonpossessory in this example since the creditor is *not* in possession of the car during the term of the security interest. II is correct. In case of default, the security agreement allows the creditor to repossess the car and sell it to apply proceeds to satisfy the debt. In this way, the creditor has rights against the debtor. The term that describes the creditor's rights against the debtor is *attachment*.

418. (C) Attachment took place Monday at Callahan's house, because that was the first moment that Callahan had any rights to the bike. For attachment to take place, the debtor must have rights in the collateral. Callahan has rights in the collateral on Monday at his house when the bike arrived, and not before even though Callahan signed the security agreement on Saturday night. Attachment refers to the creditor's rights against the debtor. The CPA exam will ask when attachment takes place. For a security interest to attach (in other words, for a security interest to be enforceable), three things must occur:

1. The debtor must have rights in the collateral.
2. The creditor must give value to the debtor.
3. There must be a signed security agreement.

The security agreement between Callahan and Lester-Glenn would be considered nonpossessory since Lester-Glenn is not in possession of the bike during the term of the agreement.

419. (C) I is correct. An example of a possessory interest would be a creditor taking possession of negotiable instruments to be used as collateral for a loan. Once the creditor has possession of the stack of notes, the creditor would have attachment and perfection simultaneously. II is correct. An example of a possessory interest would be a pawnbroker accepting goods in exchange for a loan. Once the pawn shop has possession of the goods, they have attachment and perfection simultaneously.

420. (A) I is correct. Attachment and perfection occur simultaneously when a pawnbroker lends money. The pawnbroker takes possession of the debtor's collateral, and at that moment attachment and perfection take place. Attachment refers to the pawnbroker's rights against the debtor. Perfection refers to the pawnbroker's rights against third parties whom the debtor may owe money to. A pawnbroker lending money is an example of a possessory interest rather than a nonpossessory interest. II is wrong. For a nonpossessory interest, the filing of a financing statement leads to perfection, not attachment. A financing statement is filed after the attachment has already taken place. The financing statement gives the world constructive notice of the financing arrangement between the debtor and creditor. The filing of a financing statement does *not* relate to attachment. The attachment takes place earlier when the security agreement is signed *and* the debtor has rights in the collateral.

421. (B) II is correct. A pawn shop taking possession of collateral is what the Uniform Commerical Code (UCC) refers to as a possessory interest. A possessory interest accomplishes attachment and perfection at the same time. Once Tenderloin has possession of the ring, the Tenderloin Pawn Shop has rights against Ivy and rights against third-party creditors of Ivy. Before taking possession of the ring, Tenderloin has no such rights. III is correct. When perfecting by possession, neither a financing statement nor a written security agreement is needed. Once Tenderloin has possession of the jewelry, the pawn shop has rights against Ivy and rights against third-party creditors of Ivy without the need for a written security agreement or financing statement. Note that when the security interest is possessory, no financing statement is required to perfect the creditor's interest against third parties. I is wrong. Tenderloin would *not* automatically get a security interest in the automobile; the automobile is purchased outright for cash. Tenderloin would have *no* security interest in Ivy's car.

422. (A) I is correct. Once filed, a financing statement gives the world constructive notice for five years of the financing arrangement between the parties. If the financing were to last more than five years, a continuation statement could be filed afterward. II is wrong. If the debtor moves the collateral from the state where the financing statement was filed, the original filing is valid for four months, but after a four-month grace period, the creditor would have to file a financing statement in the new state that the debtor moved to.

423. (C) I and II are both correct. A buyer in the ordinary course of business is free of any liens even if he or she knew about the liens. You don't have to ask when you go into a store whether the store finished paying for the item yet. Note: Salika would be considered a buyer in the ordinary course of business whether she was buying goods for consumer use or business use.

424. (C) I is correct. After repossession but before sale, the debtor has the right of redemption. The right of redemption involves the debtor having the right to pay the obligation in full just prior to the sheriff's auction and get the collateral back. After the auction, it's too late. II is correct. The creditor must notify the debtor of imminent sale because the debtor has the right to bid at auction.

425. (B) II is correct. There are special rules relating to consumer goods: if the consumer has paid 60% or more of the purchase price, retention by the creditor is not allowed after repossession. The creditor must sell the goods within 90 days of repossession or be liable for damages. This is because the debtor is hoping that the car sells for more than the balance owed, and if it does, the debtor would take home any surplus. I is wrong. If the car sells for less than the balance owed, Stacey would be liable for the deficiency.

426. (D) I is wrong. Special rules relate to consumer goods: if the consumer has paid 60% or more of purchase price, retention by the creditor is not allowed. The creditor must sell repossessed goods within 90 days or be liable for damages, because this would give the debtor the best chance for a surplus and the least chance for a deficiency as items tend to depreciate quickly after repossession. II is wrong. Notice must be given to the debtor before the sale because the debtor is allowed to bid. The sale must be commercially reasonable.

427. (A) I is correct. If the smart device sells for less than the amount owed, DC Appliance can obtain a judgment from Cliff for the deficiency because creditors have the right to get paid back what they are owed, provided they follow the rules relating to the collection process. II is wrong. If the smart device sells for a surplus, more than what is owed to DC Appliance, DC Appliance could *not* keep the surplus. The surplus would be given to Cliff minus any costs of collection and sale.

428. (D) II is correct. An agent owes a fiduciary duty of loyalty to the principal, but the principal can have several agents all working at once without their being aware of it. III is correct. An agent for a disclosed principal has no contract liability to third parties if the principal backs out, but an agent for an undisclosed principal would have potential contract liability if the principal backs out. I is wrong. An agency contract does *not* need to be in writing, unless the agent is selling real estate for the principal or if the agency is impossible to complete within one year.

429. (A) I is correct. An agent owes a fiduciary duty of loyalty to his principal. Stump, the agent, owes a duty of loyalty to the New York Bombers. Stump would be liable to the Bombers for breach of fiduciary duty of loyalty if he were to disclose information to any competing teams without the Bombers' consent because the Bombers are paying Stump for this information. II is wrong. While an agent owes a fiduciary duty of loyalty to his principal, a principal does *not* owe a fiduciary duty of loyalty to the agent. The Bombers could have more than one agent in Japan following Hito at the same time. The principal would owe the agent the right of compensation but not a duty of loyalty.

430. (C) I is correct. If the principal no longer wishes to be associated with an agent, notice must be given to third parties. Actual notice needs to be given to all parties that the agent did business on behalf of the principal. Actual notice to current customers will terminate the agent's actual authority to bind the principal on any new contracts. II is correct. If the principal no longer wishes to be associated with an agent, constructive notice to potential customers is required also. Constructive notice may be accomplished by classified advertisements in trade journals, etc. This will terminate the agent's apparent authority even if the third party did not read the advertisement regarding the termination. Note: notice need *not* be given if the reason for termination was due to death, insanity, bankruptcy, or destruction of the subject matter of the contract. Termination would be automatic.

431. (A) I is correct. To have a surety agreement, three parties are needed. These three parties are known as creditor, principal debtor, and co-signor. The co-signor is known on the exam as a surety or guarantor. III is correct. The agreement of surety to pay the creditor if the principal debtor defaults must be in writing, because it is a promise to answer for the debt of another. This promise is one of the contracts that has to be in writing according to the statute of frauds. II is wrong. The agreement between the surety and principal debtor may or may not be in writing and would have no effect on the surety's obligation to pay the creditor.

432. (C) Subrogation is the surety's right, after paying the creditor, to step into the shoes of a creditor against the principal debtor. If the debtor's father pays for the debtor's loan balance on a new car, the father has the right, after payment, to demand from the debtor either the money or the keys. Subrogation gives the surety the greatest chance of collecting from the debtor. (A) is wrong. Contribution would involve more than one surety contributing their share after one surety pays in full. (B) is wrong. A surety has different rights before and after payment. Prior to payment, a surety could attempt to be exonerated. If the surety was exonerated he would not have to pay, but the question is looking for a surety's right once payment has been made. (D) is wrong. *Attachment* is a term that refers to the creditor's rights, and the question asked about the surety's rights.

433. (C) I is correct. Prior to payment, the surety hopes to be exonerated. Exoneration means to be found not liable. It's not easy to be exonerated, because once the surety co-signs, the surety has primary liability. II is correct. After payment, the surety stands in the shoes of the creditor against the principal debtor. The surety can demand payment from the debtor or can demand the car from the debtor.

434. (D) The Credit Card Fraud Act deals with what happens if your card is used in an unauthorized situation, if it's stolen, and so on. If your credit card is stolen, your max liability is $50 per card if you promptly notify the credit card company upon receiving your statement balance or sooner. The debtor must act in good faith and report the issue promptly to minimize the overall damages.

435. (C) I is correct. The Equal Credit Opportunity Act prohibits discrimination in credit granting on the basis of marital status. II is correct. The Equal Credit Opportunity Act prohibits discrimination in credit granting on the basis of race and gender.

436. (A) I is correct. Liquidation involves selling all noncash assets in order to raise cash and pay all debts. Chapter 7 bankruptcy results in liquidation. In a Chapter 7 case, the debtor needs to sell all noncash assets, pay creditors, and get a discharge for the remaining debts. The business is not meant to survive a Chapter 7 bankruptcy. II is wrong. Chapter 11 is reorganization. The debtor wants to keep the struggling business alive. In the absence of fraud, the debtor is allowed to remain in charge during bankruptcy. A creditors committee is composed of unsecured creditors, and a plan gets submitted that gives the debtor more time to pay. III is wrong. Chapter 13 is for a small business owner looking to save the equity in his home. Liquidation is the last thing on the debtor's mind in Chapter 13, but it could become reality if the creditors don't get paid under the debtor's promise of a new payment plan.

437. (B) III is correct. For creditors to file involuntary bankruptcy against a debtor, unsecured creditors must prove that the debtor is not paying bona fide debts as they mature. I is wrong. If there are 12 or more unsecured creditors, then 3 or more creditors would need to file the bankruptcy petition. Since Green has only 9 creditors, only one needs to file. II is wrong. Insolvency refers to the fact that total liabilities exceed total assets. The creditors do not have to prove that Green is insolvent, but they do need to prove that Green is equitably insolvent, which is the inability to pay short-term debts as they become due.

438. (B) II is correct. The debtor is still entitled to alimony. The debtor must agree to surrender certain property to which the debtor becomes entitled within the 180 days *after* the petition is filed, but alimony is not among that property. I is wrong. Among that property that must be surrendered for the bankruptcy is life insurance proceeds. III is wrong. Among that property that must be surrendered for the bankruptcy is inherited property.

439. (C) I is correct. The trustee in bankruptcy can void any transfer made by the debtor during one year prior to bankruptcy *if* the transfer was considered a fraudulent conveyance. A conveyance would be viewed as fraudulent if it was made with the intent to hinder or delay creditors: for example, hiding assets or selling property for less than adequate consideration. Fraudulent conveyances are considered an act of bad faith and could hurt the debtor's hopes of receiving a discharge in bankruptcy, or forgiveness of debt. II is correct. A preferential transfer is also voidable by the trustee even though these transfers happen in the course of business. An example of a preferential transfer is the debtor favoring one creditor over another with payments made to that favored creditor while the debtor is insolvent. The result of a preferential transfer is that the creditor favored by the debtor receives more than he or she would have had the favored creditor been forced to wait in line in bankruptcy.

440. (B) II is correct. A Chapter 11 reorganization case may be filed voluntarily by the debtor or involuntarily by creditors. I is wrong. A trustee is *not* always appointed under a Chapter 11 bankruptcy case. Under Chapter 11 the business debtor sometimes remains in charge and other times a trustee is placed in charge of the debtor's assets. The court decides based on several factors, including the competency of the debtor.

441. (C) I is correct. A debtor could have total assets greater than total liabilities and still be unable to pay current debts as they become due. A debtor does not have to be insolvent for creditors to force the debtor into Chapter 11 bankruptcy. II is correct. The reorganization plan could be filed by the creditors or filed by the debtor, and all plans must be in by a certain date set forth by the bankruptcy judge. The goal of Chapter 11 is to give the struggling debtor more time to pay debts without the need to sell off assets. A new repayment plan will be filed by the interested parties and ultimately approved by the court.

442. (D) Secured creditors get theirs before the unsecured creditors. What happens on the CPA exam is that the secured creditors will get paid, but they won't get enough money to satisfy what was owed to them. So after they get theirs, they jump over to the unsecured creditor line. But when they get to the unsecured creditor line, they must wait at the end of that line, not the front of the line.

443. (A) Employees are given a high priority in a bankruptcy case. Of the unsecured creditors listed in this question, employees have the highest priority. It is important to note that had one of the choices been alimony, child support, or administrative costs of the bankruptcy, such as lawyer and accounting fees, those costs would have been paid ahead of employees. (C) is wrong. When assets are distributed in a bankruptcy case, certain creditors have priority over others. Secured creditors get paid the value of their security first, but if they are owed more than what their collateral sold for, they go to the end of the unsecured creditor line with no priority and wait until other unsecured creditors with a priority in that line get paid, such as employees. (D) is wrong. While unsecured taxes are given a priority, employees get paid before employer taxes get paid. (B) is wrong. In the event of bankruptcy, while customers are given a priority, employees get paid ahead of customers.

444. (B) II is correct. If the debtor acts in bad faith while in bankruptcy, this could result in no discharges at all, or discharges obtained may be revoked. An example would be fraudulent conveyances or the debtor purposefully answering the questions on the bankruptcy petition incorrectly, such as failing to explain the whereabouts of assets. I is wrong. Any creditor that the debtor fails to list will result in the debtor not getting a discharge for that one unlisted creditor. Discharges would still be available for the remaining creditors provided the debtor acted in good faith.

445. (C) I is correct. Upon filing of a petition for involuntary bankruptcy under Chapter 7, the court will appoint an interim trustee. While a trustee was optional under Chapter 11 reorganization, a trustee is mandatory under Chapter 7 liquidation. II is correct. The bankruptcy filing will act as an automatic stay and stop all collection efforts with the exception of alimony, child support, and criminal actions.

446. (C) I is correct. The SEC does not render any opinion regarding the facts contained in a registration statement. Instead, the SEC looks to see if the required information is complete. The SEC renders no opinion as to the securities value as an investment. II is correct. The registration statement will contain the following information: names of issuer, directors, officers, underwriters, and large shareholders, and description of property, business, and capitalization, description of security to be offered, certified financial statements, a balance sheet not more than 90 days old, and a profit and loss statement for five years.

447. (B) II is correct. The Federal Securities Act of 1933 states that if a corporation wants to issue securities in interstate commerce that have not previously been issued, then the securities must be registered. An exception would be when the buyers are in the same state as the seller, because no interstate commerce would apply and the federal government would have no jurisdiction. In this example, the Texas securities laws (known on the CPA exam as "blue sky" laws) would apply since all the potential purchasers live in the same state as the issuer. I is wrong. The securities would *not* need be registered with the Securities and Exchange Commission, because the purchasers live in the same state as the issuer; therefore, no interstate commerce is involved. This is known as the intrastate exemption, where the issuer and all purchasers or offerees are residents of the same state and the issuer does 80% of its business in that state.

448. (C) I is correct. The Federal Securities Act of 1933 includes common and preferred stock in its definition of a security. Preferred stock would need to be registered if being sold to the public in interstate commerce by a firm looking to raise capital. II is correct. The Federal Securities Act of 1933 includes corporate bonds in its definition of a security. Corporate bonds would need to be registered if being sold to the public in interstate commerce by a firm looking to raise capital.

449. (A) I is correct. Exemptions apply to securities issued by not-for-profit organizations. This means that a charity could issue bonds without first registering the bonds with the Securities and Exchange Commission (SEC). II is wrong. Corporate bonds, whether they are debentures or secured bonds, must be registered with the SEC prior to sale to the public in interstate commerce under the Federal Securities Act of 1933. Other exempt securities include government bonds, banks issuing securities, charities, railroads, and bankruptcy trustees. Commercial paper is exempt if it has an original maturity of less than nine months. Insurance policies and annuities are exempt.

450. (A) Issuers under Regulation D, Rule 504, may sell the shares to an unlimited number of investors. While the general rule of the 1933 act says that new issues need to be registered with the SEC, exemptions do sometimes apply. The Regulation D exemption includes Rule 504. Rule 504 limits an offering to $1,000,000 within a 12-month period. If Cramer, Inc., follows Rule 504, Cramer could sell its shares to an unlimited number of investors without registering them with the SEC prior to sale. The important points to remember about the Rule 504 exemption under Regulation D are as follows: Issuers are allowed to sell to an unlimited number of investors; both accredited and nonaccredited investors are unlimited and welcome to invest. Accredited investors include mutual fund managers, banks, hedge fund managers, and so on. Nonaccredited investors are members of the general public who want to invest and are not institutionally connected. Under Rule 504, the issuer could sell its stock to an unlimited number of both accredited and nonaccredited investors and still not have to register with the SEC, provided the dollar limit raised is $1,000,000 or less. Also under Rule 504, immediate resale of the securities is allowed. An investor who buys stock under Rule 504 can immediately sell it to another individual without violating Rule 504. (B) is wrong. If Cramer, Inc., follows Rule 504, Cramer could advertise the sale of its shares to an unlimited number of investors without registering them with the SEC prior to sale. Issuers are allowed to advertise their offering under Rule 504. (C) is wrong. If Cramer, Inc., follows Rule 504, Cramer could sell its shares to an unlimited number of investors without registering them with the SEC prior to sale. (D) is wrong. If Cramer, Inc., follows Rule 504, Cramer could sell its shares to an unlimited number of investors without registering the securities or providing the investors with a prospectus. The CPA exam often tests Rule 504 and its dollar limit of $1,000,000. If the issuer wants to raise more than $1,000,000, it cannot rely on Rule 504.

451. (C) While the general rule of the 1933 act says that new issues need to be registered with the Securities and Exchange Commission (SEC), exemptions do sometimes apply. The Regulation D exemption includes Rule 505. Rule 505 allows a corporation to issue its stock to the public without registering with the SEC. The rules for Rule 505 are as follows: The dollar limitation of Rule 505 is $5,000,000. Up to $5,000,000 can be raised over a 12-month period. Because as much as $5,000,000 is being raised, Rule 505 has more restrictions than Rule 504. While the issuer could sell the stock to an unlimited number of accredited investors under Rule 505, no more than 35 nonaccredited investors are allowed to participate. Accredited investors include mutual fund managers, banks, hedge funds, and so on. Nonaccredited investors are members of the general public who want to invest and are not institutionally connected. Having zero nonaccredited investors would comply with the rule, but 36 nonaccredited investors would violate Rule 505. Unlike Rule 504, resale of stock purchased by investors under Rule 505 is restricted and must be held for two years. It's up to the issuer to disclose the restriction to the potential investors, usually done by placing a notation or legend on the securities themselves. Unlike Rule 504, no general advertising is allowed.

452. (A) Under the Federal Securities Act of 1933, Regulation D, Rules 505 and 506, the offering needs to be made without general advertising. Rule 505 and 506 offerings are sometimes referred to as private offerings, because advertising to the general public is prohibited under these two rules. Rule 505 and 506 have a few things in common:

No advertising
No more than 35 nonaccredited investors
No immediate resale to the public

It is important to note that while Rule 505 has a dollar limit of $5,000,000, Rule 506 has no dollar limit. While Rule 506 has no dollar limit, it's important to note that Rule 506 has a provision that any nonaccredited investor who wants to invest must show that he or she is financially sophisticated. Financial sophistication refers to the fact that the nonaccredited investor understands the risk and has other money in case this money is lost. This provision is unique to Rule 506.

453. (B) Under Regulation D, Rules 504, 505, and 506 each require that the SEC be notified within 15 days after the first sale, not before the sale.

454. (B) The following must register with the Securities and Exchange Commission (SEC) per the 1934 act:

Any company that trades on a national securities exchange
Brokers and dealers doing business in interstate commerce

If not traded on a national exchange, large corporations with $10,000,000 in assets and at least 2,000 shareholders, or 500 shareholders who are nonaccredited, must also register under the 1934 act and file Form 10-K and Form 10-Q just like a large issuer.

455. (A) I is correct. Unusual events not in the ordinary course of business must be reported using an 8-K report. 8-K reports are used to report material change of events by the publicly traded company to the SEC. For example, if a board member resigns, a company must release the news in an 8-K within four days. II is correct. 10-K annual reports are required to be audited by the 1934 act and filed within 60 to 90 days of the close of the fiscal year. 10-Q quarterly reports are unaudited but required to be released under the Securities Exchange Act of 1934 within 40 to 45 days after the end of the first three quarters. III is correct. A proxy is any matter subject to shareholder vote. Soliciting proxies by use of mail or interstate commerce requires following these rules: Whomever is soliciting the proxy must state whether the proxy is being solicited by management and, if so, include annual reports for two years. Proxy solicitations must include the matters to be voted on and the place to vote. Proxy solicitations must be filed with the SEC 10 days before sending to shareholders.

456. (B) II is correct. The annual report Form 10-K must be filed by a large reporting company within 60 days after the end of the fiscal year according to the Securities Exchange Act of 1934. Certain smaller firms have 90 days to file their annual reports, but the larger companies only get 60 days. Prior to the Securities Exchange Act of 1934, corporations did not have to file an annual report. I is wrong. The Federal Securities Act of 1933 regulates initial public offerings of securities. The 1933 act does *not* regulate reporting once the shares are issued. The 1933 act regulates reporting of required disclosures for a corporation wishing to sell its stock to the public for the first time.

457. (B) Depending upon the size of the corporation, Form 10-Q is due a maximum of 45 days after the end of the quarter. Form 10-Q is a quarterly report that must be filed with the Securities and Exchange Commission at the end of the first three quarters of the fiscal year. In the 10-Q, the company's financial statements are reviewed rather than audited. Since the question mentioned that Horizons, Inc., is a small reporting company rather than large, the 10-Q is due a maximum of 45 days after the close of the first three quarters. (A) is wrong. 40 days would be the maximum amount of time that a large corporation would have to file its 10-Q. (C) is wrong. 60 days is the maximum number of days that a large reporting company has to file its annual report, Form 10-K, after year end. (D) is wrong. 90 days is the maximum number of days that a small reporting company has to file its annual report, Form 10-K, after year end.

458. (B) A party making a tender offer to purchase at least 5% of the shares of a class of securities registered under the 1934 act must file a report with the Securities and Exchange Commission (SEC). A report must also be filed by that same party to the issuer of those securities and to the exchange on which those shares trade. A tender offer is an offer to all shareholders to purchase stock at a specific price for a specified period of time. Note that the tender offer must be reported to the SEC by the party making the tender offer, not by the company being targeted.

459. (A) I is correct. The Sarbanes-Oxley Act through its Public Company Accounting Oversight Board (PCAOB) permits a registered auditing firm to perform tax services for audit clients if the tax services are preapproved by the board of directors. II is wrong. The Sarbanes-Oxley Act of 2002 prohibits many services that audit firms had previously performed for their issuer audit clients prior to 2002. Among the many prohibited services are bookkeeping, financial information system design and implementation, and actuarial services. The goal of prohibiting these services is to enhance independence of the audit firm.

460. (B) II is correct. To enhance oversight by the board of directors, the audit committee, rather than management, is directly responsible for the appointment compensation and oversight of the independent registered audit firm. The audit firm reports directly to the audit committee, and the audit committee decides whether or not to retain the independent registered CPA firm from one year to the next. III is correct. According to the Sarbanes-Oxley Act of 2002, documentation that relates to audits of publicly traded companies must be retained for seven years. I is wrong. The lead or coordinating partner and the reviewing partner must be rotated off an audit engagement every five years.

461. (D) According to the Sarbanes-Oxley Act, the audit firm cannot have employed the issuer's CEO, CFO, controller, chief accounting officer, or any person serving in an equivalent position for a one-year period preceding the audit, in order to enhance independence.

462. (D) A firm that audits more than 100 issuers annually would be inspected by the PCAOB every year. According to the Sarbanes-Oxley Act, the PCAOB must inspect registered CPA firms that regularly audit more than 100 issuers annually. (A) is wrong. According to the Sarbanes-Oxley Act, the PCAOB must inspect registered CPA firms every three years if those CPA firms regularly perform fewer than 100 audits of issuers annually. (B) is wrong. A firm that regularly performs no audits of issuers would *not* be inspected by the PCAOB. The Sarbanes-Oxley Act only has jurisdiction over publicly traded companies and their audit firms. (C) is wrong. A firm that audits more than 25 issuers annually but less than 100 issuers annually would be inspected by the PCAOB every three years.

463. (B) The CPA will likely be sued for negligence. When a CPA lacks professional care and competence during the course of the engagement, the CPA has committed negligence. (A) and (C) are wrong. For the injured party to prove that the CPA acted with gross negligence and therefore committed constructive fraud would mean that the CPA would have acted "recklessly" with regard to the rights of others, and there was no indication that the CPA acted "recklessly" in the question. (D) is wrong. Actual or common law fraud would have required the injured party to prove that the CPA acted with scienter or bad faith, that is, with intent to deceive or cheat. There was no indication of that in the facts.

464. (A) I is correct. For an injured party to sue a CPA under the 1934 act, the plaintiff would have to prove that a material misstatement or omission was included in a filed document. (This would also have to be proven if the plaintiff was suing the CPA under the 1933 act.)

II is correct. For an injured party to sue a CPA under the 1934 act, the plaintiff would have to prove that they read and relied on the false financial statements. III is wrong. For an injured party to sue a CPA under the 1933 act, the plaintiff would *not* have to prove that they read or relied on the false financial statements. All they would have to prove under the 1933 act is that a material omission or misrepresentation was included in a filed document, that they bought the stock, and that they lost money.

465. **(C)** When a CPA is liable for negligence, the CPA is liable to anyone in a class of third parties whom the CPA knows will rely or did rely on his opinion. Negligence means lack of reasonable care; a client could sue a negligent CPA because of the privity of contract between. A third party who suffers money damages by relying on the CPA's work can also sue the CPA for negligence.

466. **(A)** I is correct. To support a finding of common law fraud against a CPA, the injured party must prove that the CPA materially misrepresented facts. II is correct. To support a finding of common law fraud against a CPA, the injured party must prove an intent to deceive (scienter) on the part of the CPA. III is correct. To support a finding of common law fraud against a CPA, the injured party must prove justifiable reliance on the CPA's work and that the injured party suffered money damages by relying on the CPA's work.

467. **(B)** If the CPA is liable for fraud, the CPA can be sued for fraud by anyone who suffers a loss as a result of the fraud. To sue a CPA for fraud, the injured party must prove material misrepresentation of a fact, intent to deceive, scienter, bad faith, justifiable reliance, and damages.

468. **(D)** I is correct. To support the finding of constructive fraud on the part of the CPA, the injured party must prove that the CPA acted recklessly. You will know constructive fraud or gross negligence when you see it on the exam; if the CPA acted "recklessly," that means "gross negligence" or "constructive fraud." III is correct. To support the finding of constructive fraud on the part of the CPA, the injured party must show reliance on the CPA's work and that they suffered money damages as a result of the justifiable reliance. II is wrong. To support the finding of constructive fraud on the part of the CPA, the injured party need not show intent to deceive. The difference between actual fraud and constructive fraud is that the intent to deceive is lacking with constructive fraud. With constructive fraud, either intent to deceive is lacking or cannot be proven. It's difficult to prove that the CPA acted in bad faith, but if all the other elements of fraud are present, a finding of constructive fraud or gross negligence is often the result. Notice that constructive fraud or gross negligence is more serious than negligence, but not as serious as common law or actual fraud.

Chapter 5: Business Structures and Other Regulatory Areas

469. **(A)** I is correct. The bylaws of a corporation govern the corporation's internal management. The bylaws may be adopted by the incorporators or the board of directors. II is wrong. The bylaws are not filed with the state as part of the articles of incorporation. Corporate bylaws are *not* contained in the articles of incorporation.

470. (B) Promoters are primarily liable on preincorporation contracts they make. They remain primarily liable, even if the corporation accepts the contract. Noll (the promoter) is primarily liable for the contract made with Clark. The corporation, by using Clark's services for six months after incorporation, had impliedly accepted the contract and would be liable also. The correct answer is that both Noll and Rotondo are liable.

471. (C) I is correct. A corporate director is authorized to rely on information provided by the appropriate corporate officer. The financial statements that come from the officers of the corporation are an example of the corporate directors relying on information provided by the officers. II is correct. A corporate director is authorized to rely on information provided by the independent auditor's report. The corporate directors rely on the independent auditor's report when the board decides whether or not to declare the dividend.

472. (D) Once a dividend is duly declared by the board of directors, the stockholders become unsecured creditors of the corporation. Thus once Shea declares a cash dividend, Lucas became an unsecured creditor of Shea. (C) is wrong. A preferred stockholder is not entitled to convert preferred stock into common stock unless this right is specifically authorized. (A) is wrong. Lucas is a holder of cumulative preferred stock, not participating preferred stock. Only participating preferred stock shareholders may participate with common stock shareholders on dividend distributions. (B) is wrong. Cumulative preferred stock is usually nonvoting stock. Whether voting or nonvoting depends on the stock, not on whether dividend payments are in arrears.

473. (C) Corporations are subject to double taxation if dividends are paid. Profits are taxed at the corporate level, and if the corporation pays dividends, the dividends are taxable income for the recipient. (A) is wrong. Most privately held businesses are sole proprietorships and partnerships, not C corporations. (B) is wrong. C corporations are *not* allowed to deduct dividends paid. (D) is wrong. C corporations are not limited to only one class of stock. They can have as many classes of stock as described in its articles of incorporation. S corporations are limited to one class of stock.

474. (B) II is correct. If the shareholders have commingled their personal funds with those of the corporation, then in the event of bankruptcy, the court could hold the shareholder liable who commingled. This is common when there is one shareholder of a small C corporation who tries to run the corporation out of his personal checking account. I is incorrect. In the absence of fraud, a corporation can be formed for the sole purpose of limited liability. One of the principal reasons for choosing the corporate form over others is to obtain limited personal liability. If there was fraud involved, the court could pierce the corporate veil and hold the shareholders liable who participated in the fraud.

475. (B) II is correct. Preferred stock is considered equity securities. I is wrong. All bonds represent debt securities, not equity securities.

476. (B) II is correct. In a shareholder's derivative lawsuit, angry shareholders are suing on behalf of the corporation. The shareholder's derivative lawsuit is commonly brought against the director or officer who participated in an ultra vires act. If the corporation wins the shareholder's derivative lawsuit against the director or officer who participated in the ultra vires act, recovery of the money would belong to the corporation as an entity, not to any shareholders. I is wrong. A properly declared dividend becomes a claim against the corporation. The money from a dividend declaration is owed to the shareholders, not to the corporation. You will know a shareholder's derivative lawsuit when you see it, because the recovery would have to belong to the *corporation* and not to any individual shareholders or group of shareholders. Therefore, unpaid dividend declarations would not be the subject of a shareholder's derivative lawsuit.

477. (C) I is correct. Shareholders have the right to vote on fundamental changes in structure like a merger or consolidation. II is correct. Shareholders have the right to a reasonable inspection of corporate records unless they themselves have abused that right in the past.

478. (D) III is correct. The evidence that the parties are partners is often implied by the parties' everyday conduct. The fact that they are co-owning a business for profit will often substitute for a written partnership agreement. I is wrong. A partnership agreement need not be filed with the government. II is wrong. While you would think that all partnerships would insist on a written agreement, many partnerships begin without any agreement whatsoever and while risky, it is perfectly legal. If a dispute arises, the court asks to see the partnership agreement, and if there is none, the court then looks for evidence that the parties are partners.

479. (C) I is correct because partners are agents of the partnership and agents of each other. Each partner owes a duty of loyalty to the partnership. Since partners are co-owners of the business, when a partner acts on behalf of the business, the partner is acting both as a principal and as an agent. II is correct because partners are jointly and severally (separately) liable on all partnership debts and contract obligations. This means all partners must be sued as a group, but then after partnership assets are exhausted, whichever partner still has money can be sued individually. The term *several* means separate.

480. (A) The liability of a new partner is normally limited to the amount of his or her capital contribution to the partnership. The outgoing partner is still liable for old partnership debts and would even be liable for new debts unless the partnership gave notice of that outgoing partner's retirement.

481. (C) I is correct. Submitting to arbitration requires unanimous consent of all partners. II is correct. Admitting a new partner requires unanimous consent of all partners. Other acts requiring unanimous consent include confessing in court and disposing of partnership goodwill.

482. (D) A partner who retires, withdraws, disassociates, and so on still has liability for existing partnership debts incurred while he was a partner. The retiring partner would also be liable for new debts of the partnership unless notice of retirement is given. Actual notice of retirement would need to be given to existing creditors, and constructive notice of retirement (classified ad) would need to be given to potential creditors for Partner A to avoid liability for future firm debts. Remember, the retiring partner is still fully liable for debts incurred while he was a partner until those debts are paid off. The only way the retiring partner would *not* be liable for existing partnership debts is if released by the creditor, an unlikely situation unless there is a novation. In the case of a novation, there would be a substitution of debtors with the creditor's consent. An example of a novation would involve the creditor agreeing to release the retiring partner from existing debts and holding only the remaining partners liable. The creditor would have the power to release the retiring partner, but would be unlikely to do so.

483. (B) I is wrong. In an LLP, a partner would only be liable for torts that she herself committed and would *not* be liable for torts committed by other partners. In a general partnership, a general partner would be liable for torts committed by other partners as well as for torts that she committed herself. II is correct. In an LLP, a partner would *not* be liable for the torts committed by other partners but only for those she herself commits. In a general partnership, a partner would be liable for torts committed by other partners. LLPs are less risky than general partnerships.

484. (B) II is correct. In an LLC, losses are limited to the amount of investment, much like a shareholder in a corporation. I is wrong. The key advantage to the LLC is that the entity is treated as a partnership for tax purposes, not liability purposes. Being treated as a general partnership for liability purposes is not an advantage but a disadvantage.

485. (B) I is wrong. They will be taxed like a partnership, not a corporation, because they did *not* file articles of incorporation. II is correct. They will be taxed like a partnership because they are going to default to being a general partnership. The bottom line in an LLP or LLC is that the investor receives the tax benefits of a partnership and the liability protection of a shareholder in a corporation. This is why many new small business owners are choosing LLP and LLC over the general partnership or sole proprietorship. Since Harry, Ben, and Chico never filed with the state to be recognized as an LLP, LLC, or corporation, they would default to being a general partnership.

486. (A) I is correct. In an LLP, no tax is paid at the partnership level; the tax return is informational only, and all profits and losses flow through to the partners. II is correct. The partners may agree to have the LLP managed by just one partner or by just a few partners. III is correct. An entity such as a corporation may be a partner in an LLP.

487. (A) I is correct. A proprietorship needs no formal filing with the state. II is correct. A general partnership needs no formal filing with the state. III is wrong. LLPs do require a formal filing with the state in order to secure limited liability. IV is wrong. LLCs do require a formal filing with the state in order to secure limited liability.

488. (A) I is correct. Trusts are three and a half months after death, April 15th. Trusts must use the calendar year. II is correct. Individual returns are due three and a half months after year end, April 15th. III is correct. Partnership returns are due three and a half months after year end, April 15th, for a calendar-year partnership.

489. (A) I is correct. Workers' compensation is available even if the employee is negligent. III is correct. A negligence action could be brought against Suzy Wong, Inc., if Suzy Wong, Inc., were determined to be a third-party manufacturer of faulty equipment. II is incorrect. No negligence action can be brought against Hanson, the employer, since the employer carries the workers' compensation policy and the employee can immediately collect on the policy (even if the employee was negligent).

490. (D) II is correct. Social security tax is paid one-half by the employee and one-half by the employer. The amount that the employer pays gets deducted by the employer as part of payroll tax expense. The amount that comes out of the employee's pay cannot be deducted by either the employee or employer. I is wrong. No money comes out of the employee's pay to go toward federal unemployment. Federal unemployment is paid for 100% by the employer. The employer then deducts the amount paid for federal unemployment. A portion of payroll tax expense for the employer includes the amount paid for federal unemployment. III is wrong. No money comes out of the employee's pay to go toward workers' compensation insurance. The employer pays the full workers' compensation premium. Workers' compensation is designed to compensate an employee for job-related injury or illness without suing the employer. If the employer did not carry a workers' compensation policy, then the employer would be exposed to lawsuits from employees who got hurt while working.

491. (C) I is correct. The Americans with Disabilities Act of 1990 does *not* require companies to set up a plan to make sure they hire enough people with disabilities. II is correct. The Americans with Disabilities Act prohibits discrimination against persons with a disability in hiring, firing, compensation, or promotion. Unless the employer shows undue hardship (e.g., undue expense), the employer must make reasonable effort to accommodate someone who is handicapped, which may include modifying the facility, changing the job, or installing necessary equipment, like a wheelchair ramp or elevator. A qualified applicant with a disability is an individual who with or without reasonable accommodation can perform the essential functions of the job.

492. (D) The EEOC enforces laws regarding workplace discrimination cases. (A) is wrong. OSHA requires employers to keep records of and report serious accidents. OSHA develops standards that it enforces in the workplace for employee safety and could force an employer to purchase safety equipment from a third-party manufacturer. (B) is wrong. The FTC deals with the sale of goods and its purpose is to protect consumers, not employees. (C) is wrong. The IRS does not get involved investigating workplace discrimination cases.

493. (C) I and II are correct. ERISA allows for joint jurisdiction by the IRS and US Department of Labor with the purpose of pension regulation.

494. (D) According to the Bank Secrecy Act, financial institutions must file a CTR for each transaction in excess of $10,000, to help detect and prevent money laundering.

495. (A) I is correct. Evidence of an illegal monopoly includes the ability to control prices. II is correct. Evidence of an illegal monopoly includes the ability to exclude competition. III is correct. Evidence of an illegal monopoly includes the ability to control more than 70% market share. Market share of less than 40% will not be considered a monopoly. Market share between 40% and 70% may or may not be considered a monopoly.

496. (C) I is correct. Copyrights are good for the author's natural life plus 70 years. II is correct. Under the fair use doctrine, teachers in the classroom can bring in pages from a copyrighted book and distribute them to the class without the author's permission for classroom use.

497. (B) II is correct. The owner of the copyright can transfer ownership by sale, by rental, lease, licensing, or lending; the owner of a copyright has the exclusive right, in the case of literary, musical, and dramatic works, and motion pictures, to perform the work publicly. I is wrong. Fair use is a right that belongs to someone other than the owner of the copyright. Fair use includes using parts of the protected work without the owner's permission for purposes of teaching, criticism, news reporting, and so on: for example, a teacher making copies of a page of a copyrighted book to teach a class, and so on.

498. (B) II is correct. Patents are awarded for machines, designs, and new drugs and are good for 20 years, unrelated to the creator's life. I is wrong. Copyrights are good for the author's natural life plus 70 years.

499. (B) I is correct. To obtain a patent, an applicant must show that the invention is novel and useful. II is correct. To obtain a patent, an applicant must show that the invention is not obvious to a person who works in the field. III is wrong. There is no requirement that the invention be in a tangible medium. The work must be in a tangible medium of expression in order to obtain a copyright.

500. (D) I is wrong. $10,000 is the threshold for reporting any deposit, withdrawal, or exchange of currency. II is wrong. 15 days is the time for filing the transaction report, not 30 days.

Bonus Questions

501. (D) I is wrong. While much of the Dodd-Frank Act applies to institutions with greater than $50 billion in assets, liquidation can occur whenever the FDIC feels that the impact will hurt the economy. The institution may at one time have had assets of above $50 billion, but the banking institution may need to be liquidated now because its assets are quickly declining. II is wrong. While paying into the fund is required, no rule exists under the Dodd-Frank Act that a firm must pay into the fund for two years prior to being liquidated.

502. (B) II is correct. If the employee allows the options to lapse (not exercised), there is a capital loss based on the value of the options previously taxed. If there is a readily ascertainable value, the employee recognizes ordinary income in that amount in the year granted. If there is a cost to the employee, then the ordinary income is the value of the option minus the cost. If the options lapse, that amount previously recognized can be taken as a capital loss. I is wrong. If the options are exercised, the holding period begins with the exercise date, not the grant date.

503. (C) I is correct. A penalty of $100 may be assessed to the tax preparer who fails to be diligent with regard to whether the client is eligible for the earned income credit. The earned income credit has been widely abused for decades, and in recent years, the Internal Revenue Service (IRS) has enlisted the tax preparer as something of a gatekeeper. The tax preparer must fill out a checklist that includes computational worksheets, with the goal of determining whether the client is eligible for the earned income credit. II is correct. A penalty of $100 may be assessed to the tax preparer who fails to be diligent with regard to the amount of the client's earned income credit. The requirements for due diligence with respect to the earned income credit include eligibility checklists, computational worksheets, record retention, and inquiry of the taxpayer. The penalty for failure to be diligent will not apply if the tax return preparer can demonstrate that the preparer's normal office procedures were reasonably designed and routinely followed to ensure due diligence compliance and the failure to meet the due diligence requirements was isolated and inadvertent.